THE LEADERSHIP ASSIGNMENT

THE LEADERSHIP ASSIGNMENT

Creating Change

RAYMOND L. CALABRESE
Wichita State University

ALLYN AND BACON

Boston ■ London ■ Toronto ■ Sydney ■ Tokyo ■ Singapore

Series Editor: *Arnis E. Burvikovs*
Editorial Assistant: *Matthew Forster*
Marketing Manager: *Amy Cronin*
Editorial-Production Service: *Omegatype Typography, Inc.*
Manufacturing Buyer: *Julie McNeill*
Cover Administrator: *Kristina Mose-Libon*
Electronic Composition: *Omegatype Typography, Inc.*

Library of Congress Cataloging-in-Publication Data

Calabrese, Raymond L.,
  The leadership assignment : creating change / Raymond L. Calabrese.
    p. cm.
Includes bibliographical references (p.) and index.
  ISBN: 0-205-32183-6 (alk. paper)
1. Educational leadership. 2. School management and organization. 3.
Organizational change—Management. I. Title.
  LB2806 .C23 2002
  371.2—dc21

                                              2001053939

Printed in the United States of America

10 9 8 7 6 5 4 3 2 1   06 05 04 03 02 01

To the person who changed my life—
my friend and wife, Barb.

CONTENTS

CHAPTER SIX

Accelerate the Change Process   105

CHAPTER SEVEN

Manage Stress and Promote Acceptance of Change   128

PREFACE

This book is written for leaders who want to become change agents. Effective change agents in the midst of seeming chaos bring a sense of constructive change and order. This is a daunting task. They understand the words of James MacGregor Burns:

> The premise of this leadership is that, whatever the separate interests persons might hold, they are presently or potentially united in the pursuit of "higher" goals, the realization of which is tested by the achievement of significant change that represents the collective or pooled interests of leaders and followers.[1]

The Leadership Assignment: Creating Change is action driven. It provides eight change principles to guide the leader in creating and sustaining change. Change principle one: Prepare to lead change. Change principle two: Knowledge is power. Change principle three: Create empowering mental models. Change principle four: Overcome resistance to change. Change principle five: Lead change. Change principle six: Accelerate the change process. Change principle seven: Manage stress and promote acceptance of change. Change principle eight: Organizational renewal is perpetual change. The leader's role, as change agent, is to implement these eight principles and corresponding strategies.

Optimistically, this book advocates that change is good, that we can overcome our shared problems, and that the outcome of our collective efforts will be beneficial. Chapter Eight draws on the principles and strategies in the preceding chapters to provide seven lessons for renewing organizations. Lesson one: People are the secret to success. Lesson two: Create healthy organizations. Lesson three: Effective leadership is power. Lesson four: It's all about attitude. Lesson five: Leaders link actions and policies to change. Lesson six: Reinvent your organization—not the wheel. Lesson seven: Renewing organizations are self-actualizing organizations.

The outcome of applying these principles is organizational renewal. When a leader applies the change strategies principles and lessons in this book, he or she cultivates a learning organization that fashions and maintains organizational renewal. In essence, the leader learns to constructively develop and maintain the relationship between leadership, change, and renewal.

The Leadership Assignment: Creating Change provides change-motivated leaders with an understanding of the change process and the tools to drive change. The leader learns that leading and managing change require mastery of change principles. These change principles are grounded in the knowledge of the masters of organizational change: Kurt Lewin, Edgar Schein, Chris Argyris, and Abraham Maslow. These masters provide advice that the leader can use to make sure he or she follows the correct path to constructive change and can apply to the school setting.

Furthermore, this book addresses the critical issue of change-related stress. Change produces stress on the leader and his or her faculty. By being aware of the relationship between stress and change, the reader can actively help organizational members cope with the stress of change. The leader learns that effective change, constructively implemented, results in less stress and in personal and organizational renewal.

To aid the reader, each chapter uses a case study to illustrate critical points. The names and places used in the case studies and stories are all fictional, but each story can be found in many school settings. The main character in each case study, as well as the issues, is thematically woven throughout the chapter to show a change agent struggling with and resolving change-related issues. The reader is encouraged to reflect on the actions of the principal character. This reflection in action gives the reader insight into the case study as well as into his or her personal beliefs about the issues raised. At the end of each chapter, the reader will find Suggestions for Action, Change Factors, and Notes. The Suggestions for Action section provides practical steps the reader can take to implement the material presented in the chapter. The Change Factors table provides the reader with a chapter "how to use it" and "what it means" example for each term. In the Notes are reference citations and many Internet locations easily accessible to the reader.

ACKNOWLEDGMENTS

It is impossible to write a book like this without a great deal of assistance. I would like to acknowledge the help of many individuals. Of special note, I want to thank my wife, Barb, whose input into writing this book was invaluable. Many people at Allyn and Bacon have helped the writing process and encouraged my efforts, especially Arnis Burvikovs, acquisitions editor, whose encouragement, accessibility, and advice have been constructive and supportive. I also wish to thank Dr. Brian Roberts, editor, *The International Journal of Educational Management,* London, England, who sacrificed his time to provide timely feedback and strong encouragement. I also thank the reviewers of this book: Marva T. Dixon, Texas Christian University; Richard A. Fluck, Northern Illinois University; and Patrick Galvin, University of Utah; for their constructive advice.

NOTES

1. Burns, J. M. (1978). *Leadership.* New York: Harper & Row, pp. 425–426.

CHAPTER ONE

PREPARE TO LEAD CHANGE

Strategy ■ *Lead or Be Led*

STARTING POINT

To lead in today's society, leaders have to understand the nature of change. They must consider these basic questions: Can change be controlled or managed? Is change inevitable? How do you manage people who resist change? How do you create and sustain an environment in which organizational members embrace change? How do you assist organizational members in coping with the uncertainty associated with change?

Effective leaders consider these questions. They know that the ability to lead and manage change in an organization is critical to survival. For a half century, leadership experts have told us that employees respond negatively to authoritarian direction. Strong authoritarian leaders may get results, but their results seldom last. When they leave the organization, their changes often leave with them. Douglas McGregor, the motivation expert, stated:

> Management by direction and control—whether implemented with the hard, the soft, or the firm but fair approach—fails under today's conditions to provide effective motivation of human effort toward organizational objectives. It fails because direction and control are useless methods of motivating people whose physiological and safety needs are reasonably satisfied and whose social, egoistic, and self-fulfillment needs are predominant.[1]

Times have changed and the type of leadership that brings results needs to change. The prototypical educational leader in the emerging twenty-first century realizes that the quality of education is directly related to the vitality of the economy and national global interests; this leader is a change agent. The education profession demands it. The business sector demands it. The political sector demands it.

Leaders have a dilemma. On the one hand, they have a responsibility to lead change that results in more effective and efficient educational practices. On the other hand, they operate in an increasingly political environment. As a result, the leader must make change happen without alienating the workforce or other key

1

constituencies. A leader cannot do this with a superficial understanding of change. The leader needs to be a change expert who understands the nuances of change and then, like the conductor of an excellent symphony, orchestrates the change process through its many stages. The starting point for the leader in becoming a change expert is to understand the nature of change.

REFLECTION IN ACTION

As you read the following case study, write down the principal's guarded thoughts and feelings that he hides from his faculty. Additionally, write the changes you think need to occur for the principal to be successful.

■ ■ ■ ■ ■

CASE STUDY

Richard Jones is the new principal at Johnstown High School. The superintendent selected Jones because he has a reputation for being able to produce results and produce them fast. Jones has a well-earned reputation in the school district as the "top gun." When there is a seemingly irresolvable problem, the superintendent turns to Jones. Johnstown High School is a classic example of why the superintendent needed to turn to Richard Jones. It is a school in trouble. Achievement scores are low, teacher turnover is high, parent participation is almost nonexistent, and student attendance is the lowest in the district. Dr. Allen, superintendent of schools, asked Jones to meet with him to review the critical issues and the need for an immediate turnaround at Johnstown High School.

Superintendent Allen sat back in his chair, his desk covered with paper; he was speaking on the phone to the school board president. Richard Jones sat quietly in his chair and reviewed his planner. He pretended that he was not listening to the superintendent. He could not help, however, from overhearing the superintendent's closing remarks on the phone.

"I've got Jones in front of me right now, Mr. Jenkins. He'll get the job done. He's the best we've got."

"Richard, I don't have to tell you that the high school is in deep trouble; you've been around. I made a terrible mistake with the last principal I assigned to the school. I had community pressure to make that assignment—now I'm taking the heat. I want you to reform that school. I'll settle for no less than Johnstown High School's being recognized as an exemplary high school."

Richard Jones looked at the superintendent; he knew he was the ace the superintendent could always pull out of his sleeve. He liked his role. His words came out without a moment of reflection.

"I can do the job. It's going to take time and resources, but I'll get it done."

Superintendent Allen leaned forward, clutched his hands, and said: "You don't have time and you won't be getting any additional resources. I am under political pressure to do something about that school. You have a semester to show improvement. As far as the money goes, we had to cut teacher positions this year. I can't single your school out for special treatment."

Jones felt his heart race; he was more excited than nervous. He always liked a challenge. He looked directly at the superintendent and said: "This is going to be tough. I'll need to move rapidly with reform initiatives. Will I have your support throughout this process?"

Dr. Allen knew Jones would say yes; he always agreed with him. He could relax. He leaned back in his chair, clasped his hands behind his neck, and smiled: "Of course you will—just get the job done. I don't want the teacher union on my back; you will have to work with the union. I can't make wholesale changes in faculty assignments; you will have to make the necessary changes with your faculty. I never said this was going to be easy. I believe you're the right person to get the job done."

Jones knows that the superintendent's request is demanding. He has a mandate to lead change; yet, the lack of time and resources complicate his challenge. He understands that the superintendent chose him because he believes that he can get the job done. Jones is not naïve. He understands the trauma associated with change. He knows that he may face resentment and hostility; however, he has confidence that he can get the job done. Jones, because of the brief time frame, believes that a power-driven approach to force people to change to comply with the superintendent's request is a traditional alternative. He decides that the top-down, power-driven approach is archaic; he is going to choose a different strategy—one that involves the faculty, students, parents, and staff at Johnstown High School.

Richard Jones's choice is evidence of his wisdom. Because he made this choice, he is ready for the challenge. He will lead and manage change to construct an environment based on five essential principles inherent in the change process.

Principle one: Prepare to lead change.

Principle two: All healthy change is constructive when it conforms to pacing requirements.

Principle three: Change is personal.

Principle four: Understand the rules that guide attitudes toward change.

Principle five: The nature of change relates directly to the influence of external and internal forces.

THE NATURE OF CHANGE

Principle One: Prepare to Lead Change.   To lead change, the leader must understand change. To understand change, the leader must understand how to change. To understand how to change, the leader must personally experience the change process. Through experiencing the change process the leader identifies with the personal struggle faced by members of his organization. McDermott and O'Connor, management change experts, state: "Change is difficult, it calls for courage, yet the personal and professional rewards are great. The situation now is such that you have to change to survive. Remember the saying: there are three types of managers: Those who make things happen, those who watch things happen, and those who say, 'What happened?' "[2]

Richard Jones is the first type of leader. He is ready to make things happen. He knows, however, that change isn't easy. He is ready to learn. Take the following self-assessment with Richard Jones and evaluate your readiness for leading and managing change.

CHANGE READINESS ASSESSMENT

1. Effective change starts at the top.	True	False
2. Leaders act and employees need to follow to make change happen.	True	False
3. Employees are naturally resistant to change.	True	False
4. Effective change can start anywhere in the organization.	True	False
5. People will want to change if they understand the reasons for the change.	True	False
6. It is important to integrate the present context into any change.	True	False
7. Understanding a person's belief system has little to do with change.	True	False
8. You don't need a clear picture of the change. You just need to start changing.	True	False
9. Change is not a natural part of life.	True	False

The correct change readiness answers are True for numbers 4, 5, 6, and False for numbers 1, 2, 3, 7, 8, and 9. This assessment identifies one's personal outlook toward the leadership and management of change. The higher your readiness for change, the greater your trust in the intelligence of the employee to recognize when and where change needs to occur. The lower your score, the stronger your penchant for control over the direction and flow of change. People with a low change score believe that change starts and flows through them; their employees are the means to implementing their proposed changes.

Statement 1: Effective Change Starts at the Top—False. In learning organizations, leaders encourage change to start spontaneously at any place in the organization. Conversely, in poorly led organizations leaders often believe that they have to assume total responsibility for all change; this type of convoluted thinking isolates the leader from the rest of the organization. Consider our example: The superintendent mandates change in the high school. The principal is under pressure. The faculty, parents, and students will be on the receiving end of fast-paced policy decisions designed to change the school. If the principal operates from the premise that change starts at the top, he may have short-term success and long-term negative consequences. This solution cannot work. It may appear successful; the long-term positive effects, however, are minimal. To meet this challenge, Richard Jones has a dual task: He needs to move quickly and to have the school community buy into the change process.

Statement 2: Leaders Act and Employees Need to Follow to Make Change Happen—False. Effective leaders no longer position themselves above their employees. The effective leader recognizes that his or her attitude toward the employee is crucial to the change process. Argyris and Schon state: "We found that most people tend to be unaware of how their attitudes affect their behavior and also unaware of the negative impact of their behavior on others."[3] When the leader acts from a position of superiority and fails to respect the experience and intelligence of his employees, employees will resist change. The first step for the principal in the case study is to separate the problems. He has a professional problem in meeting the superintendent's expectations. This problem is tangential to the primary problem. The primary problem—improvement of academic performance and school climate—is jointly owned by Richard Jones, the principal, and each member of the school community.

Statement 3: Employees Are Naturally Resistant to Change—False. People resist change that they believe is not in their best interests. They cooperate with change when they believe the change will benefit them. Any resistance to change comes from the anticipated pain of learning and adapting to new behaviors. Many employees prefer to remain in a dysfunctional situation because they view it as less painful; as a result, change does not occur.

Edgar Schein, MIT management professor, states:

> Instability or unpredictability or meaninglessness is uncomfortable and arouses anxiety, what I have called anxiety 1 or the fear of changing based on a fear of the unknown. Learning how to learn may require of me the deliberate seeking out of unstable, less predictable and possibly less meaningful situations. It may also require me to become a perpetual learner with the possibility of being perpetually subject to anxiety 1. This is a situation most of us would prefer to avoid.[4]

Some people in leadership positions, although understanding the need for change, do not grasp the employee's anxiety associated with the proposed change. The leader's view of the larger picture fails to include the employee's narrower view of reality. Effective change leaders transcend the gap from the larger picture to the smaller picture so that the employee understands the relationship between her job and its impact on the larger organization. In the case study, Richard Jones understands that he must create an environment for change that facilitates the teachers' beliefs that the change is essential to personal and organizational well-being. Jones knows that as each teacher contributes to change, the school begins to change.

Statement 4: Effective Change Can Start Anywhere in the Organization—True. There is no set rule as to where to initiate change. Imagine a large ball. You can start the ball rolling by pushing the ball at any spot. The ball needs someone to push it before it starts to roll. Once it begins to roll, it gathers its own energy and the pushing becomes easier. When the leader understands that change can begin at any place in the organization, he empowers employees to act and experiment with their jobs. He allows initiatives to emerge throughout the organization. His school has the potential to become a learning organization.

This is possible if the leader is willing to discard misguided notions of perfection and permit failure to occur. Imagine a small child learning to walk and falling. The child lies on the floor, refusing to get up and walk because she bruised her knees. This is not the way of nature. The child lifts herself off the floor each time she falls and repeats the process until she learns to walk. The metaphor of a child learning to walk applies to all learning organizations. The leader understands this metaphor and encourages learned action. The leader knows that growth comes out of failure. The leader knows that organizational decline comes from the failure to try. In the case study, the principal encourages and rewards the efforts by teachers, students, parents, and staff members to transform the school. He knows that many efforts will fail. He knows that the outcome is not as important as the effort; members often learn more from failure than from success.

Statement 5: People Will Want to Change if They Understand the Reasons for the Change—True. The astute leader appreciates that knowledge is power. When the leader chooses to share knowledge, the leader creates conditions for synergistic power. Synergistic power is gestalt-like, in the sense that it is greater than the sum of its parts. It leads to the creation of a climate in which the organization's collective consciousness prepares for change. In this climate, shared knowledge prepares employees for a complete understanding of the reasons for change, thus enhancing the likelihood for their commitment to change. A complete understanding includes the rationale for the change and the consequences for continuing with current actions.

These consequences, once understood, are more likely to motivate employees to change. Knowledge alone, however, is not sufficient to maintain the change process. Kurt Lewin, the industrial psychologist, tells us that in addition to knowledge, the structure has to support the desire to change. In essence, the person and the structure interactively work together to create the conditions for change, implement the change, and sustain the change. The success of the change relates directly to the person's active involvement in the actual planning and carrying out of the change.[5] The principal in the case study recognizes that he has responsibility to help the members of his school identify the consequences of not changing in order to generate the desire to change. Once the desire is present, the school's structure adapts to support those desiring change. These members—faculty, parents, and students—then work with Richard Jones in planning and carrying out the change.

Statement 6: It Is Important to Integrate the Present Context into Change—True. The effective leader integrates past experience and the present context into the change process. Richard Jones knows that if he asks people to repudiate the past and present, he is asking them to repudiate their identity. He realizes that he can use their history and present context to fuel successful change. Embedded in the members' history and present context are their values and aspirations for the future. When the history and context connect to the change direction, members naturally gravitate toward the change. Change becomes a natural process not an imposition. Effective leadership facilitates change as a natural process by integrating the past and present into future changes.

One way the leader gains this understanding is through awareness of the multiple points of view represented in the members' consciousnesses. The leader knows that each member believes his or her point of view is valid. Adler, psychologist and communication expert, believes that the leader, if he or she is to gain a clear understanding of these multiple points of view, needs to enter nondefensively into a conversation with members. The leader seeks to gain clarification from the confluence of viewpoints. Principal Jones applies this principle by moving into a fact-finding, understanding phase. He knows this process paves the way for success.

Statement 7: Understanding a Person's Belief System Has Little to Do with Change—False. Each person's belief system is directly connected to his or her ability to change. Dilts, Allbom, and Smith, neurolinguistic researchers, state:

> Belief systems are the large frame around any change work that you do. . . . However, if people really believe they can't do something, they are going to find an unconscious way to keep the change from occurring. They'll find a way to interrupt the results to conform with their existing beliefs.[6]

Our personal and collective beliefs determine if we will change. If we decide to change, our beliefs determine the direction and extent of our change. Any sustained change must be consistent with our values and beliefs. Otherwise, the change is short-lived. The principal in the case study realizes that if he is constructively to lead change at Johnstown High School, he needs to identify and understand the values and beliefs of the school community. These values and beliefs may be different from those he espouses. If his values and beliefs are different from those of the school community, his responsibility is to find common ground and align the values and beliefs of the school community culture with any desired change.

Statement 8: You Don't Need a Clear Picture of the Change. You Just Need to Start Changing—False. Constructive change requires an intended outcome of the proposed change. A person, for example, loses weight because he has in his mind a picture of what he will look like when he is thinner. A person chooses to go to school to get an advanced degree because she has a goal as to what she will do with this advanced degree. All successful change is grounded in a clear picture of the intended outcome. Selecting appropriate change goals and gaining a clear picture of the prospective change require personal and organizational awareness of existing conditions.

Maslow, the famed psychologist, states:

> I believe that helping a person to move toward full humanness proceeds inevitably via awareness of one's identity (among other things). A very important part of this task is to become aware of what one is, biologically, temperamentally, constitutionally, as a member of a species, of one's capacities, desires, needs, and also of one's vocation, what one is fitted for, what one's destiny is.[7]

When we become aware that our existing conditions are creating conditions for pain, failure, or anxiety, we recognize that change is necessary to alter the present conditions. We now have a reason to change.

Reasons for change come from two primary motivations: (1) People are dissatisfied with their current state and desire a different state; (2) people are satisfied with their status, but they see a different state that seems to be more appealing to them. The first type of awareness is the most powerful. In many cases, personal and organizational, it relates to survival. If Richard Jones allows Johnstown High School to continue to operate the way it has for the past year, it will continue to deteriorate: Scores will continue to fall and the school climate will continue its decline. Jones knows that he can use fear as a motivation for faculty to change, but he also knows that fear is a temporary motivator. Unless he makes the attraction to a more desirable condition strong enough to overcome the faculty's satisfaction with their existing condition, he is unlikely to sustain the motivation necessary to see the change process to conclusion. He must work with members of the school community to increase their personal awareness of their condition until their dissatisfaction is so strong that they demand change to occur.

Statement 9: Change Is Not a Natural Part of Life—False.   Change is a natural part of life. It is a part of our environment; change is the thread that runs through the fabric of our lives. To live is to change. To deny the operational existence of ongoing personal, professional, social, and organizational change is to deny reality. If change is such an integral part of our lives, why do we resist it? We often resist change because we fear that we cannot control the direction or outcome of our intended change. Becoming comfortable with change takes immense trust in oneself and in life. These types of people are optimistic. They are more comfortable with change because they believe that all change leads to an ultimate positive outcome. James Loehr, author of *Toughness Training for Life,* states: "You have a much better chance of finding healthy ways to fulfill your needs when you feel positive and empowered."[8] In essence, optimism and effective leadership are two sides of the same coin.

Optimism is central to change and a crucial characteristic for a leader. The leader who provides hope to the members of his organization gives them a reason to continue to move forward in the face of seemingly overwhelming difficulties. The principal in our case study knows that he must generate optimism and cultivate an optimistic environment. His goal is to condition the members of his school to have self-confidence, have hope in the future, and recognize change as a friend. In this way, the members of the school community enter the change process comfortable that whatever the outcome, it will benefit them and the organization.

CONSTRUCTIVE CHANGE

Principle Two: All Healthy Change Is Constructive When It Conforms to Pacing Requirements.   Healthy change operates at three different stages with a specific pace at each stage (see Figure 1.1). Getting to stage 1, awareness, is slow, painstaking, and fraught with frustration. Moving beyond awareness into stage 2, the learning,

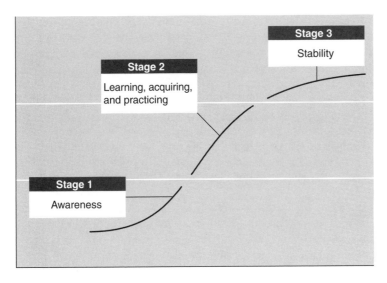

FIGURE 1.1   The Change Stages

acquiring, practicing stage, requires patience, commitment, and endurance. During this stage, change is rapid when time compression results in seeming chaos. In this stage the group struggles with replacing well-entrenched beliefs with new beliefs, attitudes, and behaviors. Once completed, the change process moves to stage 3, stability. During the stabilization period, those involved in the change process reenergize and acclimate to the changes in their work and life situations. The principal in the case study recognizes that effective change always follows this pattern. He recognizes the struggle in moving to awareness. He discerns the importance of learning, acquiring, and practicing. He is aware of the need for a stabilization period in which members of the school organization adapt and adopt their personal behaviors to the different ways of operating within the organization.

THE ORGANIZATIONAL NATURE OF CHANGE

Change, whether organizational or personal, follows similar patterns. Organizations are inanimate objects whose life comes from the members comprising the organization. These members operate in a context influenced by the organizational culture. The organization's culture originated in its original membership and evolved through the organization's history. As a result, the organization developed ways of responding to its membership and to the external world. Leaders in the organization established policies and procedures designed to make the organization survive and thrive. Critical to carrying out these policies and procedures are people who support the organization's goals. Their values are similar to those that evolved within the organization. As the organization develops, change becomes more difficult. The larger the organization, the more complex and difficult it becomes to change. Successful organizations overcome the difficulties associated with complexity by becoming learning organizations. They address the myriad of personal needs within the organization from an adaptive and generative orientation.

Peter Senge, in his seminal work on organizational learning, *The Fifth Discipline,* states:

> Real learning gets to the heart of what it means to be human. Through learning, we re-create ourselves. Through learning, we become able to do something we never were able to do. Through learning, we perceive the world and our relationship to it. Through learning, we extend our capacity to create, to be part of the generative process of life. There is within each of us a deep hunger for this type of learning.[9]

In effect, the organization recreates itself through the regeneration of the people within it. If the members of the organization understand the importance of change and continually re-create themselves, then they will understand that collective personal re-creation regenerates the organization. Once members understand the importance of personal re-creation, their motivation to change increases; they learn to embrace change.

THE PERSONAL NATURE OF CHANGE

Principle Three: Change Is Personal.   When change occurs in an organization, the members of the organization agree to change. The leader's task is to focus on the person as a way to address organizational needs. This is counterintuitive to traditional approaches to change. Historically, many people in leadership positions are taught to believe that compelling members to change is the most effective and efficient process. Imposed change, however, provides a façade of success; superficially, it appears as though the imposed change worked. The leaders in these organizations are unable to see the inherent flaws in their practice. History is replete with failed examples of imposed change attempts. The leaders of the USSR were unable to see the lack of internal acceptance of their imposed changes on millions of people. The USSR eventually dissolved. The Catholic Church in Spain used the Inquisition to force people to believe in church doctrines; the Inquisition failed. In contemporary times, some countries have imposed mandatory fundamental religious reform; eventually these hard-line reforms gradually eroded.

These political examples have their counterparts in private and public sector organizations. CEOs with strong support impose rigorous changes on workers. These CEOs learn, after it is too late, that the workers who survive undermine the CEOs' goals. Often, a leader will make numerous changes only to see the organization return to its original status after the leader moves to another position. The leader believed that his policies, practices, and actions changed the organization. In effect, only the externals changed; the internal motivation of the members of the organization remained static. The leader failed to understand that the path to organizational change is through personal change. Effective leadership calls for the leader to understand, facilitate, nurture, and guide personal change.

The leader's starting point in leading change is personal and internal. For example, I begin my change class each semester with the same activity. I take a rock and ask each student to touch and feel it. I want them to get a sense of the rock's composition. When the class finishes touching the rock, I place the rock on the floor in the center of the classroom. Under the rock, I place a $100 bill. I offer the $100 bill to any student who can transform the rock into a rose. The professor always wins! I make the point with my students that we can only change ourselves. This is the primary change lesson. This lesson, however, is not grasped by all leaders. Because of the failure to grasp the lesson, many leaders with great potential fail to accomplish their missions. They become frustrated because their goals and vision meet with continued resistance. The failures they encounter are the result of not understanding the personal nature of change.

The personal nature of change operates with a specific set of rules driven by behavior. Argyris states:

> All of us design our behavior in order to remain in unilateral control, to maximize winning and minimize losing, to suppress negative feelings, and to be as rational as possible, by which we mean laying out clear-cut goals and then evaluating our own behavior on the basis of whether or not we've achieved them.[10]

Principle Four: Understand the Rules That Guide Attitudes toward Change. The behaviors mentioned by Argyris result in five unspoken rules that guide attitudes toward change. Ironically, adhering to these rules as a source of change undermines potential constructive change.

1. We want others to change to meet our needs.
2. We change only when we believe we have no other choice.
3. We are comfortable with change when change occurs at a pace that fosters predictable outcomes.
4. We change only when we are ready to change.
5. We seldom address the real source of needed change because of our desire to avoid potential threat or embarrassment.

Five Unspoken Rules That Influence Attitudes toward Change. Rule 1: We want others to change to meet our needs. Human beings, across cultures, desire to exert control over their lives. Because of our desire for control, we attempt to make our environment predictable by requiring others to change. Richard Jones knows he has to avoid controlling behavior; otherwise, he will create an environment in which change is less likely to occur. He will quickly discover that conflict, anxiety, and power struggles become an organizational norm.

The remedy to rule 1: Leaders meet the needs of their constituents. Once the leader forgets about her needs, she focuses on the needs of the members of her organization. She ceases struggling with conflicting goals and aligns her goals with those of the organization's membership. Goal alignment builds unity out of diversity in the organization, enabling the leader to unite people in a common cause. As the leader, she intuitively understands the needs of the organization's members by becoming the people's voice. Through her actions, she elevates the members to aspire toward a higher moral and achievement-driven level. James MacGregor Burns, the noted historian, in his seminal work on leadership, states:

> Leaders most effectively "connect with" followers from a level of morality only one stage higher than that of the followers, but moral leaders who act at much higher levels—Gandhi, for example—relate to followers at all levels either heroically or through the founding of mass movements that provide linkages between persons at various levels of morality and sharply increase the moral impact of the transforming leader.[11]

Effective leaders like Richard Jones understand the symptomatic needs of the members and recognize the members' needs at a deeper, less obvious level.

Rule 2: We change only when we believe we have no other choice. Most people unknowingly resist change. They are not enemies of change, but they are unaware of their actions regarding potential change. According to neurolinguistic psychologists Bandler and Grinder, there are three primary constraints to our awareness for change: neurological, sociological, or individual.[12] Neurological constraints refer to phenomena beyond our sensory experience. Sociological constraints are cultural in nature. These constraints emerge from childhood nurturing and continually changing environmental contexts. Individual constraints become fixed patterns driven by personal histories, mental maps, and psychological and physiological DNA.

As we age, we develop fixed patterns of behaving that help us negotiate successfully through life. In this sense, we use our fixed patterns to solve problems. We face dilemmas when our fixed patterns of behavior encounter problems not easily solved by our learned behavior; this leads to unintended disastrous results. Ironically, without new learning situations, we lack the motivation to discover different patterns of behavior. Even when a new learning situation begins to manifest itself with minimal symptoms, denial overcomes the need for change. We often understand, too late, that this new learning situation requires changing or substituting a new pattern for our fixed patterns of behavior.

On a personal level, we recognize this behavior in others and ourselves. How many people do you know who refuse to quit smoking until their physicians tell them they have lung cancer? How many people do you know who refuse to alter their diets until they have a heart attack? On a professional level, many employees refuse to change until they understand the threat to their job security. The principal in the case study faces a strong challenge if the faculty in his high school do not sense the same urgency for change that he feels.

The remedy to rule 2: Leaders create a sense of personal urgency for change among members of the organization. A sense of personal urgency comes from either an internal or an external source. It is always more effective when it is internally driven. McDermott and O'Connor suggest that leaders sabotage their change efforts by reducing the sense of personal urgency for change. Leaders aware of these sabotaging activities can remove them to heighten the sense of urgency for change. These sabotaging strategies include the following:[13]

1. Ignore achievements.
2. Assume you know what is important. Do not consult members, but if you do, ignore what they say, after promising to consider it.
3. Take good results as the norm, but be extrasensitive and criticize any shortcomings.
4. Set standards that have no relevance to their work. Make many small rules and enforce them arbitrarily.
5. If they are not sure how to do a task, just tell them to get on with it. Don't let them bother you with their problems.
6. Be condescending or, failing that, sarcastic, especially in public.
7. Engineer situations whereby they develop a competitive fear of their colleagues.
8. Do not support them, but expect excellent results.
9. Take credit for their successes and blame them for failure.
10. Do not tolerate failure and make people anxious to cover their tracks. This will ensure a climate of blame and distrust and encourage political infighting that will interfere with work.

Each of these characteristics depresses the urgency for change. Members of the organization, concerned more about personal survival, think primarily in terms of self-survival strategies, without linking these strategies to the greater organizational strategy. Often, when placed in this position, members see any alternative strategy as an attack and become more rigid regarding potential change.

Rule 3: We are comfortable with change when change occurs at a pace that fosters predictable outcomes. All psychologically healthy people know that they will change. They recognize that each day brings a new context and unforeseen demands. They know that they may have to change to solve the problems presented by these demands. When we have the opportunity to recognize the new problem context, adjust our rate of change, and gradually adapt to the context, we seldom notice the change within us because the change takes place at an acceptable rate. The rate of acceptable change is also known as the Fechner-Weber Principle.[14] The principle describes a *just noticeable difference,* a point at which we begin to notice that change is occurring. Until the change rate reaches this point, we are unaware of its presence. The just noticeable difference is different for each person. Some people desire rapid change, others need an evolutionary type of change, and yet others seek a balanced approach of change. We become uncomfortable when change moves beyond our just noticeable difference. Our level of discomfort increases the further the change rate moves beyond the just noticeable difference.

The remedy to rule 3: Leaders sustain change by learning to manage the pace of change. They recognize the just noticeable difference in people as well as the collective just noticeable difference that exists within the organization. Because they can manage the pace of change, leaders have an understanding of the stress tolerance that exists within each individual and the organization. They push the limits of change while maintaining an intuitive feel for the moment to release the tension to initiate a natural recovery process. Richard Jones's challenge is to discover the balance between moving too fast and not moving fast enough. He has to discover this balance within each individual and within the organizational context. He creates change teams comprised of small cadres of people willing to change at rapid rates. These teams act as models for more reticent change members.

Rule 4: We change only when we are ready to change. Readiness for change is more a need for personal awareness for the need to change than it is for the knowledge of how to go about the change. Many leaders make the mistake of focusing on information generation as a means of preparing their organizations to change. The use of information helps members to understand the need for change; however, the members don't personalize the need for change. Because they don't personalize the need for change, many rationalize that they can change, but don't need to change. When members become aware of the need for change, they change. Psychologist and change expert Anthony de Mello states: "The most difficult thing in the world is to listen, to see. . . . The one thing you need the most is not energy, or strength, or youthfulness, or even great intelligence. The one thing you need most of all is the readiness to learn something new."[15] We stop resisting change when we recognize that change is in our best interests. Until we arrive at that point, we resist any change.

The remedy to rule 4: Effective change leaders construct a climate that encourages organizational members to gain a personal understanding of their status and weigh that understanding against the potential for improvement. The effective leader realizes that the distance from one's status to realizing one's potential is often an unconscious gap (see Figure 1.2). The leader's role is to make members aware of this gap. Until the members become consciously aware of the existing gap between their current performance and their potential performance, they remain satisfied; they believe that they are already achieving their maximum performance.

Rule 5: We seldom address the real source of needed change because of our desire to avoid potential threat or embarrassment. We avoid potential change

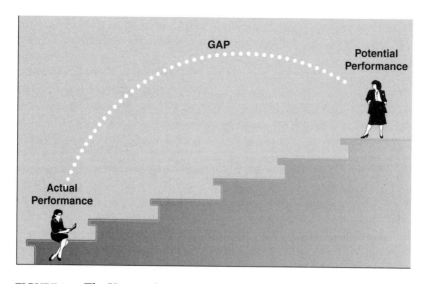

FIGURE 1.2   The Unconscious Gap

because we believe that making the change public exposes personal weakness or deficiencies. In essence, we associate potential constructive change with a personal attack on cherished values and beliefs. Our values and beliefs determine our sense of identity. Kurt Lewin, the psychologist, stated: "Only if and when the new set of values is freely accepted, only if it corresponds to one's super-ego, do those changes and social perception occur which, as we have seen, are a prerequisite for a change in conduct and therefore for a lasting effect of re-education."[16] Because we identify so closely with our personal sets of beliefs and values, we respond defensively when these beliefs and values are questioned. We believe that discarding these beliefs and values leaves us vulnerable. This is a problem for both personal and organizational change. The leader facilitating the change process often has a deep sense of frustration when confronting this problem. The effective leader recognizes that those most needing change often resist acknowledging that they are failing. Acknowledging failure is at the heart of all twelve-step change programs. The first step in twelve-step change programs is to acknowledge one's behavior and to do it publicly.

The remedy to rule 5: The leader constructs a psychologically safe environment in which members are free to question their beliefs and values without the risk of threat or embarrassment. By constructing a safe environment, Richard Jones follows the advice of Edgar Schein, "First of all we have to provide psychological safety, a sense that learning something new will not cause loss of identity or our sense of competence. I will not embark on a path that I perceive to be destructive to my sense of self-worth."[17] Creating a psychologically safe environment often means changing the organization's culture. The leader has to assess the level of psychological safety within the organization and then develop plans to maintain a level of psychological safety that allows each member the freedom to change. One effective process in creating an environment of psychological safety is to establish a set of ground rules that governs the interactions of members. Effective teachers create psychologically safe environments by making guidelines public and then making sure that all members of the class follow the guidelines. These guidelines, although unique to each context, are similar. They may apply to a classroom, faculty meeting, or committee.

GUIDELINES FOR A SAFE ENVIRONMENT
- We are a sharing group.
- We work together to construct a safe environment.
- We do not make critical statements of one another. We speak in "I" statements, not "you" statements.
- We offer advice only when requested by a member.
- We make every effort to support one another's efforts to change and construct change.
- We support each person's right to speak or to refrain from speaking.
- We recognize the importance of spontaneity.
- We do not interrupt others; we honor their right to speak.
- We respect one another by giving our full attention to each person's comments.

All groups need guidelines. Groups without guidelines create unhealthy, fear-driven environments. In these environments, members quickly learn to hide feelings, to suppress critical comments, or not to deviate from group-established norms. These groups often give the appearance of being externally healthy, but they are internally dysfunctional and decaying.

THE INFLUENCE OF EXTERNAL AND INTERNAL FORCES ON CHANGE

Principle Five: The Nature of Change Relates Directly to the Influence of External and Internal Forces.   To understand the influence of external and internal forces, the leader focuses on the influence of members' capabilities, leadership strategies, attitudes, value structures, and personality. The leader also examines organizational policy, rules, and interactions as potential sources of influence. On a personal level, each organization member's ability to change is subject to similar seen and unseen forces. The forces that we see represent the tip of the iceberg, while hidden forces drive our behavior (see Figure 1.3).

These forces interact interdependently with each other. A force that impacts one part of our being affects all parts. Eric Fromm states: "A personality and an organization are both systems that is to say it's not just a sum total of many parts, but it is a structure. If one part of the structure is changed it touches on all other parts. The structure in itself has a cohesion; it tends to reject changes because this structure itself tends to retain itself."[18] To understand change, the change process, and the reaction of the members of the organization means that we have to look beyond the symptoms to the forces that inhibit change.

Each person involved in a prospective change brings a panoply of forces affecting every decision he or she makes. The principal in our case study, for example, asks two equally capable teachers to attend a workshop to learn new teaching

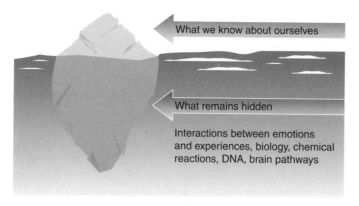

FIGURE 1.3   The Iceberg

strategies. One teacher embraces the opportunity; the other teacher responds negatively. The first teacher sees the workshop as an opportunity for growth; the second teacher views the workshop as punitive. The principal cannot understand the second teacher's reaction. He thought the teacher would appreciate an opportunity to learn something new. Each teacher's reaction to the same stimuli is different. Both bring a personal history to the interaction with the principal. The principal also brings a personal history to that same interaction. It is difficult to predict the outcome of this interaction. Only when we begin to understand each person's history, motivation, and belief system and associated nuances can we begin to discover how he or she will respond to change.

When we grasp the importance of personal understanding, we move away from seeing change as one-dimensional. Instead, we see the multidimensional aspects of change and how each individual component has a cause-and-effect relationship with all other components. Peter Senge, author of *The Fifth Discipline,* called this *systems thinking.* Leaders can use systems thinking to understand the complexity of change. Senge states that systems thinking is composed of two essential parts: "seeing interrelationships rather than linear cause–effect chains, and seeing processes of change rather than snapshots."[19]

When the leader views change as a linear response to an event, the leader's response ignores the complexity of the event and the persons involved in the event. This results in a Skinnerian approach to change. The leader links the behavior modification to a form of reward or punishment. Many organizations apply this approach. In schools, for example, when students do well, they have the promise of the honor roll, National Honor Society, or As on their report cards. When these rewards fail to motivate students, punishment becomes the primary response. Students receive the threat of failure, nongraduation, nonpromotion, and placement in nonstimulating classes. School organizations use the same approach with teachers and other employees. Behavior modification, however, has limitations. Once members become used to the reward, the reward loses its motivational power. The organization has to increase the size of the reward for it to have meaning. The same is true of punishment. The organizational use of reward and punishment as stimuli for change is similar to addiction. The addict takes drugs and receives a physical high from the drug. If the addict continues to take the drug, he or she has to increase the dose of the drug to maintain the same level of high.

When the leader sees change as emanating from interrelationships and as process driven, the leader has the opportunity to direct change and to create an environment for long-term sustained change. This is the way change works in the natural environment. The changing of the tides is a natural process whereby the tides gradually ebb and flow. The seasons gradually change from summer to fall, fall to winter, winter to spring, and spring to summer. Becoming comfortable with this natural process allows the leader to influence the change process; the leader can now take the time to understand the interrelationships that occur within the school and how the interactions within these interrelationships affect the process of change. Figure 1.4 demonstrates how this process works on curriculum revision.

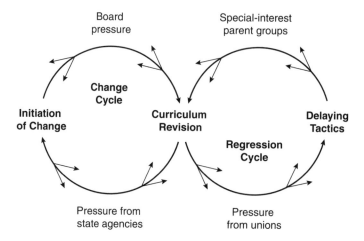

FIGURE 1.4   Interaction of Relationships

Figure 1.4 illustrates the complexity of the change process in the context of curriculum revision efforts. In Figure 1.4, we see that nearly every change process has two major factors: a change or growth cycle and a regression cycle. Kurt Lewin referred to these as force fields. Every effort to change meets a constraining effort to slow or disable the efforts to change. As the figure demonstrates, there is a myriad of players, and each player and group of players has a differing view of the situation. The leader's task is to find common ground among these views and to construct a change path that the majority of members embrace while simultaneously not disenfranchising those who oppose the change. The leader's traditional response is to increase the pressure on the change cycle, speeding up the process so that the change cycle rotates faster than the pressure applied by the regression cycle. We know from practical experience in driving our car that the car is damaged if we simultaneously apply both accelerator and brakes. We also know that a speeding car traveling down a mountain road requires the driver to apply the brakes judiciously for fear of overheating the car's braking system. The leader, understanding the interrelationship of these two cycles, learns to manage the accelerating change cycle and the regression cycle. The leader knows that neither cycle is good or bad; the cycles are created by how each member frames the change process.

CONCLUDING POINT

Richard Jones, principal at Johnstown High School, has a formidable task. Jones, however, understands the nature of change. He knows that to lead change, he must understand change. He also knows that understanding change requires an introspective look to understand the dynamics faced by each member of his school as well as the organization. Jones took the change readiness assessment and discovered that he is not ready, as he had believed he was, for change. He realized that he has a number of false notions concerning change. His awareness of his false notions is a positive start. He can replace his myths regarding change with clear knowledge regarding the nature of change. Jones now understands that change is a process more than an event. As a process, the members of his school move at their individual pace and collectively generate an organizational pace. It is up to Jones to keep the movement going. He has to facilitate the members' awarenesses of the need for change, learning, acquiring, and practice, and the stabilizing process so that the change becomes part of the school's identity. Jones is aware of the five unspoken rules that influence attitudes toward change. He quickly saw these rules in operation in other people, yet he had a difficult time acknowledging their existence in himself. Once he recognized their presence in his life and leadership style, he grasped a new level of understanding of his faculty, students, and members of his community. He now applies the change principles to each of these rules.

Jones created a safe environment at Johnstown High School. The faculty are safe to express opinions and make suggestions. He understands that there are no enemies among his faculty. He realizes that faculty, parents, and other community members will always choose to be a member either of growth-driven forces or of constraining forces. He knows that success as a leader depends on his ability to unite these two forces in the best interests of the school organization.

SUGGESTIONS FOR ACTION

- Use the change readiness assessment as a starting point for small group faculty discussions. This will allow people to voice fears and other concerns related to their readiness to change.

- Identify the growth and constraining forces in your organization. Draw a diagram such as Figure 1.4 to show how growth and constraining forces affect the change process.

- Identify strategies to diminish the fears of members of the restraining group so that they willingly release pressure from the growth cycle.

- Identify the acceptable change pace of your organization. Once you identify the acceptable pace of change, apply the construct of the *just noticeable difference* to painlessly move members into a change-driven orientation.

- Refer to Figure 1.2 and determine the gap in your organization between the actual performance and the organization's potential performance. This is an opportunity to involve faculty in a process to increase awareness of the organization's current performance level.

- Work with faculty members to create the rules for a psychologically safe environment. Refer to the rules, and remind people that when they violate the rules, the environment is becoming unstable. By monitoring the level of safety in the school environment, all members will embrace these rules as guidelines for discourse.

CHANGE FACTORS

TERM	HOW TO USE IT	WHAT IT MEANS
Belief system	Discover the belief systems of members to understand their motivations. If you can change the belief system, you can change the person.	A person's belief system is driven by the values held by the person. It is the way the person sees the world and excludes all data that challenges that view.
Change stages	The leader uses his or her understanding of the stages of personal change to facilitate change among members.	There are three basic change stages: awareness that change is necessary, learning and practicing new skills, and stability—making the change permanent.
Constructive change	The leader focuses on change that benefits all organizational stakeholders.	Constructive change benefits the person making the change and the person's environment.
Interaction of relationships	The leader understands relationship interactions to grasp all of the forces influencing change in his or her organization.	Interaction of relationships refers to the multiple forces at play in organizations. Many of these forces, often hidden, act to sabotage or retard the growth of change rate.
Optimism	The leader uses optimistic language; he or she projects an optimistic attitude toward members to provide hope.	Optimism is a learned characteristic that permits a person to view the world with hope-filled eyes regardless of the context.
Readiness	The leader assesses personal and organizational readiness to change.	Readiness refers to the predisposition that a person or organization has to change. The desire may be present, but readiness cannot occur without the will to act.
Safe environment	The leader creates a safe environment in which members are more willing to risk change.	A safe environment is one that is marked by trust. In this environment members feel free from attack and relax defensive routines.
Unconscious gap	The leader identifies the gap between actual and potential performance as the area to focus change efforts.	The unconscious gap refers to the distance between a person's actual performance and potential performance.

NOTES

1. McGregor, D. (1966). *Leadership and Motivation: Essays of Douglas McGregor.* Edited by W. Bennis and E. Schein. Cambridge, MA: MIT Press, p. 134.

2. McDermott, I. and O'Connor, J. (1996). *Practical NLP for Managers.* Brookfield, VT: Gower Publishers, p. 14.

3. Argyris, C. and Schon, D. (1974). *Theory in Practice.* San Francisco: Jossey-Bass, p. viii.

4. Schein, E. (1994/1999). Organizational and Managerial Culture as a Facilitator or Inhibitor of Organizational Learning. MIT: The Society for Organizational Learning. Retrieved August 15, 2001, from the World Wide Web: http://www.sol-ne.org/res/wp/10004.html.

5. Lewin, K. (1948). *Resolving Social Conflicts.* New York: Harper & Row.

6. Dilts, R., Allbom, T. and Smith, S. (1990). *Beliefs: Pathways to Health and Well-Being.* Portland, OR: Metamorphous Press, p. 3.

7. Maslow, A. (1971). *The Farther Reaches of Human Nature.* New York: Penguin, p. 31.

8. Loehr, J. (1994). *Toughness Training for Life.* New York: Plume, p. 134.

9. Senge, P. (1990/1994). *The Fifth Discipline: The Art and Practice of the Learning Organization.* New York: Doubleday, p. 14.

10. Argyris, C. (1999). *On Organization Learning* (2nd ed.). Malden, MA: Blackwell Business Publishers, p. 232.

11. Burns, J. M. (1975). *Leadership.* New York: Harper & Row, p. 455.

12. Kostere, K. and Malatesta, L. (1989). *Get the Results You Want.* Portland, OR: Metamorphous Press.

13. Direct quote from McDermott and O'Connor, *Practical NLP for Managers,* pp. 126–127.

14. Leri, D. (1997). The Fechner Weber Principle. *Mental Furniture #10.* Retrieved August 15, 2001, from the World Wide Web: http://www.semiophysics.com/mentfurn.htm.

15. de Mello, A. (1992). *Awareness.* Edited by J. Francis Stroud. New York: Image Books, p. 28.

16. Lewin, *Resolving Social Conflicts,* p. 66.

17. Schein, E. (1994/1999). Organizational and Managerial Culture as a Facilitator or Inhibitor of Organizational Learning. The Society for Organizational Learning.

18. Fromm, E. (1994). *The Art of Listening.* New York: Continuum, p. 68.

19. Senge (1994), *The Fifth Discipline,* p. 73.

CHAPTER TWO

KNOWLEDGE IS POWER

Strategy ■ *Knowledge Acquired from the Change Masters Fuels the Capacity to Change*

STARTING POINT

Effective leaders acknowledge that society is growing increasingly complex. Russell Ackhoff, management expert, stated:

> Because of the increasing interconnectedness and interdependence of individuals, groups, organizations, institutions, and societies brought about by changes in communication and transportation, our environments have become larger, more complex, less predictable, in short more turbulent.[1]

In essence, successful leaders, in touch with turbulent times, accept the notion that circumstances change. In my book, *Leadership Through Excellence*, I state:

> Change surrounds us. It always has been a part of the human situation. The difference between today and fifty years ago, is that change has accelerated to the point where we can often no longer anticipate change, but must adapt to it as part of the natural flow of life. Those who adapt to change will survive and thrive in the future.[2]

Those who understand the nature of change recognize that change is a complex and dynamic process. Change is a process requiring the leader's full attention and commitment. To lead change, twenty-first century leaders release previously held conceptions regarding leadership as vertical and isolated. They no longer consider change static, ordered, and easily manipulated. In addition to leading change, they act as facilitators and managers of change. Twenty-first-century leaders, to survive and thrive, need to understand change and the change process to further the aims of the organization.

REFLECTION IN ACTION

As you read the following case study, write down the principal's guarded thoughts and feelings that she hides from her faculty. Additionally, write the changes you think need to occur for the principal to be successful.

CASE STUDY

Gillian Broner, principal of Sunset Elementary School, leads a veteran faculty. Faculty members average twenty years of experience in her school. Gillian has been principal of Sunset for three years and feels a sense of frustration at introducing any form of change. Her initial efforts to lead change resulted in passive resistance at best and the feeling of being patronized by the faculty at worst.

At one time, Gillian considered herself a visionary leader; now she believes that the faculty has turned her into a manager. Gillian still believes she knows what should be happening at her school; however, she feels helpless in convincing people to join her cause. Listen to a conversation Gillian had with two respected teachers.

Gillian sat with the teachers in the teachers' lounge. After the preliminary small talk, Gillian summoned up her courage and said, "We have really got to change. The state department has new requirements for student achievement. We need to meet these mandates."

Mary, a first-grade teacher, replied, "Do you think the teachers in this school are incompetent?"

"I didn't say that the teachers were incompetent. I believe I said we need to change." Gillian could feel the tension rising in her stomach. She felt beads of perspiration on her forehead and under her arms.

Joan, another first-grade teacher, had her arms clasped tightly across her chest. She glared at Gillian, "If we're not incompetent, why should we change? I think we're doing a great job; don't you agree?"

"Yes, the teachers are doing a great job. It is just that the new requirements require different strategies."

"Gillian, do you hear what you are saying?" said Mary. "If we're doing a great job, and you admit that, why do we have to change? Besides, if you want us to change our working conditions, you'll have to take up your issues with our union. It's salary negotiations time."

Gillian smiled, changed the subject, and moved the conversation to a discussion about the teachers' grandchildren. After the meeting, Gillian stared out the window and wondered why she even met with the teachers.

Gillian's situation is common among leaders. She knows the what, why, and how to change as well as the direction the change should take. She is sure of the constructive consequences of her intended change plans. The faculty, however, are divided regarding her proposed changes. To her face, various faculty agree with her changes and then passively resist; other faculty openly resist any efforts to change; still others unquestioningly endorse the changes.

We can sense Gillian's thoughts as she considered setting up this meeting: They are the two most respected teachers on my staff. The parents love them and other teachers will do whatever they tell them to do. If I can get them to agree to my change plans, the rest will be easy.

Gillian's expectations for this meeting were high. She has excellent communication skills and the faculty like her as a person. Gillian had an internal and external reaction to Mary's comment: "Do you think the teachers in this school are incompetent?" She immediately felt a surge of anger and resentment. She forced a smile, not letting either teacher know that she was angry. She thought, I can't let them see my anger. I may need their help later on. What can I say to move them to my side of the table?

Any hope she had fell apart when Joan stated, "If we're not incompetent, why should we change? I think we're doing a great job; don't you agree?" Gillian's heart sunk; depression was not far behind. She knew she had lost. She knew that these two teachers were not going to change or to help her get other teachers to change. How stupid can I be, she thought, to agree with these teachers. I fell right into their trap. Now I can't ask them to change. Chapter Two focuses on the change principle that knowledge is power.

LEADERSHIP AND CHANGE

Leaders like Gillian understand that constructive change depends on the leader. They feel that the context dictates change; they rationalize that some environments change more readily than others. This is a leadership myth. Successful leaders know that change is inevitable and they make change possible.

As much as Gillian wants to change her school, if she lacks the leadership characteristics to lead, facilitate, and manage change, she will continue to feel frustrated. It may be that Gillian is unaware of her leadership deficits. Awareness is the start of the change process. As we become aware of the choices in our lives, we increase our options and improve the likelihood that we will make good decisions. This is true on an organizational level as well as a personal level. Unhealthy people and organizations operate with a zero-sum paradigm. For example, a principal operating with a zero-sum paradigm states: "Either we will implement this program in its entirety or we will totally discard it." This type of zero-sum thinking leads to little change and disastrous results. For these people, there is only one alternative and that is the opposite of their choice. They are unaware of the array of alternatives.

The lack of awareness extends to all aspects of our lives. We can sit in a room reading a newspaper and be unaware that our child sits in a corner, depressed. We can drive to work unaware that we are speeding. Awareness means to be mindful and to live in the present moment aware of the choices that the present moment has to offer. It also means that we are aware of our limitations as well as our strengths. Once we are aware of our limitations, if we are psychologically healthy, we take responsibility for those limitations and transform them into strengths.

Do you have the characteristics necessary to lead, facilitate, and manage change? The following assessment can increase your awareness of these abilities. Take the assessment along with Gillian Broner and see what you learn about your ability to lead, facilitate, and manage change.

PERSONAL ASSESSMENT ON PRESENCE OF LEADERSHIP CHARACTERISTICS THAT FACILITATE CHANGE[3]

1. I am open to multidimensional communication patterns.	Yes	No
2. I view people as the primary impediment to change.	Yes	No
3. The welfare and concerns of the members of my organization are not as important as my vision.	Yes	No
4. I get angry. It is normal, and I do not let it interfere with my work or work relationships.	Yes	No
5. I like to keep a tight control on every aspect of the organization. I feel better when I know that my employees finish tasks on time.	Yes	No
6. I like to delegate and share decision-making power with the members of the organization.	Yes	No
7. I can take or leave this organization and its members. They need my leadership skill; I do not need them.	Yes	No
8. You have to manipulate people to get things done.	Yes	No
9. If things fall apart, I am willing to take the blame; after all, I am the leader.	Yes	No

When Gillian took the Personal Assessment on Presence of Leadership Characteristics, she gained personal insights into her attitudes and behavior that contributed to her frustration in facilitating change in her school. Let's examine her assessment.

Multidimensional Communication Patterns

Gillian answered yes to item 1, I am open to multidimensional communication patterns. She is an active listener. She pays close attention to body language and other nonverbal signals. She makes sure that she understands what people mean by the words they use. She realizes that the same word often has a different meaning to different people. She knows that effective communication is a complex task. Adler states:

> In communicating, either in words, gestures or overall body language, we are seeking to get nearer to the "territory" of reality, but, more practically, we are trying to bridge the gap between our map of what is real and the map of the other person. Consequently, congruence between maps, or perceptions, and the transfer of understanding, rather than the futile quest for "reality," is our objective. And this is how we need to approach communication.[4]

This is an area of strength for Gillian.

People as the Primary Impediment to Change

Gillian answered yes to item 2, I view people as the primary impediment to change. Gillian's response limits her leadership effectiveness. Effective leaders know that organizational change happens with and through the members of the organization. Imposed change is temporary and leads to the creation of organizational resistance. The resistance, often covert, sabotages efforts at change and polarizes the leadership from the members of the organization. People are not the primary impediment to organizational change; Gillian's attitude toward her faculty is her primary impediment. When Gillian's attitude changes, she will find that the teachers suddenly become more cooperative and work with her to improve Sunset Elementary School.

Welfare and Concerns of the Organization's Members

Gillian answered no to item 3, the welfare and concerns of the members of my organization are not as important as my vision. This is an area of strength for Gillian; she gives primacy to people's needs. Gillian realized that her actions and beliefs were not congruent. According to McDermott and O'Connor, there are at least ten ways that people in leadership or managerial positions suppress organizational growth. Leaders suppress change when[5]

1. They regard any new idea suspiciously and insist that approval be a complicated process.
2. They give ambiguous messages.
3. They freely criticize others and withhold praise.
4. They blame individuals for problems.
5. They demand results and establish unattainable targets, introduce penalties, and reprimand those who make mistakes.
6. They exercise high levels of control.
7. They surprise people with their decisions to change and reorganize.
8. They manipulate the flow of information and deny legitimate access to appropriate information.
9. Their short- and long-term goals conflict.
10. They act rigidly, adhering to outdated rules.

Each of the above items impedes organizational growth. When these suppressing tactics are present in the organization, the welfare of each member suffers. Successful leaders know that organizational change takes place with the permission of the members of the organization. When leaders connect to the welfare and concerns of the members of the organization, members are more likely to trust the leader and support the leader's efforts to initiate change. Douglas McGregor asserts: "A fair amount of research has pointed up the fact that resistance to change is a reaction primarily to certain methods of instituting change rather than an inherent human characteristic."[6] The faculty in Gillian's school quickly recognized that her vision and goals took precedence over their welfare and concerns. As a result, they justified their resistance to her efforts to reform school practices.

Anger and Work Relationships

Gillian answered yes to item 4, I get angry. It is normal, and I do not let it interfere with my work or work relationships. This is a strength area because she is aware of her anger and keeps it under control. When we are unaware of our emotions, we are not in control of them. James Loehr, author of *Toughness Training for Life*, proposes that the first step to emotional control is to listen and analyze the messages that emotions are communicating. Emotions, when treated as messengers, lose their power to control our behavior.[7] When we are unaware of our emotions, we react according to previously learned behavioral patterns to various stimuli, often regretting our actions.

Control

Gillian answered no to item 5, I like to keep a tight control on every aspect of the organization. I feel better when I know that my employees finish tasks on time. This is a challenge area for Gillian. If she, however, maintains tight control to the point that it restricts faculty involvement and growth, it becomes a limitation. If she remains aloof from the change process and allows faculty to drift it also is a limitation. It is a strength as long as Gillian maintains a balance between the two polar extremes.

Effective leaders understand the necessary balance between tight and loose control. They know that absence of control produces anarchy and that total control produces robot-like performance. Psychologist John O'Neil maintains in *The Paradox of Success*

> Long-distance winners understand that true power lies in being able to let it go; they have learned how to do this, and when. For such men and women, the act of letting go provides a positive charge, enhancing their personal as well as professional strengths. Success sustainers also know that the exercise of control contains inherent risks of self-inflation, and must be carefully monitored, directed to specific goals beyond personal gratification.[8]

Gillian's hands-off approach allows her to maintain control over a program she wants to change. She needs to know more about the judicious application of control and its relationship to change.

Shared Decision Making

Gillian answered no to item 6, I like to delegate and share decision-making power with the members of the organization. This is a limitation for Gillian. Gillian recognizes that her espoused theory of believing in shared decision making is different from her theory-in-use. She has to learn to trust members of her organization or find that her ability to lead and manage change is severely limited. To date, however, her efforts to empower faculty to share in decision making are negligible. She knows that sharing in decision making is an act of trust. She does not trust her faculty. She feels that any faculty-driven decision will benefit the faculty, not the students. The faculty believe that Gillian does not trust them. As a result, they withhold critical information as well as participation.

Learning to trust requires letting go of control. It means that the leader recognizes a member's ability and has confidence in the member to successfully carry out a task without direct oversight. Successful leaders know that trust is an essential ingredient to effective leadership and constructive change.

Leaders and Members

Gillian answered no to item 7, I can take or leave this organization and its members. They need my leadership skill; I do not need them. Gillian's attitude is a strength area; she had little hesitation in answering no. She cares deeply about people. She lets go of hurts and can move forward in reconstructing damaged relationships. She understands that relationship building is at the core of leadership and change.

The famed psychologist Carl Rogers declared:

> If I can create a relationship . . . which I am by real feelings and by a warm acceptance of a liking for the other person; by a sensitive ability to see his world and himself as he sees—then the other individual in the relationship will experience and understand aspects of himself which he has previously repressed; will find himself becoming more integrated, more able to function effectively; will become more similar to the person he would like to be; will be more self directing and self confident; will become more of a person, more unique, more self expansive; and will be able to cope with the problems of life more adequately and more comfortably.[9]

Rogers places responsibility for relationship building on the person desiring to create the relationship. Relationship building is essential to creating a change-producing environment. It is at the core of leading, facilitating, and managing change.

Manipulation

Gillian answered no to item 8, you have to manipulate people to get things done. This is another strength area for Gillian; she knows that manipulation, even at its best, is using people without their knowledge to further one's best interests. At its worst, manipulation furthers the best interests of the manipulator without regard for the people being manipulated. Every person has felt the sting of manipulation. When we recognize that we are being manipulated, we respond negatively to the manipulator. We may ignore it because we suffered no injury, but we remember the manipulator. This person loses our trust and more importantly his integrity. The effective leader is honest with others, and when the leader is not able to communicate a complete truth, the leader informs others that there is a certain confidence that he or she is bound to protect. Leadership without integrity is an illusion.

Faculty Respect

Gillian answered yes to item 9, if things fall apart, I am willing to take the blame; after all, I am the leader. This is an area of strength for Gillian. The faculty respect her for her willingness to assume responsibility and for decisions that need her final approval. If failure occurs, she needs to work with the faculty member; however, she as the leader answers for the failure to her superiors. She remembers Yate's comment about failure in *Beat the Odds:*

> You've failed many times, although you may not remember. You fell down the first time you tried to walk. You almost drowned me the first time you tried to swim, didn't you? Did you hit the ball the first time you swung at bat? Heavy hitters, the ones who hit the most home runs, also strike out a lot. R. H. Macy failed seven times before his store in New York caught on. English novelist John Creasey got 753 rejection slips before he published 564 books. Babe Ruth struck out 1,330 times, but he also hit 714 home runs. Don't worry about failure. Worry about the chances you miss when you don't even try.[10]

She knows that her faculty, if given permission to try, will learn to be successful and learn to trust her leadership. Her belief in her ultimate responsibility for her school provides faculty with reassurance that they will not become scapegoats.

Taking the Personal Assessment on Presence of Leadership Characteristics That Facilitate Change makes it easier to understand why it is so difficult to bring about change. Gillian is like you or me. She is a composite of strengths and limitations. She is aware that she can no longer ignore her limitations and concentrate solely on her strengths. If she does, she compromises her leadership effectiveness. She will lead effectively when there is a match between context and her skills. She needs the ability to lead, facilitate, and manage change in every context. As part of her plan of growth to overcome her deficiencies, Gillian focuses on learning more about change and the change process. Gillian doesn't want to stymie her professional growth. She makes plans to develop professional growth strategies that will transform her limitations into leadership strengths.[11]

LEWIN, SCHEIN, ARGYRIS, AND MASLOW'S INFLUENCES ON CHANGE LEADERSHIP

Learning from Lewin

Psychologist Kurt Lewin's work is the basis for much of today's change theory.

> Few people have had as profound an impact on the theory and practice of social and organizational psychology as Kurt Lewin. . . . The power of Lewin's theorizing lay not in a formal propositional kind of theory but in his ability to build "models" of processes that drew attention to the right kinds of variables that needed to be conceptualized and observed.[12]

Leaders can learn from Lewin's work by applying the following principles that are directly applicable to the leader who wants to lead, facilitate, and manage change.[13]

BASIC PRINCIPLES FOR LEADERS
- Knowledge alone has no impact on change.
- If a person's perception of reality is faulty, education alone will not change that person's perception.

- Real change takes place simultaneously at three levels: conscious, subconscious, and testing levels.
- Change must be freely chosen and accepted.
- Forced change results in conscious and subconscious hostility.
- People cannot learn when they are being attacked.
- No change can take place unless the hostility to the new set of values is released.
- Successful change is directly proportional to the degree that the person changing participates in the planning and implementation of the change.
- Change in a person requires a change in the person's knowledge, beliefs, values, standards, emotional attachments, perceived needs, and real needs.
- Change can happen only if the person's environment supports the desired change.
- New values accepted by the person undergoing the change process have to conform to the person's superego if the change is to be successful.

Lessons from Lewin's Work for the Leader.   We can condense these change principles into three basic lessons for the leader: (1) Create an environment supportive of the change you desire. (2) Real sustained change requires that the people involved in the change must be involved in the planning and implementation of the change. (3) Change is a process that involves reeducation.

Lesson 1: Create an Environment Supportive of the Desired Change.   Leaders who understand this lesson know that although ideas and vision are important, an environment that supports those who want to change is even more important. The leader has to create and sustain an environment in which members considering change do not face loss of ego identity or of the values they bring to the organization. This type of environment doesn't force change; it allows change to happen. When the environment nurtures change among members, members willingly test the change and slowly adapt to the change. Through this process, they adopt the values inherent in the change environment and substitute them for the values they currently hold. They learn how these new values more constructively meet their needs.

Schein, who was influenced by Lewin, explains how Lewin's theory works:

> The true artistry of change management lies in the various kinds of tactics that change agents employ to create psychological safety. For example, working in groups, creating parallel systems that allow some relief from day to day work pressures, providing practice fields in which errors are embraced rather than feared, providing positive visions to encourage the learner, breaking the learning process into manageable steps, and providing on-line coaching and help all serve the function of reducing learning anxiety and thus creating genuine motivation to learn and change.[14]

The means to accomplishing this task requires the suspension of judgment and acceptance of each faculty member. The essential change takes place in the leader, not the faculty. When the leader suspends judgment, the faculty have no reason to be defensive and are more open to the flow of external information.

Lesson 2: Real Sustained Change Requires Involvement of Those Participating in the Change. Wholehearted involvement in the change process leads to lasting and effective change. Faculty involvement in planning and implementing change allows faculty to experience change on three levels: conscious, subconscious, and testing levels.

On the conscious level, faculty cognitively engage in the proposed change. Cognitive engagement in change creates subtle changes at the subconscious level. Even while the conscious mind struggles to grasp the intricacies of the change and the learning associated with the change, the subconscious mind begins to adapt to the change by creating new neural pathways. Imagine learning to brush your teeth with your nondominant hand. Your brain initially sends signals to brush your teeth in the same manner as you did with your dominant hand. The feedback the brain receives is that the original message is no longer valid. The brain then begins to create neural pathways until you can brush your teeth as well with your non-dominant hand as with your dominant hand.

Testing the change application reinforces changes taking place at the subconscious level. When the faculty member tests new values and matches the new values with his superego's expectations, it becomes easy to change. We can imagine this happening in an interracial faculty team in which one member of the team does not value diversity. The goal of the change effort is to assist this team member to embrace values consistent with diversity. The team, working on a project, invites the resistant member to participate. When the member makes proposals related to his values (antidiversity), the other members refrain from attacking (they created a safe environment). Instead, they show how the member's attitude is harmful to people and in violation of a superego value espoused by the member (fairness). The member begins to test the adoption of new values in his work with the team. He discovers that they are much like him. He drops his previous values and assumes the values held by the group. He becomes a spokesperson for encouraging diversity in the school.

Lesson 3: Change Is a Process That Involves Reeducation.   Reeducation is critical to the change process. Those participating in change need to "unlearn" past ways of acting and behaving and learn new ways of acting and behaving. This concept is critical for the leader desiring to lead and manage change.

Change is not an event; it is a process. Change happens over time; those who successfully change experience the reeducation process. Lewin tells us that in order for people to change they need to be reeducated and the reeducation has to result in the change of their knowledge, beliefs, values, standards, emotional attachments, perceived needs, and real needs. Lewin uses the terms *unfreezing, changing,* and *refreezing* to symbolize the change process.

Unfreezing is the reexamination, for validity, of currently held beliefs and values. Changing is the actual substitution of one behavior for another through the acquisition of new information and skills. Refreezing is making the new change a permanent part of the person's actions and behavior.

Changing requires the acquisition of new knowledge and skills. The new knowledge and skills have to demonstrate to the person undergoing the change that the change is beneficial to him or her. Some leaders make the error of suggesting that the important focus is on the effects in the classroom. Although that focus is ultimately important, the teacher will not accept the changes until he or she recognizes personal benefit. Once the teacher recognizes personal benefit, the teacher is ready to make the change permanent.

Refreezing is the solidification of change. This requires coaching, support, and patience with the person undergoing the change. If refreezing does not occur, change is short-lived. Imagine a teacher, for example, attending a dynamic teaching workshop at which her attitudes about teaching are disconfirmed and replaced with new attitudes. The teacher returns to school and implements new strategies and tactics. She even contacts the workshop presenter for guidance. Her grade-level teachers, however, rebuke her for the new methods and tell her that these new methods just don't work. The teacher quickly loses interest in the change and reverts to prior practice. The change was short-lived. Conversely, the same teacher returns to her school and finds her colleagues excited about her new strategies and tactics. The teacher becomes a source of knowledge for her colleagues. They reinforce the changes in this teacher, and in turn the teacher inspires them to change.

Learning from Schein

Edgar Schein's work focuses on organizational development and psychology. Schein's ideas about change draw heavily on Lewin's work. Schein integrates Lewin's work into examining organizational culture and organizational learning. From Schein's work, we discover basic principles related to the facilitation of organizational change through the encouragement of a generative learning environment.

BASIC PRINCIPLES FOR LEADERS
- Human change is an intense, psychologically animated, complex process involving conscious and subconscious levels of the mind.
- Change begins when there is dissatisfaction with one's present condition.
- If change is to occur, a sense of survival anxiety must exist.
- People and groups resist change when their fear of change outweighs their perceived need to change.
- Leaders can lead, facilitate, and manage change by reducing the fear associated with change to be less than the perceived need to change.
- Anxiety related to learning is the essential restraining force for change to take place.
- Sufficient psychological safety must exist if change is to occur.
- Organizational members learn something new through semantic redefinition, cognitive broadening, and the creation of new standards of judgment.
- For change to occur, the learner becomes skilled at how to change from observing effective models or from scanning.
- Organizations are composed of three separate cultures, which are often misaligned.
- The most effective way to understand a system is to try to change the system.

Lessons from Schein's Work for the Leader.   If we condense these basic principles derived from Schein's work, we generate four lessons to apply to the change process. (1) Leaders must become immersed in change. (2) Leaders exercise well-honed change-management skills. (3) Leaders align the three school cultures to create an environment conducive to change. (4) Leaders create and sustain parallel systems to foster learning and change.

Lesson 1: Leaders Must Become Immersed in Change.   If the leader proposes change from a detached distance, she will never understand the driving and restraining forces at play within her school. When the leader proposes change, she sets into motion a set of driving forces; she is often unaware that a set of restraining forces also exists. Many leaders, unaware of the restraining forces, intensify pressure on the driving forces, hoping to make their proposed changes succeed. This appears to be successful; it gives the leader a sense of victory in the change process. In the end, the change fails because the leader either failed to recognize the restraining forces or ignored the restraining forces and attempted to overwhelm them.

When the leader is immersed in the change process, she understands both the driving and restraining forces. By understanding the restraining forces, she realizes that the most effective way to change the organization is not by increasing the pressure on the driving forces for change, but by reducing the pressure of the restraining forces. Schein states: "We can concentrate on making the learner feel more comfortable about the learning process, about trying out new things, about entering the perpetual unknown."[15] Therefore, the leader's focus on reducing anxiety among those undergoing change in the organization reduces the restraining forces.

Lesson 2: Leaders Exercise Well-Honed Change-Management Skills.   Schein associates learning with change. He believes that learning organizations have specific characteristics when compared to organizations that seem stagnant. The leader who wants to lead, facilitate, and manage change can work to ensure that these characteristics are present in his organization. These characteristics include[16]

- A common concern for people (faculty, students, and parents)
- A belief that the faculty can and will learn and value learning and change
- A belief that change is possible and that the faculty can determine their destiny
- A commitment to diversity of people, thought, opinions, and attitudes to stimulate creativity and generative learning to spark change
- A commitment to creating open and far-reaching communication patterns
- A commitment to foster collaborative efforts to think systemically to examine multiple forces, short- and long-range consequences, and feedback loops
- A belief that interdependence is growing and independence is waning

The leader, by integrating these elements into the mundane activities of the school day, gradually transforms the school into a learning organization, capable of solving problems and sustaining change. These elements become the bedrock for organizational change. The consistent application of these elements creates an organizational culture that seeks to learn, embraces change, and moderates restraining organizational forces.

Lesson 3: Leaders Align the Three School Cultures to Create an Environment Conducive to Change.   Schein identifies three cultures that exist in every organization: executive, engineer, and operator. Each school also has these three cultures. The aims, patterns of communication, and allegiance of members of these cultures are different from one another.

The executive culture represents administration. These are the people responsible for the operation and sustained life of the school. Administrators have more in common with other administrators than they do with the members of the other two cultures within their school. They develop patterns of thinking, communication, and allegiance aligned with other school administrators, regardless of location.

The engineering culture represents department chairpersons, lead teachers, and people in supervisory positions such as athletic directors or special education coordinators. These people drive the school's fundamental technologies. They coordinate programs, monitor curriculum implementation, and manage the school's day-to-day operations. Members of the engineering culture operate in a buffer-type zone between the executive and operator cultures. They are responsible for the maintenance and transmission of the school's culture. If you were to imagine the school as a body, the engineering culture is the heart and arteries of the system.

The operator culture represents the school faculty. The operator culture delivers the operational production of the organization. The school faculty engage students in classrooms, deliver instruction, maintain order, and provide the basis for student achievement. The issues daily faced by teachers are far different from those of the other two cultures. Teachers' concerns focus on students and the ability of the teacher to deliver instruction to students.

For the leader to lead, facilitate, and manage change, he must understand the fundamental nature of these three cultures. Each culture has a different set of assumptions and beliefs about the other cultures. Each culture maintains a separate vocabulary and way of solving problems. In many organizations, these cultures are misaligned and communication nonexistent.

In schools in which the leader aligns the three cultures, people work together for common goals, and a sense of community exists within the school. The most effective strategy that the leader can employ to foster cultural alignment is to increase the level of meaningful dialogue within and between cultures. When we choose to enter into a dialogue with members of other cultures, we temporarily set aside our thoughts and assumptions of the other cultures. Physicist and philosopher David Bohm states: "A person whom we consider an enemy is an enemy only because of our thoughts. In general, our thought requires us to see based on memory and respond based on memory without really knowing what is really happening."[17] It is through dialogue that we learn about other people and their beliefs, assumptions, and ways of seeing the world. The leader takes responsibility for initiating the dialogue and as a result fosters the movement toward organizational cultural alignment.

Lesson 4: Leaders Create and Sustain Parallel Systems to Foster Learning and Change.
Parallel systems exist within all learning organizations. Schein states:

> If one studies organizational transformation, one finds that in every case the orga-
> nizational learning first began in an individual, then diffused to a group, and only
> gradually diffused from the group into the main body of the organization. Observ-
> ing this process carefully from a clinical perspective reveals that the group which
> initially learns becomes a parallel system.[18]

According to Schein, the leader must be a member of the parallel system for
the rest of the organization seriously to consider the proposed change. The parallel
system, operating with the leader's sanction, acquires new skills and implements
change on a micro basis. As the parallel group's skill level increases, it recruits and
attracts new members. The new members are taught the skills by their peers who
serve as models of the new behavior. Eventually, the parallel system grows to the
point that it constitutes a majority, making school-wide change an accepted fact.

Learning from Argyris

Chris Argyris is the James B. Conant Professor, Graduate Business School, at Harvard University. Argyris's work focuses on organizational learning and change.
His models for explaining organizational learning are essential pieces of change
knowledge for the leader.

BASIC PRINCIPLES FOR LEADERS
- People operate with a theory-of-action comprised of an espoused theory and
  a theory-in-use.
- Organizational learning occurs primarily as single-loop learning.
- Double-loop learning is essential to an organization's long-term effectiveness.
- Exclusive use of a model I theory-in-use makes it difficult to move to model
  II behavior.
- Within organizations, there are defensive routines that prevent a true appraisal
  of existing performance.
- Communication patterns within organizations prevent the acknowledge-
  ment of existing performance.
- Awareness of behavior is the starting point for change.
- Changing individual behavior and performance are at the core of improving
  organizational performance.
- A person's theory-in-use can be assessed only through observation of the per-
  son's behavior, not the person's description of the behavior.
- A participant must be involved in the change process to understand the
  change process.

Lessons from Argyris's Work for the Leader.   If we condense these basic principles derived from Argyris's work, we generate four lessons for the leader. (1) Differences exist between single- and double-loop learning. (2) Defensive routines are
eliminated. (3) Change occurs at the theory-in-use level. (4) Taboo subjects are
identified and openly discussed.

Lesson 1: Differences Exist between Single- and Double-Loop Learning. Single- and double-loop learning are essential in learning organizations. Leaders use single-loop learning to set patterns, establish routines, and resolve mundane problems. Single-loop learning is a linear response to problem-solving symptoms. In the case study, Gillian, when faced with a problem, uses single-loop learning. She meets with two faculty leaders hoping to convince them to support needed changes. Gillian's approach to this problem is soft. She presents her case, tries subtle pressure, and when opposition surfaces, she backs off and changes the subject.

The teachers developed a counterstrategy to subvert Gillian. Gillian is stuck with little hope for change unless she moves from single-loop learning to double-loop learning. Argyris states:

> I have coined the terms "single-loop" and "double-loop" learning to capture this crucial distinction. To give a simple analogy: a thermostat that automatically turns on the heat whenever the temperature in a room drops below 68 degrees is a good example of single-loop learning. A thermostat that could ask, "Why am I set at 68 degrees?" and then explore whether or not some other temperature might more economically achieve the goal of heating the room would be engaging in double-loop learning.[19]

Gillian, by employing double-loop learning, examines the values governing her actions. She realizes that maintaining peace is more important to her than is change. This is a difficult realization for Gillian. All along, she believed she was the change agent and the faculty resisted her efforts. Now, because she has the courage to examine her own motives, she can change. She chooses to place change ahead of peaceful coexistence. As a result, her actions change. She is now willing to risk making the teachers feel uncomfortable and ask them to reflect on their motivations and the potential consequences for not changing. This will be difficult for Gillian; she knows she has to change if faculty are to change.

Lesson 2: Defensive Routines Are Eliminated. Effective leaders recognize organizational defensive routines and move to eliminate them. Argyris studied more than 6,000 people and discovered that defensive routines are universal across cultures, countries, people, and organizations. We use defensive routines to refrain from examining our personal and organizational behavior. Consequently, we fail to understand how that behavior leads to negative consequences. Argyris believes that problems associated with learning and change result from the failure to deal with the potential embarrassment and threat linked to disclosing marginal performance, ineptitude, and gross errors. Instead, most people cover up embarrassing situations because it is easier than confrontation. Examine the following to see how defensive routines inhibit learning and change.

Michael Stone, a sixth-grade teacher, is liked by the entire faculty. They perceive him to be friendly, energetic, and cooperative. Michael has significant classroom control issues. The principal consistently rescues Michael. She transfers students from his class and allows Michael to refer students to the office for problems that Michael should handle. Michael is a burden to the principal, but because Michael is so well liked, she chooses to look the other way. She doesn't want to hurt

Michael's feelings. The result is that Michael doesn't grow. Resentment toward the principal grows among faculty. Michael's students continue to receive a substandard education.

Using the same situation, imagine Gillian Broner, principal, responding differently. Gillian asks Michael to meet with her after school. Gillian greets Michael at the door, thanks him for taking time to meet with her, and then motions for Michael to take a seat. Gillian sits across a coffee table from Michael. For all appearances, it seems to be an informal meeting.

"Michael, let's talk about the classroom management issues you're having."

"I'm not having any problems in my classroom. If I have a problem, I send the student to the office and you take care of it. I appreciate your assistance."

"That's exactly what has happened for the past two years. That's what we need to discuss. Michael, your referrals to the office are creating an unnecessary burden for the administrators and a morale problem among teachers."

Michael becomes defensive. His smile is gone. He folds his arms across his chest. His back stiffens and he sits erect in his chair. He doesn't look at Gillian. He stares out the window for a moment and responds: "Fine, I won't send any more students to the office. I'll just let them reign out of control in my classroom."

"That's not going to work, Michael. That's not acceptable to me, the parents, students, and you."

Michael shifts around in his seat. He is uncomfortable. He looks at his watch and realizes only minutes have passed. He knows he promised Gillian that they could meet for forty-five minutes. "The problem is the kind of students you assign to me. If I got the good students, I wouldn't have any problems."

"That's not true, Michael. The students you have are not having problems in other classes. Let's focus on you."

"I'm a good teacher. You're attacking me. I feel uncomfortable."

"I'm not attacking you. I'm trying to help you. You need to work with me so you can change."

"I don't know what to do. I don't know how to control these kids."

Gillian Broner had to work through Michael's defensiveness. It was not an easy process. Every leader, like Gillian, faces similar situations. Unless the leader recognizes the defensive routines employed by the teacher and has the courage to challenge these routines, change is impossible.

Lesson 3: Change Occurs at the Theory-in-Use Level. Each person has a theory-of-action. Theories-of-action have espoused theories and theories-in-use. Espoused theories relate to how we believe we act. They are the ideal way in which we see ourselves. Psychologist Karen Horney states:

> Conscious or unconscious, the image is always in large degree removed from reality, though the influence it exerts on the person's life is very real indeed. What is more, it is always flattering in character, as illustrated by a cartoon in the *New Yorker* in which a large middle-aged woman sees herself in the mirror as a slender young girl. The particular features of the image vary and are determined by the structure of the personality.[20]

Espoused theories may differ widely from theories-in-use. A person, for example, may believe that he is kind, although his theory-in-use demonstrates an arrogant, manipulative person. When confronted with his behavior, he reacts defensively because he recognizes only his espoused theory and not his theory-in-use. Argyris and Schon state:

> We cannot learn what someone's theory-in-use is simply by asking. We must construct his theory-in-use from observations of his behavior. In this sense, constructs of theories-in-use are like scientific hypotheses; the constructs may be inaccurate representations of the behavior they claim to describe.[21]

The path to change is to make the person become aware of his behavior and its extended consequences. Once he is aware of his behavior and extended consequences, he will be ready to acknowledge the discrepancy between his espoused theory and his theory-in-use. If you try to change a person's espoused theories, you attempt to change the person's self-identity. Most people will actively resist any attempt to change their espoused theories. Change, according to Argyris, takes place at the theory-in-use level.

Lesson 4: Taboo Subjects Are Identified and Openly Discussed.   Most organizations operate at a level at which members get along with each other and the leader gets along with members. On the surface, the organization appears to be a happy family. In most organizations, this is far from fact. Underneath the calm surface unresolved issues sit ready to explode. Argyris refers to these issues as undiscussable. Further, he discovered that within these social and professional groups, most people are unwilling to discuss why they cannot discuss the undiscussable. Members who venture into these taboo areas risk sanctions from the leader or members of the staff. A faculty member who states, "Why do we have to do it this way?" is likely to hear, "Because this is the way we've always done it." If the faculty member pushes his case, he faces increased resistance. If the faculty member asks, "Why is everyone resistant to talking about this?" he faces overt or covert sanctions. One senior class adviser, for example, was told by faculty members to stop sponsoring senior class activities because the faculty adopted a work-to-rule strategy in their negotiations with the school board. The adviser questioned this strategy, saying it wasn't fair to the senior class. The faculty refused to discuss the issue. When the senior class adviser continued sponsoring activities, the faculty shunned her; she resigned at the end of the year.

Effective leadership discusses the undiscussable. When undiscussable issues arise and faculty members avoid discussion, the effective leader encourages conversations related to why the issues are undiscussable. Learning organizations do not recognize taboo areas; everything is open to discussion.

Learning from Maslow

Abraham Maslow profoundly influenced thought on human behavior and motivation. Maslow brought a unique approach to psychology. Rather than asking the question, what's wrong? he asked, what's right? Maslow believed that if you want to find out how to become the best, look at the best and see what they do and who they are, and then model them. His research led him to identify self-actualizing people and the behaviors that self-actualized people consistently apply throughout their lives. His innate belief in the goodness of human beings led him to postulate that all people have an instinctive pull to becoming physically, psychologically, and spiritually healthy. It is from his profound optimistic belief in the desire of human beings for health that we gain deep insights into the change process.[22]

BASIC PRINCIPLES FOR LEADERS

- If leaders are to encourage change, they have to accept the members of their organizations with their inherent hereditary, constitutional, and temperamental differences.
- The leader's primary change focus is to help the organizational members grow to self-fulfillment.
- The leader creates an environment conducive to change by providing full access to the truth through available information.
- The leader must seek self-actualization as well as encourage other members of his organization to do the same.
- The leader assists members in overcoming the Jonah complex. This is a fear of greatness and the fulfillment of one's destiny.
- The leader helps others to change by facilitating their growth toward full potential.
- Change is a process of becoming aware of the present so that goals can be set to achieve one's destiny.
- Our environment determines, to a great degree, our ability to change and to maintain any substantive change.
- True change begins within the person and emanates outward.
- Before a person can change, that person has to have a set of life-sustaining values.

Lessons from Maslow's Work for the Leader. If we condense these basic principles derived from Maslow's work, we generate four lessons for the leader. (1) The leader promotes self-actualization. (2) Change is internally driven. (3) The leader facilitates change by constructing a positive relationship with the person desiring to change. (4) The leader eliminates the Jonah complex.

Lesson 1: The Leader Promotes Self-Actualization. Maslow asserts: "Operationally, this notion means that under good conditions, people can be expected to manifest such desirable traits as affection, altruism, friendliness, generosity, honesty, kindness, and trust."[23] Maslow believes that people are good and want to succeed. They do not go to work with the express purpose of subverting the leader's change efforts. Given this premise, the primary role for the leader, as change agent, is not to change people, but to create the optimum environment for human growth. Once the leader creates this environment, people will no longer be defensive and revert

TABLE 2.1   Personal and Organizational Elements That Act as Barriers to Growth and Change

ELEMENTS THAT ACT AS BARRIERS TO GROWTH AND CHANGE

1. Loss of zest for life (depression and cynicism)
2. Meaninglessness
3. Inability to enjoy work or people
4. Indifference to what is happening
5. Boredom
6. Life ceases to be intrinsically worthwhile and self-validating
7. Existential vacuum
8. Spiritual illnesses and crises, dryness, staleness
9. Sense of being useless, unneeded, of not mattering, ineffectuality
10. Hopelessness, apathy, defeat, cessation of coping, succumbing
11. Feeling totally controlled
12. Ultimate doubt. Is anything worthwhile? Does anything matter?
13. Despair, anguish
14. Joylessness
15. Futility
16. Cynicism, disbelief in, loss of faith in, or reductive explanation of all high values
17. Aimless destructiveness, resentment, vandalism

Source: Adapted from Maslow, A. (1971). *The Farther Reaches of Human Nature.* New York: Penguin, p. 308.

to the defensive routines that Argyris observes. Instead, they will automatically seek personally and professionally beneficial avenues.

Consider Gillian's situation. Gillian's school environment is toxic. A toxic organization sustains a specific set of ingredients that stunt growth. Maslow, in Table 2.1, indicates the elements that can be found in people and organizations that resist learning, growing, and changing.

Because Gillian's school environment is toxic, the members of her faculty fear risking new teaching strategies. They know, under present conditions, that they are likely to be treated as scapegoats by faculty ringleaders if they cooperate with Gillian's change plans. They are unsure of Gillian's reaction if they fail. They wonder if they can master the skills to be successful. If Gillian works to create a growth-oriented environment by having the faculty openly, and in a safe setting, talk about their fears, she will alleviate faculty fears and increase the number of risk takers.

Lesson 2: Change Is Internally Driven.   Maslow believes "In general, there is a reciprocal relationship between psychological health and McGregor's Theory Y kind of management. . . . This is to say that people who are healthier are more apt to hold to Theory Y in their spontaneous and instinctive management policies."[24] The effective change leader realizes that change begins with individual awareness. Only when the individual has an awakening experience can she freely choose to change. The leader works to create the correct conditions for the awakened experience by providing information, reflective discussions, and optimistic encouragement.

Lesson 3: The Leader Facilitates Change by Constructing a Positive Relationship with the Person Desiring to Change.   Maslow believes that change occurs when the leader creates an I–Thou experience with the other person; the person feels loved and accepted, and has a sense that he is worthy.[25] The effective leader understands that sound relationships are at the heart of all social institutions. The more we understand our interconnectedness, the more we understand our need to master the art of relationship building.

The leader builds successful relationships by creating an environment of unconditional acceptance. In our case study, Gillian feels frustration and anger toward the two teacher leaders who resisted her suggested changes. If Gillian reverses course and accepts these two teachers unconditionally, she will discover the teachers' fears masked by their bravado. If she accepts the two teachers unconditionally and moves to establishing a relationship, the two teachers will develop the confidence to share their fears with Gillian. Only then can Gillian work with the teachers to overcome their fears and freely embrace change.

Lesson 4: The Leader Eliminates the Jonah Complex.   Maslow believed that many people who have a depth and breadth of talent never achieve their talent because they harbor an innate personal belief like that of the biblical figure of Jonah: They fear their potential. The potential they have remains dormant. The person is alive, but never fully lives. The leader works to raise levels of aspiration among faculty, students, and staff. She challenges them to expect more from themselves. She doesn't let them settle for less than the full realization of their potential. The effective leader realizes that the healthy person always seeks to grow, change, and embrace new challenges. Accordingly, the leader acts as a catalyst so that the student, teacher, or staff member is growth oriented. Creating a school full of psychologically, physically, and spiritually healthy people generates conditions for continuous renewal.

CONCLUDING POINT

Gillian has a challenge. She considers herself a change agent who has a history of successfully bringing about change. Now, Gillian is more reflective. She assesses the change that she led in her previous positions and realizes that the change was temporary. Everything she did is now back to the way it was before she led those organizations. At first she thought she was superior to those who succeeded her; now she realizes that she did little to institutionalize change. She knows that the changes were externally imposed and not internally embraced. Gillian wants this situation to be different. Unlike her previous positions in which she had little opposition, she now has organized opposition that causes her to feel as if she is walking a tightrope. Fortunately, Gillian has help. The resources to be a successful change agent exist. She can apply the principles of Lewin, Schein, Argyris, and Maslow. Each approaches change differently; yet there are strong similarities among the different approaches. Gillian knows that organizational change begins with the individual. She knows that individuals will change when they are aware of their need to change. She also realizes that her primary task is to create an environment that is psychologically safe, is growth oriented, and works to benefit members.

SUGGESTIONS FOR ACTION

- Use the Personality Assessment on Presence of Leadership Characteristics That Facilitate Change to gain insights into your attitudes and behaviors.

- To what extent do you, as leader, act to suppress change or stifle the development of a learning environment?

- Identify the level to which you build relationships within your school. Commit yourself to building new relationships and improving those that already exist. Relationship building takes work, but the investment returns large dividends.

- Create a psychologically safe environment for members. Ask members to set ground rules and to identify what they feel are issues that they have previously considered undiscussable.

- Apply Argyris's concept of single- and double-loop learning. Begin by asking faculty to identify the governing values in a problem context and then ask what other governing values might be more appropriate.

- Ask the faculty to work with you in a self-assessment of the school's cultural attitudes toward administrators, teachers, students, and parents. Identify the difference between espoused values and the theories-in-use at work in your school.

CHANGE FACTORS

TERM	HOW TO USE IT	WHAT IT MEANS
Awareness	Leaders are cognizant of the present moment, assessing the steady stream of oncoming data so that they can appropriately direct change.	Awareness means living in the present moment by being aware of what is happening at any exact instant.
Dissatisfaction	Leaders create a state of dissatisfaction with the present status of the organization so that members willingly embrace the desire to change.	Dissatisfaction is a psychological state in which the person is no longer satisfied with his current state. As a result of this disequilibrium, the person moves to create a state of homeostasis, resulting in constructive change.

Double-loop learning	The leader resists efforts at the simple solution (single-loop learning). Instead, the leader focuses on examination of the governing values underlying decisions to make a better decision.	Reflective learning whereby members examine the governing values driving their decisions. It is a process governed by the asking of "Why?"
Espoused theory	The leader identifies the espoused theories of members of the organization and moves to align espoused theories with theories-in-use.	Those theories driven by governing values and communicated to others as to what is important in a person's life.
Parallel systems	The leader organizes small groups to implement change on a small scale parallel to the organization with the hope that the parallel system will eventually expand to encompass the entire organization.	The term refers to independent groups of people who operate within and yet apart from the system. The actions of these groups complement the organization and are used to test potential change.
Reeducation	Leaders facilitate the learning process whereby members learn new skills to replace outdated skills.	A term introduced by Kurt Lewin to indicate the need for new learning to replace staid ideas.
Self-actualizing	The leader helps to create an environment in which members seek to fulfill their potential.	A term coined by Maslow indicating a level of peak performance that demonstrates the maximizing of high levels of superior human qualities.
Semantic redefinition	The leader understands that people communicate through words. The leader helps to redefine terms so that they no longer act as stumbling blocks to growth.	This term, applied by Edgar Schein, refers to the reframing of words or terms. A problem, for example, is redefined to mean a challenge or opportunity and not an obstacle.
Theory-in-use	The leader watches members' actions to determine behaviors. Personal behaviors describe a person's theory-in-use, which is often different from the person's espoused theory.	The actual behavior of a person indicating his or her actual governing values.
Zero-sum paradigm	Identify instances in which the zero-sum paradigm is in play and move to expand alternatives.	A paradigm in which choices are forced between two alternatives. This creates winners and losers.

NOTES

1. Ackhoff, R. (1981). *Creating the Corporate Future: Planned or Be Planned For.* New York: John Wiley, p. 4.

2. Calabrese, R. L. (2000). *Leadership through Excellence: Professional Growth for Leaders.* Boston: Allyn & Bacon, p. ix.

3. Adapted from a list of characteristics of aggressive managers by Elbing, C. and Elbing, A. (1991). *Do Aggressive Managers Really Get High Performance?* Glenview, IL: Scott Foresman Professional Books.

4. Adler, H. (1996). *NLP for Trainers.* New York: McGraw-Hill, p. 50.

5. McDermott, I. and O'Connor, J. (1996). *Practical NLP for Managers.* Brookfield, VT: Gower Publishers.

6. McGregor, D. (1966). *Leadership and Motivation: Essays of Douglas McGregor.* Edited by W. Bennis and E. Schein. Cambridge, MA: MIT Press, p. 134.

7. Loehr, J. (1994). *Toughness Training for Life.* New York: Plume.

8. O'Neil, J. (1993). *The Paradox of Success: When Winning at Work Means Losing at Life.* New York: G. P. Putnam's, p. 106.

9. Rogers, C. (1956). *Becoming a Person.* Austin, TX: The Hogg Foundation for Mental Hygiene, pp. 6–7.

10. Yate, M. (1995). *Beat the Odds.* New York: Ballantine Books, pp. 305–306.

11. See Calabrese, *Leadership through Excellence,* for a detailed professional growth process for leaders resulting in the generation of a personal professional growth plan.

12. Schein, E. (1999). Kurt Lewin's Change Theory in the Field and in the Classroom: Notes Toward a Model of Managed Learning. MIT: The Society for Organizational Learning. Retrieved March 17, 2000, from the World Wide Web: http://learning.mit.edu/res/wp/10006.html.

13. These principles are taken from the following work: Lewin, K. (1948). *Resolving Social Conflicts: Selected Papers on Group Dynamics.* New York: Harper & Row.

14. Schein, E., Kurt Lewin's Change Theory in the Field and in the Classroom: Notes Toward a Model of Managed Learning. MIT: The Society for Organizational Learning. Retrieved March 17, 2000, from the World Wide Web: http://learning.mit.edu/res/wp/10006.html.

15. Schein, E. (1994/1999). Organizational and Managerial Culture as a Facilitator or Inhibitor of Organizational Learning. MIT: The Society for Organizational Learning. Retrieved March 20, 2000, from the World Wide Web: http://learning.mit.edu/res/wp/10004.html.

16. Adapted from Schein, E., ibid.

17. Bohm, D. and Edwards, M. (1991). *Changing Consciousness.* San Francisco: Harper & Row, p. 144.

18. Schein, E. (1994/1995). Learning Consortia: How to Create Parallel Learning Systems for Organization Sets. Retrieved March 20, 2000, from the World Wide Web: http://learning.mit.edu/res/wp/10007.html.

19. Argyris, C. (1999). *On Organizational Learning* (2nd ed.). Malden, MA: Blackwell Business Publishers, p. 127.

20. Horney, K. (1945/1992). *Our Inner Conflicts: A Constructive Theory of Neurosis.* New York: W. W. Norton, p. 96.

21. Argyris, C. and Schon, D. (1974). *Theory in Practice.* San Francisco: Jossey-Bass, p. 7.

22. See Maslow, A. (1971). *The Farther Reaches of Human Nature.* New York: Penguin.

23. Maslow, A. (1996). *Future Visions: The Unpublished Papers of Abraham Maslow.* Edited by E. Hoffman. Thousand Oaks, CA: Sage Publications, p. 83.

24. Maslow, A. with D. Stephens and G. Heil. (1998). *Maslow on Management.* New York: John Wiley, p. 97.

25. Maslow, A. (1970). *Religions, Values, and Peak-Experiences.* New York: Viking Press.

CHAPTER THREE

CREATE EMPOWERING MENTAL MODELS

Strategy ■ *Break Away from the Pack*

STARTING POINT

The principal turned to his assistant and said, "I just don't understand why these teachers don't see the need to change."

The assistant principal replied, "Maybe they see things differently."

Knowledge of mental models allows the leader to recognize the map that each member follows. Each of these maps operates within the framework of organizational maps. Neurolinguistic psychologists, however, are quick to point out that the map is not the territory. Physicist David Bohm suggests that many people follow their map as if it were the only map. A map, however, can act as a guide if the person considers the facts and does not rely solely on assumptions.[1]

Many researchers refer to these maps as mental models. Johnson-Laird, mental models researcher, states:

> Mental models provide a unified account of deductive, probabilistic, and modal reasoning. People infer that a conclusion is necessary—it must be true—that it is probable—it is likely to be true—if it holds in most of their models of the premises, and that it is possible—it may be true—if it holds in at least one of their models of the premises.[2]

Each person operates with a series of mental models to make sense out of his or her context. Likewise, organizations also operate with mental models. These models are part of the organization's culture. Each person in the organization creates a map of the organization. He uses his map to make sense as to how the organization works, its direction, as well as its policy application, symbols, and myths. These maps are mental models representing complex realities. Peter Senge states:

> The inertia of deeply entrenched mental models can overwhelm even the best systemic insights. This has been a bitter lesson for many a purveyor of new management tools, not only for systems thinking advocates. But if mental models can impede learning—freezing companies and industries in outmoded practices—why can't they also help accelerate learning?[3]

Mental models allow us to conceptualize what we believe to be reality. Imagine, for example, that each night as you enter your house you place your car keys on a hook near the garage door. This practice has taken place for so long that it is a thoughtless habit. On this day, you are engrossed with a problem that occurred at work. You enter your home, walk directly to your study, and absentmindedly place your keys on a bookshelf. An hour later, you decide to go to the grocery store. You can't find your keys. In frustration you shout, "Who took my keys? I left them on the hook." Your mental model told you where to locate your keys. In most instances, the mental model is accurate. In this instance, it is inaccurate.

Our mental models are closely connected to our identity; this close association prevents us from recognizing the existence of other mental models.[4] As a result, they prevent us from seeing what actually exists. For example, two school administrators observe the same class at the same time. One school administrator observes lack of organization, direction, and goals. The other sees a classroom with organized chaos, in which students move freely about, collaborate, and significant learning occurs. Two administrators report contradicting observations.

The identification of mental models is an important starting place for leading, facilitating, or managing change. Once the leader understands the concept of mental models, he can identify these models and manage them to lead the change process. The complexity increases because each organization has a number of simultaneously operating mental models within this complex situation; each organizational member, including the leader, operates with a personal set of mental models adding even more complexity. No wonder change is difficult! Learning about change starts with understanding mental models. Recognizing and understanding the function of mental models facilitate entrance into the organization's relational side. Here, the leader uses mental models as a guide to lead, facilitate, and manage change.

REFLECTION IN ACTION

As you read the following case study, write down the principal's guarded thoughts and feelings that he hides from his faculty. Additionally, write the changes you think need to occur for the principal to be successful.

■ ■ ■ ■ ■

CASE STUDY

Dr. Timothy Peerless is principal of Astin High School. It's 4:30 P.M. Monday. The site-based decision-making committee meeting has been going on for nearly an hour. Dr. Peerless's strategy seems to be working perfectly. He has saved the most difficult issue for last. He hopes the members are tired and ready to leave. All they have to do is to agree with him and he can start making the changes he wanted to make since his appointment two years ago.

Dr. Peerless shuffled through some papers and looked at the clock. "I know it's late, but I have one more item to discuss. I reviewed our achievement test scores for the past five years and I am detecting an alarming trend: Our scores, although good by comparison with similar schools, are not getting better. I want to institute a complete curriculum revision. Of course, I'll select a steering committee to help me with this project, and we'll keep this committee informed of our progress."

Mike Johnson, English department chairperson, couldn't wait to respond. His jaws tight and hands clenched as his voice rose with anger, "Now just wait a minute. This wasn't on the agenda. What are you trying to do? The English achievement test is in six weeks. Why don't we try what has worked so well in the past? We'll drill the students on vocabulary and ask the teachers in other disciplines to emphasize vocabulary in their classes. If all teachers increase the number of writing assignments to the students, we'll be able to improve our scores."

One of the teachers on the committee, Louise Sitowski, a well-known ally of the principal, responded. "Mike, that sounds like a short-term solution. We need to think long term. It won't hurt to give Dr. Peerless our endorsement."

"Louise, we don't have time to think long term; the test is in six weeks. Did you already forget?"

Pauline Curtis, mathematics department chairperson, supported Mike Johnson: "I think that Mike is right. We need to move fast. My teachers will cooperate. We can talk about Dr. Peerless's new idea at our next meeting."

Dr. Peerless sat frozen. He didn't want to demand that they implement his proposal. He needed the department chairs' support on the upcoming achievement test.

Mike Johnson, sensing Dr. Peerless's tentative behavior, asserted: "That settles it; I'll draft a plan and give it to Dr. Peerless to distribute to the faculty."

Dr. Peerless sat passively. How did he let this meeting get out of control? This was no solution. Finally, he spoke: "Mike, I appreciate your willingness to develop a plan for this year. With all due respect, your plan is only a temporary solution. I want a long-term solution, something that will move all of our achievement scores up a notch."

Pauline Curtis gave Mike Johnson a slight kick under the table indicating that she wanted to speak. She knew that Dr. Peerless and Mike Johnson were on philosophically different paths. "Sure, it's a solution. You're missing the point, Dr. Peerless. We are going back to what has always worked and it will work again. Let's finish the meeting. It's been a long day for all of us."

The room was stone silent. Dr. Peerless did not receive encouragement. He felt trapped. He felt that he had no other options. He looked at the group and stated: "Let's make it work. Achievement testing is important in this state. Our reputation is on the line."

How many leaders face situations comparable to that of Dr. Peerless? Let's listen to Dr. Peerless as he reflects on his situation: What am I going to do? Why can't they see the big picture? Don't they know that what they are proposing is only a Band-Aid approach? When I mention the bigger picture, they give me their standard line, "This worked before and it will work again." I'm not sure it will work again; yet, I need their support for my other initiatives. Maybe it will work; maybe we will get by this problem.

Dr. Peerless doesn't understand that the mental models his department chair-persons are following are different from his mental models. When people recognize only their own mental models without acknowledging the existence of competing mental models of equal and possibly superior value, they create conflict conditions. Conflict occurs over simple definitions and fixed ideas of intended outcomes. In this environment, change is unlikely to occur when members' positions become frozen. Kurt Lewin stated that the first step in change occurs in the unfreezing of held attitudes and assumptions. Chapter Three focuses on the principle of recognizing mental models. This principle, when followed, will allow the leader to reconstruct the organization's traditional maps.

RECOGNIZING MENTAL MODELS

A mental model is a device that each of us subconsciously builds. We draw from a set of mental models to address stimuli that we receive from a variety of contexts. For example, you are walking down a city street at night and you see a couple, apparently in love, walking toward you. Your brain, always active and always scanning the environment, recognizes this pattern and tells your conscious mind not to worry. You continue to walk down the street, perhaps smiling at the couple as you pass. What if the couple you approach appears to be fighting and one person pulls a knife? Your subconscious alerts your conscious mind and you have a different response. You call for help, someone calls the police, and you start screaming at the attacker. Both people stare at you and wonder why you are screaming. What occurred was a bartering session and one person pulled a pen out of his pocket and challenged the other person to sign a bill of sale. The gesturing was part of their culture. You are embarrassed. Your mental model inaccurately assessed the situation. You approached each of these situations with a predisposed strategy. You had no time to reflect or anguish over your decision. Your actions, driven by your mental model, set your behavior into motion, which in turn produced the embarrassing consequences.

Peter Senge states: "Our mental models determine not only how we make sense of the world but how we take actions. . . . Why are our mental models so powerful in affecting what we do? In part, because they affect what we see."[5] Because people comprise organizations, such as a school, the mental models of the organization's members determine how the school responds to its context. Dr. Peerless discovered a mental model in his organization: The quick fix is the most effective way to operate. Dr. Peerless recognizes that understanding this mental model and the others that exist in his organization is at the heart of change.

PURPOSE OF MENTAL MODELS

Mental models have three primary purposes: protection, overcoming anxiety, and efficient functioning.

Mental Models and Protection

Mental models serve as protection in the sense that they respond immediately to any perceived threat, much like in the case study. Our response to the threat is unique. As we created our mental model, we learned through experience and the trial and error associated with experience what worked and what did not. When strategies attached to a mental model worked and we removed the threat, we reinforced our mental model. When strategies failed, depending on the intensity of the failure, we altered our mental model because we did not want to experience the pain associated with the failure. We also create mental models out of knowledge. We apply the cumulative knowledge we gain in situations in which we perceive threat; if the knowledge we applied works, we write that information into the mental model program. If the knowledge fails, we continue to search for new knowledge that resolves the problem.

Mental Models and Overcoming Anxiety

The appropriate use of mental models protects us from our perceived personal struggle to survive. This is an evolutionary process inherent in all species. As we evolve physically, politically, socially, and spiritually, we realize that survival means learning to live in harmony with others, our environment, and ourselves. This is called social capital. According to Putnam, "Social capital refers to features of social organization, such as networks, norms, and trust, that facilitate coordination and cooperation for mutual benefit. Social capital enhances the benefits of investment in physical and human capital."[6]

To the extent that we are out of harmony with others, our environment, or ourselves, we experience anxiety related to survival. Einstein stated: "All human beings . . . are prisoners of their own egotism, they feel insecure, lonely, and deprived of the naïve, simple, and unsophisticated enjoyment of life. Man can find meaning in life, short and perilous as it is, only through devoting himself to society."[7] Einstein speaks of the importance of interconnectedness as a way out of anxiety. Mental models of healthy people and healthy organizations find ways to create and sustain interrelated connections.

In those situations in which anxiety is a norm, we can accurately assume that the person or organization is not whole. If anxiety becomes prolonged, we become depressed, suffer panic attacks, and in severe cases are unable to function. Because a primary function of human beings is to seek health, we form mental models to assist us in avoiding anxiety. Most mental models that seek to avoid anxiety frame themselves around control. Control is a typical human defensive routine that allows us to attempt to determine the outcome.

In a professional sense, we desire to control our circumstances to reduce instances of risk or humiliation. Whenever we fear risk or humiliation, our minds immediately put a previously successful mental model into operation to reduce the threat. Consider the case study: Here the two department chairpersons, without hesitation, reverted to a previously successful strategy. They did not stop to consider whether the effectiveness of the strategy permanently eliminated the problem. They applied a mental model that eliminated the immediate threat. This was their primary response.

Mental Models and Efficient Functioning

Mental models enable us to function efficiently by acting as adaptive learning instruments. The model constantly adapts to changing contexts by acquiring and processing new information. It becomes increasingly complex over time as it addresses numerous similar situations. This is part of its efficient nature. The mental model's efficient design prevents us from relearning each time a new situation arises. For example, as a child we learn to compete with other children in simple games. In a game of checkers, we learn that we do not move our red checker in front of a black checker and allow the black checker to jump. We learn to avoid being jumped and simultaneously gain strategic advantage over our opponent. As a result, we form mental models about competition. We learn what we had to do to win in competitive childhood games. We also learn the types of behaviors that contribute to losing. Because we desire to win more than to lose, our mental models form constructs for competitive situations. As we grow older, we apply our competitive model in situations that require us to compete. The more attention we pay to any of these models, the more complex the model becomes and the more effective its application.

MENTAL MODELS IN ACTION

All mental models operate the same way (see Figure 3.1). Visualize an air control tower at a busy airport. The air controller is constantly monitoring the radar screen. The screen continuously scans the environment for hundreds of miles to track the

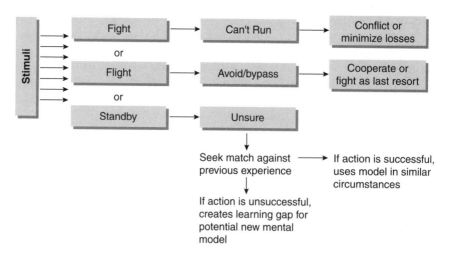

FIGURE 3.1   **Mental Models in Action**

movement of aircraft. The air controller is in constant contact with the aircraft. Our minds work similarly. Each of our senses, like the air controller's radar, continuously scans our environment. This happens whether we are aware or unaware of what we are doing. A mother of young children, while sleeping, ignores the sound of cars passing by her home. She ignores a distant siren or a cat howling outside her window, but she jumps up the moment she hears her baby cough in the next room. Even though the mother slept soundly, her senses scanned the environment screening incoming stimuli. Her prevailing mental model was to take care of her child. When her child made an unusual sound, her mental model moved immediately into action.

Our operating systems work constantly in the background monitoring the environment. As the stimuli arrive, they go through an initial screening to classify the stimuli as threats, nonthreats, or undetermined. If we classify a stimulus as a threat, we move toward three options: We fight, we prepare for flight, or we implement a mental model that handled a previously similar situation. If we choose to fight, our mental model immediately assesses the situation and provides a series of strategic options. If the forces against us are too strong, our mental model provides strategies that seek compromise and the minimizing of losses. If our primary mental model is to avoid the conflict and turn toward flight, the model generates strategies on bypassing, prolonging contact, or avoiding the situation. If we previously experienced a similar situation, we apply a mental model that successfully resolved that situation to dispose of the perceived threat.

We encounter obstacles when a new situation does not match our mental models. We are not sure how to proceed. Instinctively, like the department chairpersons in the case study, we revert to an old model. Subconsciously, we are looking for a solution that matches the new context. If our mental model resolves the situation, learning occurs. We now know that we can successfully use this mental model in similar circumstances. If our mental model fails to dispose of the situation favorably, we have a mismatch between our mental model and the new context. A gap exists between what we know and what we need to know to resolve the situation. In this situation, through trial and error and the accumulation of new knowledge, we create new learning. As a result, either we add to an existing mental model through the process of adaptation or we generatively create a new mental model to address the new context. Some people refuse to close the gap between what they need to know to resolve the context and what they know. These people condemn themselves to replicate nonproductive behavior, frequently resulting in negative consequences.

In our case study, Dr. Peerless has a mismatch between his mental model and the response of the site-based decision-making team to the problem situation. Dr. Peerless's operational mental model was to strategically wait until the meeting was nearly over, present the problem, offer a nonthreatening solution, and seek immediate closure. The department chairpersons, however, had a different mental model; they chose to ignore long-term solutions in favor of a short-term solution. Dr. Peerless has a gap between his existing mental model and this problem context. If he fails to close the gap through new learning, Dr. Peerless will continuously face frustration. The change needs to take place in Dr. Peerless, not in the department chairpersons. Most leaders focus their change efforts on the external resistance to change; however, the astute leader recognizes that the place for the most effective change is within the leader, and the locus of control is in adapting or creating a new mental model to handle the problem context successfully.

GOVERNING VARIABLES

Governing variables determine the mental model that we use in any context. These variables operate below the surface of our consciousness. They tend toward an idealized image. The variables project and defend our idealized image. A school, for example, that projects an idealized image of producing outstanding scholars will defend itself against any intrusion on that image. One high school in an affluent part of San Antonio, Texas, has a reputation for academic excellence. Because of changing demographic patterns, the school's population changed over the years. The teachers, however, fought to maintain the idealized image by teaching as if they had the same students. The teachers and administrators ignored a student dropout rate until the state department of education classified the school as a low-performing school. This embarrassment triggered important changes in policy and behavior.

Governing variables are tied directly to our idealized image; our idealized image aligns with our self-image. These variables operate to make sure that our self-image is not hurt by ordering mental models into action to defend the self-image. Although our governing variables are unique, researchers such as psychologist Karen Horney and organizational development expert Chris Argyris indicate that patterns of governing variables exist. According to Karen Horney, each person has a primary worldview.[8] Some people move toward people, others move against people, and others move away from people. People who move toward others believe that the world is a friendly place. Those who move against people believe that the world is an unfriendly place. Those who move away from people are ambivalent and desire to be left alone. Although each of us operates in all three spheres, we function primarily out of one model. Argyris suggests four different governing variables: maximize control, maximize winning and minimize losses, suppress feelings, and rationalize behavior.

To understand how governing variables influence mental models, we integrate Horney's model with that of Argyris (See Figure 3.2).

Figure 3.2 illustrates Horney's three primary personality styles and Argyris's representation of human behavior. Each of Argyris's behaviors can occur within

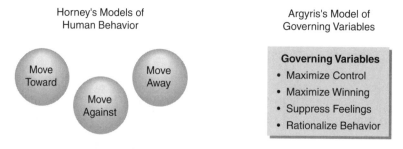

FIGURE 3.2   Governing Variables and Mental Models

each of Horney's personality styles. The manner of behavior is different within each personality style. For example, people who move toward others will seek to maximize control by collaborating and helping others. They will ingratiate and manipulate people into doing what they want done. Those who move away from others seek to maximize control by maintaining personal independence.[9] In each case, the governing variables suggested by Argyris are incorporated into specific mental models driven by each individual's personality. In other words, we might have the same end in mind, but our paths to the acquisition of that end are different. Understanding individual personality styles helps us to identify the motivation inherent in governing variables. It also helps us to realize why people don't understand what we want to do, or if they do understand, why they disagree with what we want to do. In effect, understanding personality style enables the leader to identify the mental models being used by the members of his organization.

MENTAL MODELS IN ORGANIZATIONS

Organizations also have mental models. Organizations are learning organisms, constantly adapting to a changing environment. An organization begins with a set of mental models; over time, the organization's original set of mental models changes through adaptation and new learning. Organizations that adapt their mental models to meet current and future demands survive, whereas those that hold on to outdated mental models become a memory. In the last fifty years, for example, buggy factories became automobile manufacturers, the corner grocery store gave way to the supermarket, the prairie gave way to the city, the slide rule gave way to the calculator, and wire-driven technology is giving way to wireless technology. Organizations that are unaware of what is developing around them soon find themselves in positions in which they are unable to adapt rapidly, which raises the question of their survival.

These organizations attempt to interpret the world with outdated mental models. As a result, they ignore the incoming data as irrelevant or apply the prevailing mental model to the incoming data provoking an inaccurate response. Our case study provides an excellent example. The department chairpersons are unable to see the external threat posed by static test scores. They are unaware of the relationship of the test scores to the community's future willingness to support a much needed bond issue. The chairpersons have a shortsighted vision with little relationship to long-term consequences. Peter Senge, learning organization expert at MIT, states:

> I am increasingly convinced that this lack of implementation is not the result of poor management. Rather, the process of adoption fails because the new ideas are at such variance with mental models currently accepted by the organization. More specifically, new insights fail to get put into practice because they conflict with deeply held internal images of how the world works, images that limit us to familiar ways of thinking and acting. That is why the discipline of managing mental models—surfacing, testing, and improving our internal picture of how the world works—promises to be a major breakthrough for building learning organizations.[10]

Mental Models in Schools

Schools, like other organizations, employ mental models. A mental model may act as a regressive agent and prevent schools from embracing substantive and sustained change. Figure 3.3 represents a systemic look at a change attempt in a school organization. This figure, still incomplete, demonstrates the complexity associated with organizational change. In the figure we examine the panoply of forces driving and restraining change. The problem, according to Senge, is not the people, but the way we look at change. If we continue to view change individually, according to Senge, then we will continue to blame people without considering the real source of the problem, the systemic issues that will cause the same problem continually to reappear. Systemic considerations make change look more like a swirling river than a quiet pool.

The complexity of this figure helps us to understand the field forces that Lewin emphasizes affect change. In this mental model, the driving forces, those desiring change, are in *italics*. The restraining forces, those resisting change, are underlined. In this case, the administration feels the driving forces for change coming from the state department of education, school board, community, parents, and private sector. The administrators apply the driving forces for change to teachers and students. The teachers resist the administration's driving force for change. The resistance is natural. It emanates from the teachers' culture, identity, union, and fear of the unknown. The students also resist. They apply their restraining forces against teachers and parents. The school administrators, faced with mounting

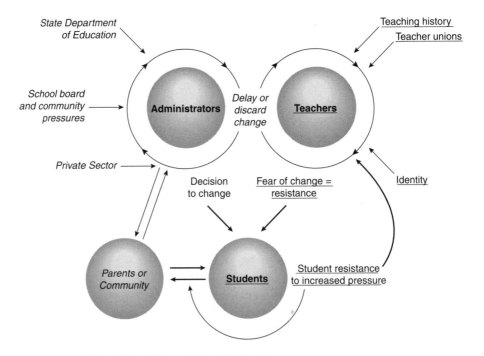

FIGURE 3.3   **Prevailing Change Mental Model**

pressure, discard, delay, or opt for a satisficing strategy. In satisficing strategy the problem solvers adopt the first seemingly satisfactory option. They fail to take the time to generate and consider other alternatives. In our case study, Dr. Peerless allows his group to adopt a satisficing strategy.

The result is a classic battle for control and clear description of the contest for dominance between driving and restraining forces. A power struggle usually results in administrators negotiating the rate of change in exchange for a reduction in the level of resistance. Administrative action forces teachers to negotiate with students over the rate of increased work in exchange for student compliance and productivity. A large general contract between administrators and teachers governs these negotiations. The administrator also negotiates with individual teachers, applying leverage when possible. As a result, some teachers will apparently agree to change whereas others will not. Consequently, although the espoused theory of administrators and teachers focuses on student achievement, their theory-in-use focuses on the governing variables of control over the work environment. In this model, the school administrator acts as more of a manager than a leader and more of a facilitator than a visionary.

Fortunately, the leader does not have to fall into this trap. He can learn from Kurt Lewin. Lewin teaches that personal change requires the person to acquire a new knowledge base. Acquiring this new knowledge base compels the person to learn how to do things differently, think differently, and view the context differently. When the person acquires this type of learning, the person's knowledge base, beliefs, values, standards, emotional attachments, and personal desires change. In effect, the person becomes a new creation with different ways of seeing reality. The person's change results in the acceptance of a new culture that the person develops and creates for himself.[11] The leader, as change agent, acts as a facilitator of the learning process. The leader creates new conditions in which change becomes a viable option for each person affected by it.

Leaders who facilitate the learning process identify driving and restraining forces within the organization. When driving and restraining forces are ignored, the struggle for control dominates. The effective leader moves beyond the control game by identifying mental models and the driving and restraining forces at work in the mental models. She then concentrates on reducing the level of resistance rather than concentrating on increasing the pressure of the driving force.

IDENTIFYING MENTAL MODELS, DRIVING FORCES, AND RESTRAINING FORCES

The identification of mental models, driving forces, and restraining forces is a cooperative and reflective process. The leader moves the faculty toward greater awareness of existing conditions. The leader knows that each condition is a symptom. He uses these symptoms to facilitate a learning process designed to identify the sources of the symptoms. The sources for symptoms are both organizational and individual. They are individual in the sense that the interactions between and among members of the school organization create or destroy a climate conducive to constructive change. They are organizational in the sense that the organization, over time, takes on an individual identity as members enter and leave. The organization develops an established way of accomplishing tasks and fits new members into this process. Identifying existing symptoms and their source is a critical first step, yet their identification is impossible without the presence of two essential organizational characteristics: honesty and trust.

Honesty and Trust

Honesty and trust allow organizational members to identify accurately the organization's theories-in-use. Trust is essential because members who do not trust will refuse to name existing theories-in-use if they feel that they will be the objects of reprisals. We have all heard of individuals in corporations who were "whistle-blowers." They described the illegal behavior of the organizations and how the organizations' members covered up this behavior. When they brought the behavior to the attention of the public, the organizations fired the members for being honest. The organizations' behavior sent a significant message to the members: Don't be honest and don't describe our theories-in-use. In a news report taken from the *St. Louis Post-Dispatch,* the dangers of being a whistler-blower were made clear.

> "There are things that many of them go through, like post traumatic stress syndrome. And if they don't get fired, often they will be stuck where they are. Promotions just don't happen," he said.
>
> Jeff Ruch, executive director of Public Employees for Environmental Responsibility in Washington, said that Donald Sweeney [whistle-blower] is in many ways atypical. Ruch's group has been helping Sweeney.
>
> "He is not a biologist, a botanist or an earth scientist, the people who usually step forward. He comes from the 'dismal science,' and there aren't a lot of economists that become whistle-blowers," he said.
>
> Ruch said that he advises people not to blow the whistle because the costs to them, both personally and financially, can be great.[12]

When trust doesn't exist, people are reluctant to name existing theories-in-use. Instead, they opt to describe the organization's espoused theories, that is, the behavior that matches the organization's ideal. They describe espoused behavior in relationship to organizational activities, themselves, and their colleagues. If there is a blatant mismatch between a colleague's espoused theory and its theory-in-use, members, in general, find an excuse to explain the difference. For example, a teacher's behavior toward students may be clearly abusive. The teacher's colleagues and administrators espouse theories that would not allow abusive behavior. They, however, do not address the teacher's behavior, but speak of the stress in the teacher's private life. Their theory-in-use ignores or denies the existence of the teacher's abusive behavior.

Creating Climates of Trust.   Trust within the organization creates the conditions for honesty. According to psychologists McDermott and O'Connor, members trust the leader when they see that the leader's actions and words are consistent. Trust, although built by integrity, requires the leader to treat people as if they were trustworthy. People who do not trust other people do not trust themselves.[13] Where mistrust exists, people are prone to act defensively. Mistrust becomes a primary source for the withholding of vital information and support.

Each member of the school organization is responsible for contributing to a trust-filled environment. To the extent that each member makes a commitment to creating this environment, members will trust each other. Conversely, a single member can disrupt and destroy a trust-filled environment. The leader, committed to leading through change, understands that a trust-filled environment is central to his efforts. The leader employs several strategies. He honestly examines his actions to make sure that each action builds trust. He creates dialogue opportunities with the members of his organization and community. He focuses on the process and not on the outcome. He eliminates behaviors that separate, segregate, or punish.

The effective leader who creates a trust-filled environment recognizes that trust flows from her personal interactions with others, the observation of her behavior, and of her ability to sustain her integrity in a myriad of contexts. The effective leader creates an environment of trust by increasing opportunities for dialogue. It is through dialogue that the leader brings diverse groups of people together to generatively create mutually beneficial conditions. According to the Global Dialogue Institute,

> If the world is to benefit from the tremendous creative power of the different cultures and religions and diminish their potentially destructive forces, we must join together, regardless of faith, ideology, or culture to confront the threats to the world: injustice, violence, poverty, and the destruction of the global ecosystem. By engaging in dialogue, holders of different worldviews and believers of different faiths can learn from each other, and change. Through dialogue, we can promote better understanding of and creative cooperation among cultures and religions, while acknowledging and accepting their differences.[14]

Dialogue is at the heart of trust. When members of the organization join in dialogue, they express their opinions and feelings knowing that those receiving the communication actively listen without making judgment. Nothing is hidden. Suppressed issues are brought to light. Dialogue is difficult because people identify with the issue and it forces the members of the organization to discuss what is uncomfortable. Swidler states:

> In dialogue, each partner must listen to the other as openly and sympathetically as s/he can in an attempt to understand the other's position as precisely and, as it were, as much from within, as possible. Such an attitude automatically includes the assumption that at any point we might find the partner's position so persuasive that, if we would act with integrity, we would have to change, and change can be disturbing.[15]

Dialogue requires members to commit to seeking mutual understanding. It places responsibility on each member to raise unresolved issues. In this sense, dialogue is open, honest, and free from attack. It is the only way through seemingly irresolvable issues to a common understanding.

The leader encourages dialogue by focusing on the process rather than the outcome. By focusing on the process, the leader creates conditions in which bias drops, members set aside their natural defensive reactions, and learning occurs. Focusing on the process centers on human relationships and the understanding that goes into building those relationships. It is out of relationship building that the process allows members to work in solidarity. Members learn to cooperate to achieve mutually beneficial outcomes conducive to change. Psychologist Eric

Fromm believes that the interpersonal relationship between the person trying to facilitate change and the person wanting change is crucial to the whole process.[16]

The effective leader recognizes that trust cannot be built in an environment in which members build political coalitions, operate with cliques, or base membership in groups on biased criteria. He knows that this type of behavior sets up a continuous struggle for domination and power. Groups take turns at ruling and implementing specific agenda-driven goals. These goals, once implemented, never receive the full support of the group, because the minority waits until they become the majority and bring their agenda forward. The effective leader knows that there is a better way.

Reflective Awareness as a Means of Identifying Mental Models

Reflective self-awareness connects us to the present moment. It allows us to examine our current actions and the consequences that result from these actions. In reality, both the past and the future do not exist. If we are to connect to what we are doing individually and to what we are doing organizationally, we examine our current actions. We become aware of our decisions, attitudes, rules, and actions. If we examine each of these areas in a detached, nonjudgmental way, we gain insight into the mental models that drive our personal and organizational behavior.

Through reflective self-awareness, the person or organization identifies the driving and restraining forces inherent in their mental models. Otherwise, the focus remains on symptomatic issues, not on the real area for change. In our case study, for example, neither Dr. Peerless nor his department chairpersons are aware of the mental models that drive their behaviors. Both agree on the outcome; they disagree only on the means. The department chairpersons want a quick fix, while Dr. Peerless, still focusing on the scores, wants to ensure that scores continue to improve over time. He disagrees with the quick fix, yet he feels too politically insecure to address the issue with his department chairpersons. If Dr. Peerless and the department chairpersons were aware of their driving and restraining forces, they would discover common ground and move to a constructive and mutually beneficial outcome. Identifying the driving and restraining forces requires reflective self-awareness grounded in trust and honesty.

Driving forces control the direction of flow within the organization. These forces may be reasons, people, political pressures, values, or beliefs. The restraining forces operate to mediate the direction and speed of flow. Imagine yourself jogging. The driving force motivating your jogging may be to improve your health, lose weight, reduce stress, or maintain your physical condition. The initial restraining force may be the weather, time commitments, or a sense of lethargy. Once you start running, your body loosens up, you run a little faster, and at some point you may feel you could run forever. All the while, your brain is sending signals to your muscles; your muscles accumulate lactic acid and begin to fatigue, you begin to sweat, your temperature rises, and you realize that you need to end your run. Your restraining forces eventually overwhelm your driving forces. The pattern of interaction of driving and restraining forces in this example perseverates in many other forms. In our case study, for example, Table 3.1 illustrates the same type of interaction among the driving and restraining forces.

TABLE 3.1   Identifying Driving and Restraining Forces

GROUP/PERSON/ ORGANIZATION	DRIVING FORCES	RESTRAINING FORCES
Dr. Peerless	Pressure from the superintendent State mandates on achievement testing Personal reputation Personal ambition Parental ambitions for children to go to selective colleges	Reluctance of department chairpersons to consider long-term view Perceived need to cooperate with department chairpersons Desire to maintain cordial relationships Desire not to disturb morale at a critical time
Department chairpersons	No desire for extra work Reliance on past methods that worked Time pressures Pressures from department faculty Sense of power from longevity in school system	Principal's pressure Some faculty members who desire substantive change Pressure created by state mandates

Dr. Peerless's frustration comes from the reluctance of his department chairpersons to consider change. After examining the driving and restraining forces, Dr. Peerless realizes that his department chairpersons do not fear change. Their anxiety results from time pressures and a perceived belief that faculty members don't want to change. Dr. Peerless realizes that he has to change his strategy and discover strategies to assist his department chairpersons in reducing the faculty members' fear of change. He has to be cognizant of the real and perceived time and work load demands of the department chairpersons. Dr. Peerless now feels better about the short-term solution proposed by the department chairpersons. He decides to live with this solution and begin to plan strategically for long-term substantive change.

Reflective self-awareness in identifying the mental models that harbor the driving and restraining forces takes great courage because we have to identify our behavior and acknowledge responsibility for the consequences of our behavior. For change to occur, a behavior has to be dropped and replaced with another behavior. MacDonald and Bandler, change researchers, state: "If behavior is the consequence of a learned response, then change requires that something else be learned in its place."[17] Identifying our mental models and their driving and restraining forces requires reflection on our behavior and the consequences produced by that behavior. It also requires us to examine the forces that produce our behavior. Once we identify these forces, we learn to control the direction and pace of change in our lives and in our organizations.

Reflection in Action

Reflection is at the core of change. Reflection is a tool that effective leaders use to examine beliefs, theories of action, or organizational purpose. According to Dewey, reflective thought "is the active, persistent, and careful consideration of any belief or supposed form of knowledge in the light of the grounds that support it and the further conclusions to which it tends."[18] Reflection, as it applies to the discovery of mental models, focuses on the present; it does not purposefully delve into the past. Reflection requires that the leader accurately perceive present circumstances. The leader must be aware of his biases and other filters that obscure the present reality. Donald Schön states:

> By organizational inquiry, I mean the business in which individual members of the organization think about problems, talk about them, design experiments, probe situations through interactions with one another and in ways that leave residue that can be embodied in organizational artifacts, such as files, memories, maps and programs for future organizational life. I think that organizations don't learn, people do. But people can learn on behalf of organizations; and individual learning becomes organizational when it results in change of organizational theory of action, embodied in organizational artifacts.[19]

Reflection becomes a group activity when the group collectively examines its present state, reflects on how it arrived at its present state, and visualizes where the journey leads if current mental models are retained. For an organization to become a healthy learning organization, reflective practices by individuals as well as the collective membership are essential. In either case, the process of reflection operates in a detached, nonjudgmental, fashion. By removing judgment from the observation of behavior, the observer sees the action with clarity. If the observer judges the action as good or bad, the observer immediately stops observing and continues to judge based on a preconceived standard that may or may not be appropriate or accurate. W. Timothy Gallwey, writing in his best-selling book, *The Inner Game of Tennis,* states: "What I mean by judgment is the act of assigning a negative or positive value to an event. . . . Thus, judgments are our personal, ego reactions to the sights, sounds, feelings and thoughts within our experience."[20]

In our case study, Dr. Peerless employs a reflective strategy. He says, "Let's look at our achievement scores. Is there a pattern?"

Ms. Sitowski responds: "Our scores seem stagnant."

Dr. Peerless: "Let's brainstorm all the possible reasons for this stagnation."

Each member of the group focuses on brainstorming. Dr. Peerless refrains from judgment. Instead, he alters the group's focus and allows members to engage in the discovery process. This process requires the leader to have the skill, the patience, and the belief that the members, if properly led, can discover their mental models and choose to revise those mental models that restrain growth.

CONCLUDING POINT

Dr. Peerless found himself caught in a trap he did not consciously create. He followed the steps of other leaders. Dr. Peerless became a victim to personal and organizational mental models. As soon as Dr. Peerless questioned his mental models and those of his organization, he ceased to be a victim. He never thought of the concept of mental models, but the more he reflected on this concept the more he realized that he operated with a number of mental models. These mental models dictated how he interacted with his wife, children, neighbors, church members, and colleagues. He had a mental model that fit every situation. He recognized that the continuance of outdated mental models forced him to control the behavior of others, to fit them into his mental model. In his efforts to control others, he employed a variety of tactics from the use of power to manipulation. Sometimes, when his tactics seemed to fail, he tried to negotiate and minimize his losses. As he reflected, he realized that some of his mental models were outdated. It was time to change.

Dr. Peerless now understands the usefulness of updated and effective mental models. He realizes that his school has mental models that need to be updated. The most effective way to update mental models is through reflective self-awareness and reflection in action. Dr. Peerless found reflection in action a little awkward at first, but persisted in honing his skills. He discovered that his department chairpersons and faculty members are not enemies but members of his team, fully invested in making their school a learning organization based on trust and honesty. He began to change. In changing, Dr. Peerless realized he was stimulating the change process within his school.

SUGGESTIONS FOR ACTION

- Assess the level of psychological safety in your school organization. Is your environment toxic or healthy?

- Consider a major problem that you are facing. What is the mental model that drives the problem and its potential solution? Draw the mental model so that its construction looks similar to Figure 3.3. Continue to construct the model until you understand what is occurring in the problem and solution construction.

- Consider a present issue faced by your school or school district. Can you determine the driving and restraining forces that are influencing this issue? Where can you apply leverage to influence this model? Can you determine where you have been applying leverage? Is it possible for you to discover common ground between your driving and restraining forces and those who have a different perspective as well as different driving and restraining forces?

- Do you take time for reflective self-awareness? Take ten minutes each day to get in touch with your context. Determine what you feel emotionally and physically. Listen to your breathing. Become aware of the sights and sounds around you. This practice will soon translate into action as you become more aware of what others are feeling and saying. You will live more in the present moment.

- Practice reflection in action with the members of your school faculty and other school groups. Reflection in action is a gentle way of examining the present context and entering into the discovery of the reasons for the current context and the consequences for maintaining the identified mental models.

CHANGE FACTORS

TERM	HOW TO USE IT	WHAT IT MEANS
Defensive routine	The leader identifies personal and organizational defensive routines as a means of reducing resistance to change.	Defensive routines refer to those organizational and human actions that are put into play whenever a person or the organization feels the risk of threat or embarrassment.
Dialogue	The leader moves the level of communication from discussion to dialogue as a means of having members of the organization understand the values and motivation behind one another's actions.	Dialogue is a communication process by which people work toward mutual understanding and each member raises unresolved issues.
Idealized image	The leader identifies the gap between the idealized image and the current state to encourage new learning and change.	The idealized image is that image we have of the organization or ourselves that is not based on reality but on the ideal that we would like to be. It is the cause of problems when people believe they are their idealized image.
Mental model	The leader identifies the mental models in use by the organization and members as a primary means to understand the human and organizational forces affecting change efforts.	A mental model is a subconscious cognitive construct used to make sense out of a context. Mental models may be based on erroneous as well as factual information.
Reflection in action	The leader examines the context and reflects on how the context evolved and on the forces at play within the context; aware of this data, the leader acts based on his or her reflection.	The art of examining the context and the influence of personal filters on the interpretation of that environment and then acting accurately and appropriately as demanded by the situation.
Social capital	The leader acts to increase the social capital among members in the organization. By increasing social capital, the leader adds to the "glue" that holds the organization together.	Social capital refers to the connections within the organization that make people feel connected to one another; it is the bond that ties human beings to each other in a common cause.
Trust	A primary leadership task is the building of trust. Trust is the substance that the leader will use to gain member consent to change.	Trust is the bond established between people by which each person believes the other will act in his or her best interests.

NOTES

1. Bohm, D. and Edwards, M. (1991). *Changing Consciousness*. San Francisco: Harper & Row.

2. Johnson-Laird, P. (2000). The Mental Model Theory of Thinking and Reasoning. *Mental Models Website*. Retrieved August 14, 2001, from the World Wide Web: http://www.tcd.ie/Psychology/Ruth_Byren/mental_models/theory.html.

3. Senge, P. (1990/1994). *The Fifth Discipline: The Art and Practice of the Learning Organization*. New York: Doubleday, pp. 177–178.

4. Quinn, R., Faerman, S., Thompson, M., and McGrath, M. (1996). *Becoming a Master Manager: A Competency Framework*. New York: John Wiley.

5. Senge, P. (1990/1994), *The Fifth Discipline*, p. 175.

6. Putnam, R. (Spring 1993). The Prosperous Community: Social Capital and Public Life. *The American Prospect* 13. Retrieved August 14, 2001, from the World Wide Web: http://www.prospect.org/archives/13/13putn.html.

7. Einstein, A. (1970). *Out of My Later Years*. Westport, CT: Greenwood Press, p. 128.

8. For a more detailed explanation of the application of Karen Horney's personality types and an instrument that defines your type drawn from her typology, see Calabrese, R. (2000). *Leadership through Excellence: Professional Growth for Leaders*. Boston: Allyn & Bacon, ch. 3.

9. See Calabrese, ibid., for a complete discussion on these three personality styles. Calabrese provides a self-scoring instrument to identify one's dominant personality traits.

10. Senge, P. (1992). Mental Models: Putting Strategic Ideas into Practice. *Planning Review* 20, no. 2: 4. Retrieved August 14, 2001, from the World Wide Web: http://deming.ces.clemson.edu/pub/tqmbbs/tools-techs/menmodel.txt.

11. Lewin, K. (1948). *Resolving Social Conflicts*. New York: Harper & Row.

12. Lambrecht, B. (March 19, 2000). Whistle-Blowers Often Find Their Chosen Path Is Traumatizing; One Adviser Even Warns Against Coming Forward. St. Louis, MO: *St. Louis Post-Dispatch*, p. 8A.

13. McDermott, I. and O'Connor, J. (1996). *Practical NLP for Managers*. Brookfield, VT: Gower Publishers.

14. Global Dialogue Institute. *Power of Deep Dialogue*. Retrieved August 14, 2001, from the World Wide Web: http://astro.temple.edu/~dialogue/case.htm#0.

15. Swidler, L. (1983). The Dialogue Decalogue: Ground Rules for Interreligious, Intercultural Dialogue. *Journal of Ecumenical Studies*. Retrieved May 2, 2000, from the World Wide Web: http://astro.temple.edu/~dialogue/Antho/decalog.htm.

16. Fromm, E. (1994). *The Art of Listening*. New York: Continuum.

17. MacDonald, W. and Bandler, R. (1988). *An Insider's Guide to Sub Modalities*. Cupertino, CA: Meta Publications, p. 7.

18. Dewey, J. (1910/1933). *How We Think: A Restatement of the Relation of Reflective Thinking to the Educative Process*. New York: D. C. Heath, p. 118.

19. Schön, D. (1996). Learning through Reflection on Conversations: In Conversation with Donald Schön. *Capability Volume* 2, no. 2. Retrieved August 14, 20001, from the World Wide Web: http://www.lle.mdx.ac.uk/hec/journal/2-2/1-2.htm.

20. Gallwey, W. T. (1974/1997). *The Inner Game of Tennis*. New York: Random House, p. 20.

CHAPTER FOUR

OVERCOME RESISTANCE TO CHANGE

Strategy ■ *Conquer Change One Step at a Time*

STARTING POINT

The superintendent of schools was meeting with a fellow superintendent from a neighboring district. It was obvious he was deeply troubled. He looked at his friend and said, "We just had board elections. Four incumbents were ousted. I have a whole new majority to educate; if only I had stability I might be able to make a difference."

The superintendent in the neighboring district leaned back in his chair and smiled, "Jim, relax, things change."

Everything changes. The inevitability of change is written onto all that exists. We are born. We age. We die. These are inevitable changes; however, there are changes that we control. We can choose to change to improve our career, health, happiness, and security. Whether we change depends on us. We also experience changes that are neither inevitable nor chosen by us. A department chairperson, for example, arbitrarily decides to change a department member's teaching assignments. The teacher balks at the proposed change; the department chairperson refuses to negotiate; then the teacher files a grievance to reverse the decision.

Many leaders, like the department chairperson in the previous example, feel frustrated because the people most needing to change resist efforts to change. Instead, the leader often considers only two options: Impose change against the will of the membership or settle for minimal change that has little, if any, long-lasting impact on the organization or its members. In either case, the leader exerts an immense amount of energy to generate and sustain minimal movement. Many leaders with charismatic power sustain imposed change with their charisma. When they leave, their charisma and the changes leave with them. Leaders lacking charisma become progressively more frustrated and subject to burnout. They clearly see what needs to be done. They communicate the consequences of continuing on the same path. The members of their organization may smile or nod in agreement; yet they remain oblivious to danger and continue on the same path.

The leader, unable to orchestrate or sustain the necessary change, is frequently blamed for the failure of the school staff to change.

Unfortunately, people still look for charismatic leaders to guide them out of troubled waters. Charisma, however, has little to do with constructive and sustainable change. It has a lot to do with infusing people with energy for short periods of time. Leaders, regardless of levels of charisma, can be effective change leaders. Rosabeth Moss Kanter, professor of business administration at Harvard Business School, states: "The most important things a leader can bring to a changing organization are passion, conviction, and confidence in others."[1] Leaders use these attributes if they are to be catalysts for change. Moreover, leaders understand the stages of change. They intuitively know that change operates in stages. They have a command of the stages of change; they know their role and its inherent subtleties in each stage of change.

REFLECTION IN ACTION

As you read the following case study, write down the superintendent's guarded thoughts and feelings. Additionally, write the changes you think need to occur for the superintendent to be successful.

■ ■ ■ ■ ■ ▬▬▬▬▬▬▬▬▬▬▬▬▬▬▬▬▬▬▬▬▬▬▬▬▬▬▬▬▬▬▬▬▬▬▬▬▬

CASE STUDY

Dr. Janell Waterman was appointed superintendent of schools two months ago at East Borough School District. Her predecessor retired after serving for twenty-one years. The relationship between the previous superintendent and school board was amicable until last year. A majority of the school board, with support from the business community, believed that student achievement performance was stagnant. Board members became concerned that school administrators had grown too powerful during the previous superintendent's tenure and that little, if anything, could be done to influence the district's educational policies. Board members realized their chance when Superintendent Michael Rivera retired. The school board members unanimously agreed that they wanted a person to bring new life, new energy, and new leadership and who would be dedicated to bring change to the district. They were determined to hire a superintendent with a record of accomplishment for leading change. They chose Dr. Waterman as their change agent. They requested that Dr. Waterman report to them in two months with her change plans.

It was now time for her report. The school board changed the location of the meeting to accommodate a large crowd. The auditorium was crowded with parents, teachers, administrators, teacher union officials, community leaders, and media representatives. When asked by the board president to make her plans public, Dr. Waterman responded:

"I plan to reorganize the entire administration of the school district. I will accomplish this through reassignments, retirements, and staff reductions. No administrator's position is safe in this district. The sole criterion for appointing and retaining an administrator will be results."

(continued)

CASE STUDY CONTINUED

There was applause from the community members and parents. Administrators sat stone-faced with arms folded across their chests. Some teachers smiled. Dr. Waterman continued:

"My plans for change extend beyond the administration. Each teacher's past performance in the district is under review. I will not tolerate substandard classroom performance. It is the teacher's responsibility to make sure that students succeed. I am instituting a mandatory performance review for teachers. Each teacher will have performance goals tied directly to the state achievement tests. Teachers failing to reach their goals will undergo retraining. If the retraining fails to produce intended results, I will initiate efforts for dismissal."

Again, the community members and parents applauded. Nearly one-third of the teachers and their union representatives staged a walkout. Some teachers booed and others jeered. The chairperson of the school board called for a ten-minute recess.

How does a leader balance the demand for change from the political body with the resistance to change from within the organization? Dr. Waterman knows that the school board wants change. She is aware that the district has changed little in the past twenty-one years. Prior to the meeting, she felt that her best chance for change was to go to the school board in a public meeting with an aggressive agenda. She felt that a slow, piecemeal approach had no chance of success. As she made her presentation, she heard applause to her comments. Her confidence rose. I know what this community desires, she thought. As she continued speaking, she read the nonverbal language of the board members and sensed their support of her ambitious agenda. She wasn't prepared for the booing or the jeers from the teachers, nor was she ready for the rapid change in body language from the school board members.

A metaphor that we can use to help understand this situation is that of the growth stages of agricultural crops. Crops respond differently at different stages to the stress from lack of water or to excessive water. Imagine that the amount of water applied to the crops is the amount of change that Dr. Waterman proposes to the school board and district. Some crops, based on their specific needs and stage of development, adapt to heavy watering. Similarly, the community members, parents, some administrators, and teachers respond favorably to the heavy emphasis on change. Some crops, however, need little water at their stage of development. If they receive excess water, they will atrophy. Some members of the community feel overwhelmed with the change agenda. Their initial reaction is to react defensively. They see Dr. Waterman's ambitious plan as a personal attack on their professional identities.

Human beings are psychologically complex. Each person responds differently to the same stimuli. Every stimulus is interpreted individually. What one person thinks is wonderful, another finds intolerable. Understanding the stages of change requires us to examine these stages from a human as well as an organizational perspective. Chapter Four focuses on the principle that change occurs in stages. This principle, when followed, allows the leader constructively and successfully to move members, based on their change readiness, from one stage to the next.

HOW WE THINK ABOUT CHANGE

Analytical and Analogical Reasoning versus Analytical or Scientific Reasoning

Change is difficult. Dr. Waterman is learning that lesson. One reason that it is difficult is due to the prevailing practice of using only analytical thinking patterns to resolve problems. The application of analytical thinking patterns to problem solving is consistent with the prevailing cultures in Western civilization. The general pattern in Western culture is that to understand the whole, one understands the parts because the whole is the sum of the parts. This is scientific thinking. We naturally separate parts from the whole as a way of understanding each part. When we understand the part, we reunite it with the whole.

Tom Peters, professor of architecture and history, maintains: "Scientific thinking follows scientific method. The goal is to discover knowledge, and such thinking deals with concepts, hypotheses and theories, all abstractions. Scientific method is linear and hierarchical and aims to be independent of the thinker's personal and cultural value system so that results can be repeated by anyone."[2] In essence, our culture conditions us to operate from the premise that what we observe happening follows specific identified or discoverable patterns. On a natural level, we know that when a child builds a sand castle as the tide is ebbing, the child's delight will soon turn to disappointment as the tide returns engulfing the sand castle. On an organizational level, we operate from a similar premise. Many people, for example, believe that increased pressure on employees increases the rate of production and the quality of production. In organizations as in nature, we operate from a culturally taught imperative that there is a cause to every effect. Dr. Waterman operates with this perspective. Figure 4.1 illustrates this pattern.

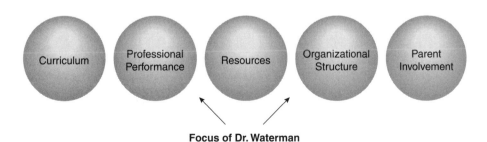

FIGURE 4.1 Analytical Thinking

Dr. Waterman wants to lead change in her school district. She knows that her district is a large and complex organization. Not wanting to overwhelm herself, she has chosen to concentrate her efforts in two areas: faculty performance and organizational structure. Dr. Waterman operates on the assumption that these two areas are the primary source of district problems. By initiating change in these areas, she feels, the entire system changes. Dr. Waterman is acting analytically. She separates the different components of the school district and then selects the two components she believes will have the greatest impact on the organization and its members. This type of thinking and acting often has beneficial results. It also can have disastrous results. It works when the leader managing the change intervention localizes the impact of the intervention. It doesn't work when the leader fails to recognize the multiple forces at play in the school system. In essence, the leader is blind to the existence of the other forces.

We are learning that there are other ways of thinking and perceiving to complement our prevailing thinking model. We know that the scientific method of interpreting reality is one way and that it is not always accurate. John Dewey stated:

> While many empirical conclusions are, roughly speaking, correct; while they are exact enough to be of great help in practical life; while the presages of a weather wise sailor or hunter may be more accurate, within a certain restricted range, than those of a scientist who relies wholly upon scientific observations and tests; while, indeed, empirical observations and records furnish the raw or crude material of scientific knowledge, yet the empirical method affords no way of discriminating between right and wrong conclusions. Hence, it is responsible for a multitude of *false* beliefs. The technical designation for one of the commonest fallacies is *post hoc, ergo propter hoc;* the belief that because one thing comes *after* another, it comes *because* of the other."[3]

Analogical Reasoning

Aside from the scientific method of thinking, we can interpret reality through analogical reasoning. Analogical reasoning attempts to discover similarities in seemingly dissimilar objects. It is a creative approach to discovery and problem solving. In this sense, it is highly applicable to the leader who desires to lead and manage change. Geoffrey Broadbent, architect, claims: "Analogical design occurs away from the physical material which is to be used in the construction. Instead, the designer uses an analogue, such as a drawing, to describe intentions. Allowing many variations to be tried on paper before choosing one to be constructed."[4] In analogical reasoning, the leader does not focus on the outcome. Focusing on a fixed outcome moves the leader away from analogical thinking to scientific thinking. It becomes cause-and-effect driven. The leader concentrates on a field of unlimited possibilities. The leader knows some possibilities, while an infinite number of possibilities await discovery.

Dr. Waterman could have avoided the problems resulting from her presentation to the school board by using an analogical process. In Figure 4.2, Dr. Waterman

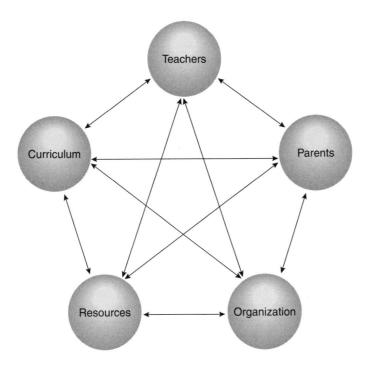

FIGURE 4.2 Analogical Reasoning

no longer compartmentalizes the elements in her school district. She now sees that each element exerts an influence on each of the other elements. When she chooses to intervene with one element, she affects all others. Scientific or analytic thinking doesn't recognize that multiple relationships simultaneously occur within complex organisms. Dr. Waterman begins to think differently. She knows the kind of reaction she wants to generate among members of the school community. Knowing this, she can simulate interventions at various parts of her system and examine the reaction of the whole system to the intervention.

As she becomes adept at analogical reasoning, she applies appropriate analogies to her system. She imagines her school district as a human body. Visualizing the school district as a human body allows her to understand the relationship between and among the multiple elements in the district. She realizes that the human body needs to be healthy to function efficiently. Similarly, she realizes that her district needs to be healthy to function efficiently. She knows that a human body with lower back pain may not function or, at best, functions below peak performance. Knowing this, she withdraws her strategy to focus solely on the curriculum. As an alternative, she can work with the school community to create a healthy organization, leaving the actual outcome open to the unlimited possibilities that extend from her analogy.

STAGES OF CHANGE AND ANALOGICAL REASONING

The discovery of this infinite number of possibilities through analogical reasoning follows a specific sequence:[5]

- Collecting information
- Processing collected information
- Waiting for unexpected insights
- Transferring insights to the context
- Validating the accuracy of the insights
- Integrating valid insights into permanent practice

Collecting Information

The primary derailer for change agents is initiating change without thoroughly understanding the system, system components, system culture, and system's members. The leader generates this problem by narrowly focusing on the problem and compartmentalizing its specific aspects. If the leader focuses on the perceived problem context, she operates from a fixed position. Her narrow attention draws intention of purpose. As a result, she commits the organization's resources to the perceived problem context. Dr. Waterman's current approach works when she correctly identifies the target.

Another approach is to operate without specificity, allowing numerous possibilities to arise. During this primary stage, the leader purposely remains unfocused. She allows the data to filter through her experience and knowledge base. She trusts in her intuition that a synergistic, creative insight will occur.

Processing Collected Information

The processing stage is similar to the farmer who plants wheat and sees no results for a month. All the while, the seeds are germinating and spreading a root system into the soil. The seed's growth is hidden from the farmer. The leader's processing stage, like the farmer's effort, represents significant hidden work. Each person involved in the acquisition of information allows the information to ferment. Just as grapes need time to turn into wine, the acquired information needs time to transform into creative insights. This is known as liminal space. "At the heart of this experience is the social-psychological construct of 'liminality.' From the Greek *limnos,* meaning 'threshold,' liminality describes an in-between time when what was, is no longer, and what will be, is not yet. It is a time rich with ambiguity, uncertainty, and the possibility of creative fomentation."[6]

The knowledge gained by the leader works creatively within his mind. He is, in a sense, no longer the same person as he was before he acquired the knowledge. He has not, however, arrived at a new position because he has yet to integrate his knowledge. He is in liminal space. Liminal space is essential to change. It allows our organizing properties to sift, sort, and integrate our knowledge with past experience and knowledge base.

Waiting for Unexpected Insights

Unexpected insight is the "aha" experience. It happens all of a sudden without pre-planning. The leader may be walking through the cafeteria, sitting at her desk, or reading a memo when the flash of insight occurs. This "aha" experience is the reason why effective leaders focus on the process and not outcomes. It is in the processing of information, sharing of ideas, and struggling to understand and reconciling opposing points of view that unexpected insights occur. It is a burst of creative activity with insights into the problem context that were not apparent moments before. A junior high school principal led a two-year study to transform his junior high school into a middle school. His transition team struggled for nearly a year with the organizational design of the school. Some members wanted to retain the traditional academic structure of the junior high school. Other members wanted to embrace an elementary school structure. He resisted the call for votes. Instead, the principal and his team met weekly to discuss the various ideas and concepts. During the eighth month of meetings, the principal recalled, a group member suggested a new kind of structure. There was a long silent pause. The group realized they had been presented a structure that no one had previously conceptualized; this insight stimulated a period of heightened creativity. A new model emerged integrating the components of both groups. The principal and his team experienced unexpected insight.

Transferring Insights to the Context

The leader needs to know how to transfer the new information to the existing system. Too often, the leader moves rapidly into implementation, believing that the results will prove he is right. Unfortunately, this leader adds to the existing chaos and creates more disruption and disorganization than existed prior to his enlightened motives.

Edgar Schein suggests a path the leader can use in transferring new information to members of his organization. He believes that an organization must have embedded into its normal operational design a system that empowers the organization and its members to learn, change, and adapt to changing contexts. Schein states: "When we are in a reflective mode, we are creating within ourselves a 'parallel system' in which we can experiment, contemplate, and reframe our thoughts and, thereby, allow new thoughts to arise. When we 'practice' we are creating a 'parallel system' in which to test new behavior, allow ourselves to make errors, repeat desired responses until they become habitual."[7] A parallel system allows the system time to understand the new information and to learn how to process the new information. It also allows the leader time to test the new information to make sure that it works (see Figure 4.3).

In Figure 4.3 the organization operates with a parallel system. The parallel system acts as a vendor of new information, ideas, and models. It integrates its new information on a small scale and communicates, at a grassroots level, the goals, objectives, methodology, and outcomes of its efforts. The parallel system is in constant communication with the larger organization. It uses this opportunity to teach others and to show them the benefits of the new information. Members of

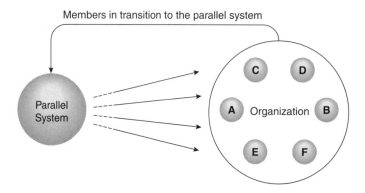

FIGURE 4.3   Parallel System at Work

the organization, subunits A, B, C, D, E, and F, maintain their current practices. They are acquiring critical information relevant to the system's components, while the parallel system is transferring information. If the parallel system reports success, other members begin to move toward the parallel system. The size of the parallel system begins to grow and the size of the organization correspondingly shrinks. When the parallel system reaches a critical mass, it transcends the organization and becomes the organization.

Validating the Accuracy of the Insights

Sending information from the parallel system to the larger organization is a primary goal of the parallel system. The members of the larger organization observe the theories-in-action of the parallel system. They take a wait-and-see attitude to determine if the parallel system's espoused theory matches its theory-in-use. They also wait to see the outcomes of the parallel system and then match the outcomes to internal pictures of how they view their role within the organization. They reject any outcome, positive or negative, that is not consistent with their idealized professional self-image. They embrace any outcome, positive or negative, that draws them closer to their idealized image of professional self. In effect, they have to understand the personal benefits that the new information coming from the parallel system provides. A teacher, for example, wants to know whether the new model operating in the parallel system provides more work with little benefit or provides a commensurate professional benefit in terms of stature, prestige, and rewards. If it provides the latter, the teacher will move toward accepting the parallel system.

Integrating Valid Insights into Permanent Practice

Integration of valid insights is the nucleus of analogical reasoning. The members of the parallel system have a responsibility to assist members from the primary organization in discovering similarities in values, goals, and vision. When the parallel system operates with analogical reasoning, it moves toward the primary organization. It works with members of the primary system to build links from one system to the other. The more links created, the faster information travels. The faster information travels, the quicker the pace of learning and change.

Dr. Waterman can use the stages associated with analogical reasoning to revise her change strategy. She, however, has significant leadership experience and recognizes that even with an effective process to move toward change, some people still refuse to learn. How does Dr. Waterman work with people who refuse to listen? The starting place for Dr. Waterman is in understanding the personal struggle that people have with change. Elisabeth Kübler-Ross's work on death and dying speaks to this struggle.

GRIEVING OVER CHANGE

Effective leaders recognize that there are no enemies. Those who apparently resist constructive changes proposed by the leader are often arbitrarily placed in an enemy camp. They are not enemies; in nearly every case, their resistance to change is driven by a fear of the unknown. Psychologist David Viscott states: "No one can deal with fears of the unknown for it is fear without limitations. It contaminates judgment and paralyzes. Fearing the unknown complicates life and defeats the very purpose of fear. The fear of the unknown always expands."[8]

The change resister feels secure in his current situation, although that situation may be dysfunctional or harmful. The current situation presents a predictable way of living. The change resister learned how to cope with the vagaries of his situations as they arose. He now finds it difficult to let go of the familiar and embrace the new. When change is required of him, he finds himself having to discover and process new information, testing an unpredictable and strange environment, and considering the possibility of failure. The first step in understanding the grieving process, especially that of the change resister, is to recognize that each person experiences resistance to letting go of a familiar behavior, object, or belief.

Each of us, throughout our lives, experiences a continual attraction and aversion toward objects. When our attraction is strong, we overcome pain associated with our aversion. For example, do you remember when you learned to ride a bicycle? You had an attraction to the freedom, fun, prestige, and social experience that riding a bicycle brought to you. You also had an aversion to falling. You grasped the handlebars, watched the pedals, and focused your eyes directly in front of your bicycle. You found it difficult to maintain your balance without external help.

The parent helping you learn to ride experienced the same attraction and aversion to the change that was happening to you. On one hand, this parent experienced excitement because you were growing up, your motor skills were developing, and you were gaining independence. On the other hand, this parent experienced aversion. Your parent knew that you would no longer always be close to the house; you would now venture further into a world over which the parent had little control.

You had to let go of your fear of falling so you could learn to ride. Your parents had to let go of their fear of your changing so you could develop into a normal adult. Normal, well-adjusted people overcome their aversion to change, yet even normal well-adjusted people fear change. Psychologist Karen Horney states: "Behind the fear of changing are qualms about changing for the worse . . . [or] a fear of being unable to change."[9] When conditions force change on an unwilling person, expect resistance. After all efforts at resistance fail, she will grieve for the loss of what once belonged to her. In normal, well-adjusted people, the grieving process has a natural beginning and end; life continues. In others, their grieving process is persistent, a focal point of activity, and sometimes held to the point of obsession.

Managing the Grieving Process

Elisabeth Kübler-Ross, physician and renowned expert on grieving, provides us with the five stages of grieving.[10] Kübler-Ross's five stages include

1. Denial and isolation
2. Anger
3. Bargaining
4. Depression
5. Acceptance

Each stage has applicability in any organization undergoing change. Identifying these stages allows us to understand the personal turmoil people experience when letting go of a familiar way of acting. The teacher who is asked to change grade-level assignments, the student transferred to a new school, the principal asked to implement a new program, and the secretary given a new assignment all experience these five stages of grieving when they are asked to change.

The grieving process, when properly managed, allows the leader to gradually bring all members closer to acceptance. By viewing the grieving process as a series of challenges, the leader progressively moves members closer to full acceptance of the change. In Figure 4.4, the effective management of the grieving process moves systematically toward the acceptance of change. Initially, at stage one, denial, the obstacle seems insurmountable. As each obstacle is surmounted, the barriers seem less intimidating; the process becomes easier. The grieving member gradually lets go of her attachment and moves on with her life. This is the healthy process of living. Healthy people and healthy organizations grieve over loss and then move on, constructively creating their destiny.

FIGURE 4.4   The Grieving Process

The leader who understands these stages has a greater degree of empathy for the members of his organization. He is able to counsel, console, and guide them through the change process. The depth and length of their grieving is proportional to the intensity of their attachment.

Stage One: Denial and Isolation.   Denial is a defense mechanism that prevents people who need to change from facing the fact that they have to change. Often, what is clearly visible to others is invisible to the person needing the change. The teacher whose poorly taught class is due to his lack of preparation denies that his classes are poorly prepared. Instead, he attributes the students' poor performance to parents or the students' attitude. This is denial. The principal is also in denial when she believes that three years of continued decline in English achievement scores indicates no problem.

The person in denial isolates herself from people who bring her attention to the reality of her situation. She finds solace in associating with those who are also in denial or with those who, although well intentioned, refuse to hold her accountable for her action. The latter response is known as codependency. Anne Wilson Schaef and Diane Fassel in their seminal work, *The Addictive Organization,* state: "Denial prevents us from coming to terms with what is going on before our very eyes. When we will not let ourselves see or know what is happening, we pose no threat to the continuation of a dysfunctional system, and we perpetuate a dishonest system."[11]

The leader will always have people in the organization who deny the personal need for change or the organization's need to change. The strategy of last resort is that of force. A teacher, for example, may refuse to maintain control over his classroom. Little learning takes place. The principal's efforts to assist the teacher are ignored. The teacher continues to act as if there is no problem. The principal has little choice but to remove the teacher to maintain a healthy learning environment. The principal who hopes the teacher will eventually change is in denial of the teacher's prolonged, harmful behavior.

A more effective strategy is to move the person out of denial. The effective leader does not resort to anger or other forms of emotional response. She presents objective, irrefutable data and requires the person in denial to take responsibility for his actions. Psychologist Kurt Lewin termed the first response *the principle of concreteness.* He stated:

> Only what is concrete can have effects. . . . Effects can be produced only by what is "concrete," e.g., by something that has the position of an individual fact which exists at a certain moment; a fact which makes up a real part of the life space and which can be given a definite place in the representation of the psychological situation.[12]

The effective leader understands that facts do matter. She uses facts to replace anger, emotional responses, or arbitrary threats. If Dr. Waterman relies on facts, she educates faculty and administrators to the need for change by presenting them with accurate data concerning the state of the school district. The school community may not want to hear these facts, yet it must consider them. Using this approach, the need for change emerges from the school community.

When people refuse to listen to facts and continue to deny the reality of the context, the leader needs to act. One strong action is to make sure that those who understand the present context do not act with complicity by codependently supporting the actions of the person in denial. The person in denial must face the consequences of his actions. A poor mathematics teacher who refuses to accept the objective data related to his teaching receives negative performance reviews as a step in the process toward termination. In the majority of cases, careful collection of data and its objective presentation is enough to move a person from the denial stage. Once out of denial, he realizes he has to change; that does not mean, however, that he is ready to accept change.

Stage Two: Anger.   Once the leader moves members out of the denial stage, she encounters the members' anger. The anger that members feel is related to their fear of change, fear of having to acquire new skills, or frustration associated with not having a voice in change planning. The leader, being the focus of change, becomes the recipient of the members' displaced anger. Psychologist Gordon Allport states:

> It seems to be undeniably true that man's instinctive response to frustration is aggressive assertiveness in some form. An infant when balked will kick and scream. Under anger, it certainly shows no sign of love or affiliation; its reaction is random and wild. The infant attacks not the true source of the frustration, but any object or person who crosses its path. Throughout life the same tendency persists for anger to center upon available rather than upon logical objects.[13]

The anger that many members of the school community feel at proposed changes is a coping mechanism to deal with their fear of change. In other members, the anger relates to an experience that may or may not be in the conscious memory of the member. Even though the member is not conscious of his motivation, his experience continually triggers an angry emotion anytime the member is asked to change.

A principal reported the following story that demonstrates anger associated with externally imposed change and how this anger was projected onto the principal. The voters in a northeastern state passed tax-limiting legislation. The day after the public vote, the superintendent called all administrators and informed them that their faculty positions were reduced by one-fourth. This principal had to develop recommendations reducing his faculty of 120 members to 90. The principal worked with department chairpersons and other senior faculty, but could appease no one. As word leaked out to faculty of the impending recommendations, faculty stopped speaking to the principal, his car was vandalized, and faculty began a petition to request his removal. This principal could not bring peace to his faculty. He had to weather the storm of anger.

Elisabeth Kübler-Ross states: "In contrast to the stage of denial, this stage of anger is very difficult to cope with from the point of view of family and staff. The reason for this is the fact that this anger is displaced in all directions and projected onto the environment at times almost at random."[14] The leader must manage the anger that members generate because of the imposed or impending change. Dr. Waterman, for example, will increase the anger and frustration level of the members of her school community if she denies that the anger exists or seeks to stifle the emotion associated with anger. She has to provide an appropriate venue in which members release their anger.

One venue is an open meeting at which each member can voice his or her opinion without threat of reprisal. The leader who holds an open meeting needs to set guidelines to ensure psychological safety (see Guidelines for a Safe Environment, Chapter One). Unfortunately for the leader, she has to allow angry statements directed at her to be part of the discussion. She must refrain from defensiveness and be gracious for any comments. After all, she is a learner, and there may be some information offered by members that can constructively influence her change proposal. Her openness to learning, although not abating the anger, will gain the respect of the members of her organization.

The more opportunities that the members of the organization have to express anger in constructive ways, the less need they will have to use anger as a defensive reaction. Once members realize that change will happen and that their anger interferes with the inevitable results of change, they suppress their anger and focus on adapting to the evolving context. Even members who refuse to let go of their anger realize that their anger isolates them from those who accept the change. They soon realize that they no longer have support. If they are to survive, they have to change or leave to find a context more in line with their values.

Stage Three: Bargaining.   Members, when faced with inevitable change, attempt to capitalize on benefits and curtail losses. They realize that they are unable to prevent the change. Although they have not accepted the change, they try to undermine it through a negotiation process. The negotiation process centers on self-interests. This self-interest-driven process creates alliances banding together into special-interest cliques. The objective of these cliques is to gain political advantage and either stop the change process or control its direction and duration.

Many change-resistant members learn that persistent criticism and self-righteous anger take an emotional toll on the leader. As a result, the leader accepts a partial change when she could have had the entire change. If she is unsure of her vision or position, she will sacrifice hard-won gains by seeking peace over justice. She is reluctant to stay the course. There is another alternative, however, available to the leader.

The leader, as an effective negotiator, understands her value and vision boundaries. If her boundaries are unclear, she'll have no idea as to what she can and cannot concede. She will either become rigid, making no concessions, or weak, making many concessions. Her personal outcome will be frustration and resentment toward the members of her school community. She will also cause resentment among her supporters. In the end, they will view themselves as supporting the wrong leader.

Explicit value and vision boundaries increase her flexibility. She can concede some issues important to faculty members without altering her values or vision. Dr. Waterman, for example, may allow a central office administrator about to be reassigned to a school principal's position to choose from multiple selections that meet the criteria for the assignment set by the superintendent. The central office administrator feels he has won a small victory. Dr. Waterman's value and vision boundaries remain untouched.

Stage Four: Depression. Butler and Hope, a psychologist and a physician, state:

> Sigmund Freud saw depression as a reaction to loss. The idea that anxiety is a reaction to threat and depression a reaction to loss is one that has proved useful over the years. . . . The usefulness of this idea is that it helps you to think about what losses might be important in causing and sustaining the depression. . . . They may be losses of status or hope or self-image.[15]

Once members move out of the bargaining stage, they enter into a period of depression. Depression is normal for those who lose something to which they attributed great importance. Ignoring a member's depression is to ignore the reality of imposed change.

People who suffer from depression may feel sad, defeated, worthless, or helpless. "These feelings may exacerbate both physical and psychological symptoms. Depressed people have little energy or desire to be active. Depression also involves a loss of self-esteem and concomitant feelings of inadequacy."[16] The source of their loss is unique as are their symptoms. Some members, who feel betrayed, see the change as eroding their power base, and yet others, who are highly competitive, view any change as a loss. Each experiences a sense of failure at not being able to control the outcome.[17]

The effective leader understands that depression is part of the grieving cycle. He makes sure that he creates a support network for members experiencing depression. Sometimes professional help is essential to help people move from depression. For most people, active listening, patience, reducing the threat associated with change, and linking long-term personal benefits to the change create conditions to move members from depression to the final stage.

One strategy is to create a support group for members suffering from depression. The team is led by a trained psychologist and is comprised of people who are experiencing depression. Support groups are an effective way to help people who are struggling with similar circumstances to become healed.

Stage Five: Acceptance. The final stage, acceptance, is one at which members accept the change as inevitable and constructively work to adapt to the change. In this stage, members who resist the change have had the time and opportunity to come to grips with their grieving process; they now accept the change as inevitable.

There are two types of acceptance: passive acceptance of one's fate and proactive integration of acceptance by constructively redesigning one's destiny. Passive acceptance is harmful. It is symbolic of hopelessness and alienation. It is a warning sign that the member who passively accepts the change feels powerless and is willing to operate in an existential vacuum. The member acts as a fatalist unable to do anything about his or her life. Conversely, the member who integrates each stage rises to a new level of wisdom. No longer naïve, the member realizes that things change; to live is to constructively engage the change forces that surround one's life. Viktor Frankl, psychologist, poignantly states:

> By declaring that man is responsible and must actualize the potential meaning of his life, I wish to stress that the true meaning of life is to be discovered in the world rather than within man or his own psyche, as though it were a closed system. I have termed constitutive characteristic "the self-transcendence of human existence." It denotes the fact that being human always points, and is directed, to something, or someone, other than oneself—be it a meaning to fulfill or another human being to encounter. The more one forgets himself—by giving himself to a cause to serve or another person to love—the more human he is and the more he actualizes himself.[18]

The effective leader creates conditions for acceptance by encouraging participation, providing ongoing professional development, encouraging failure, and story sharing.

ACTIONS THAT CREATE CONDITIONS FOR THE ACCEPTANCE OF CHANGE

Encouraging Participation

Members who passively accept change are likely to withdraw. They no longer resist, but their lack of participation contributes to overall organizational dysfunction. There is a reason for the member's withdrawal. The member feels hurt, betrayed, or remains locked in a lower stage of the grieving process. The effective leader encourages the withdrawing member to restate her feelings in a safe environment while simultaneously requiring her participation. The more she participates, the more she will forget her pain and constructively embrace the change.

Providing Ongoing Professional Development

Providing ongoing professional development bolsters acceptance by eliminating a primary cause of change resistance: the person's fear that he does not have the skills to make the transition or that he does not have the aptitude to learn the skills required to complete the change successfully. Consider how many teachers resist integrating the rapid advances in technology into their classrooms. Their resistance occurs even when modern technology is available. Systematic and ongoing professional development is an antidote to fear.

The leader cannot take for granted that his faculty has the requisite skills to implement significant changes. Instead, the effective leader provides empowering professional development. Empowering professional development is meaningful, focused, and personal. It is meaningful because it addresses the immediate needs of the person receiving the training. It is focused because it deals specifically with a learning target necessary for personal and professional growth. It is personal because it is a source of professional growth and higher levels of self-esteem.

Encouraging Failure

The wise leader understands human nature and knows that human beings learn most effectively through trial and error. Tom Peters, management expert and consultant, states: "There's little that is more important to tomorrow's managers than failure. We need lots more of it. We need faster failure. It is fair to say that if we can't increase the gross national failure rate, we're in for a very rough ride indeed."[19] When teachers fail in trying to implement new changes, it means that they are willing to work with the change, to learn about the change, and to acquire the skills necessary to make the change. As with all newly acquired skills, there is a learning curve. Few people learn to ride a bicycle on their first try; they have to acquire the skill. It takes a clarinetist virtuoso years of practice and struggle to attain world-class level of performance and stature. Similarly, the teacher learning new skills goes slowly as she practices what she is learning. At first, her progress is marked more by failure than by success. As her learning rate increases, her success rate surpasses her failure rate. She now practices her skills automatically. She fully integrates her new learning into her past experience.

Story Sharing

An overlooked but essential part of creating conditions for acceptance is the communal act of story sharing. Teachers, business leaders, religious leaders, and community builders increasingly recognize the value of story sharing. Dolly Haik-Adams Berthelot, story sharing consultant, states:

> Since the most primitive campfires and throughout history, stories have helped teach, influence, and bind people together. Stories have fostered the understanding—of self, of others, and of life—which is vital to progress. Such understanding is sorely needed today, as we struggle to live and work together and progress toward common goals.[20]

The leader facilitates the story sharing process. These are stories of struggle as well as of success. These are stories of grieving as well as of joy. The story sharing process is a synergistic event that enhances creativity, collegiality, and community. Through this process, members identify with one another. Each person recognizes that stories, although unique, share common patterns. They recognize that the suffering associated with change is common and shared. In essence, story sharing becomes a healing and liberating experience for the group.

CONCLUDING POINT

Dr. Waterman initially followed her predetermined behavioral script. This script, in the past, always was efficient and effective. She was given a job to do by the school board and she was determined to complete the job. The reaction of the teachers, community members, and some of the administrators shocked her. She felt that everyone wanted change; after all, that's why the school board had hired her. She took each issue, separated the pieces, discovered the broken part, and developed a solution. It always worked, yet this time she knew she had to change. Her script no longer worked. She realized that all of her professional life she looked analytically at issues. She now knows that she has to change to lead change.

Dr. Waterman had the wisdom to understand that change begins within the change agent and then moves into the organization. Dr. Waterman realized she had to move from analytical thinking to analogical thinking if she were to be successful. This was a new way of thinking about issues. She was a coalition builder; she counted votes and made sure she was always on the winning side. Now, her context changed; she had to bring opposing sides together in a common cause. She realized that she would always have a predisposition toward analytical thinking, but now, as she developed her analogical reasoning skills, she would improve her leadership capabilities. She was determined to change her organization into a learning community committed to continuous growth in the service of its stakeholders.

Dr. Waterman learned that people have difficulty with change. She previously believed that those who resisted her change efforts were either fools, enemies, or blind to the realities of the context. She now understands that many people develop attachments to the way they teach, where they teach, and with whom they teach. It isn't easy to let go of an attachment. A grieving process is necessary. As a leader, she realizes, she has to lead the grieving process through compassion, insight, patience, and toughheartedness. Dr. Waterman is ready to be a change leader in her school district.

SUGGESTIONS FOR ACTION

- Examine an issue you tried to change in the past. Did you do it analytically or analogically? Were the results divisive or did they build a sense of community? Reflect on how you can improve your change process.

- Identify subordinates or colleagues whom you consider enemies. Identify commonalities that you have with them. Choose one issue that separates you from them. Use this issue to work analogically with them so that the issue is mutually resolved.

- Reflect on a subgroup in your school organization. Do you understand the motivation of each member of this subgroup? What is propelling some members forward toward the change? What is holding other members from embracing the change?

- Create a parallel system within your organization. Allow the parallel system latitude to fail. Also, allow easy access to the parallel system by other members of the organization. Use the parallel system to teach your organization how to change a specific issue.

- Consider a recent change. Can you identify the grieving stage for each member of your organization? Once you identify these stages, move to assist grieving members to shift closer to acceptance in a constructive personal and professional way.

- Are there teachers, staff members, or students in your school who would benefit from a professionally led support group? Identify these people and establish a support group.

CHANGE FACTORS

TERM	HOW TO USE IT	WHAT IT MEANS
Analogical reasoning	The leader seeks to find similarities between dissimilar objects as a means of bringing about unity. The leader, for example, will look for common issues between English teachers and social studies teachers to promote more effective teaching.	Analogical reasoning is a thinking process designed to help the person look at the whole and see places of connection.
Analytical reasoning	The leader uses analytical reasoning to understand the details embedded in problems and contexts. It is a linear, rational, and logical skill that can be acquired.	Analytical thinking is scientific reasoning applied to problems and contexts. It separates the whole into its components and then examines each component separate from the others. A person uses either deductive or inductive reasoning to reach a conclusion.
Change stages	The leader understands the six stages associated with change knowing that the stages occur in sequence and cannot be ignored. The leader guides members through each of the change stages.	Six sequential stages are associated with change: collecting information, processing collected information, waiting for insights, transferring the insights to the context, validating the accuracy of the insights, and integrating valid insights into permanent practice.
Grieving process	The leader assists faculty in working through the grieving process as faculty members let go of cherished behaviors.	A five-stage process for grieving over loss. The five stages include denial, anger, negotiating, depression, and peaceful acceptance.
Story sharing	The leader uses story sharing as a way to promote understanding among faculty, students, and parents. Through story sharing, the leader encourages stakeholders to listen to each other's successes and fears related to change.	Story sharing is a communication process that is used to promote understanding. Through story sharing people discover commonalities in values and life experiences.

NOTES

1. Kanter, R. M. (Summer 1999). The Enduring Skills of Change Leaders. *Leader to Leader,* no. 13. Retrieved May 5, 2000, from the World Wide Web: http://www.pfdf.org/leaderbooks/L2L/summer99/kanter.html.

2. Peters, Tom F. (1998). How Creative Engineers Think. *Civil Engineering* 68, no. 3: 48–51.

3. Dewey, J. (1910). *How We Think: A Restatement of the Relation of Reflective Thinking to the Educative Process.* Boston: D. C. Heath, p. 145.

4. Broadbent, G. (1973). *Design in Architecture: Architecture and the Human Sciences.* New York: John Wiley. Retrieved August 14, 2001, from the World Wide Web: http://www.arch.usyd.edu.au/~rob/study/DesignInArchitecture.html.

5. O'Donoghue, D. An Integrated Model of Analogy for Creative Reasoning. Retrieved August 15, 2001, from the World Wide Web: http://www.compapp.dcu.ie/~tonyv/MIND/diarmuid.html.

6. Schaetti, B. and Ramsey, S. (1999). Transition Dynamics: The Global Nomad Experience, Living in Liminality. *Mobility.* Retrieved August 14, 2001, from the World Wide Web: http://www.transition-dynamics.com/liminality.html.

7. Schein, E. (1995/1999). Learning Consortia: How to Create Parallel Learning Systems for Organization Sets. MIT: The Society for Organizational Learning. Retrieved March 20, 2000, from the World Wide Web: http://learning.mit.edu/res/wp/10007.html.

8. Viscott, D. (1996). *Emotional Resilience.* New York: Harmony Books, p. 74.

9. Horney, K. (1945/1992). *Our Inner Conflicts.* New York: W. W. Norton, p. 153.

10. Kübler-Ross, E. (1969). *On Death and Dying.* New York: Macmillan.

11. Schaef, A. W. and Fassel, D. (1988/1990). *The Addictive Organization.* San Francisco: Harper & Row, p. 62.

12. Lewin, K. (1936). *Principles of Topological Psychology.* Translated by F. Heider and G. Heider. New York: McGraw-Hill, pp. 32–33.

13. Allport, G. (1954). *The Nature of Prejudice.* Reading, MA: Addison-Wesley, p. 343.

14. Kübler-Ross, *On Death and Dying,* p. 51.

15. Butler, G. and Hope, T. (1995). *Managing Your Mind.* New York: Oxford University Press, p. 238.

16. Benson, H. and Stuart, E. (1992). *The Wellness Book: The Comprehensive Guide to Maintaining Health and Treating Stress-Related Illness.* New York: Fireside, pp. 210–211.

17. See Viscott, *Emotional Resilience,* pp. 297–298.

18. Frankl, V. (1959/1984). *Man's Search for Meaning.* New York: Touchstone, p. 115.

19. Peters, T. (1988). *Thriving on Chaos: Handbook for a Management Revolution.* New York: Harper & Row, p. 316.

20. Berthelot, D. (1989/1996). The Value of Story Sharing. Retrieved May 17, 2000, from the World Wide Web: http://www.berthelotconsulting.pen.net/drdolly/story.htm.

CHAPTER FIVE

LEAD CHANGE

Strategy ■ *Be Forward Looking—*
Recognize Shifting Paradigms

STARTING POINT

The Japanese monkey, *Macaca fuscata*, has been observed in the wild for a period of over 30 years. In 1952, on the island of Koshima, scientists were providing monkeys with sweet potatoes dropped in the sand. The monkeys liked the taste of the raw sweet potatoes, but they found the dirt unpleasant. An 18-month-old female named Imo found she could solve the problem by washing the potatoes in a nearby stream. She taught this trick to her mother. Her playmates also learned this new way and they taught their mothers, too. This cultural innovation was gradually picked up by various monkeys before the eyes of the scientists. Between 1953 and 1958, all of the young monkeys learned to wash the sandy sweet potatoes to make them more palatable. Only the adults who imitated their children learned this social improvement. Other adults kept eating the dirty sweet potatoes. Then something startling took place. In the autumn of 1958, a certain number of Koshima monkeys were washing sweet potatoes—the exact number not known. Let us suppose that when the sun rose one morning there were 99 monkeys on Koshima Island who had learned to wash their sweet potatoes. Let us further suppose that later that morning the hundredth monkey learned to wash potatoes. Then it happened! By that evening, almost everyone in the tribe was washing sweet potatoes before eating them. The added energy of this hundredth monkey somehow created an ideological breakthrough! However, a most surprising thing observed by these scientists was that the habit of washing sweet potatoes then jumped over the sea. Colonies of monkeys on other islands and the mainland troop of monkeys at Takasakiyama began washing their sweet potatoes.[1]

This story, whether myth or fact, suggests an important, yet overlooked characteristic of change: When a critical mass of members agree to change, the entire organization automatically changes. Gustavsson and Harung, European management researchers, call this phenomenon the collective consciousness of the organization. They state:

By a collective consciousness, we mean the wholeness formed by the members of an organization coming together. It is the characteristics of this Gestalt—the wholeness that is more than the collection of its parts—that define the phase, or level, of development of the organization. We can define the collective consciousness as the sum total of the level of being of the members. All the individual consciousnesses contribute to this overall quality, and it is therefore the net resultant of all the individual levels of personal development. It is this aggregate level of *being* that defines the quality of *doing*, and consequently all the influences put into the environment by the members of an organization. We therefore suggest that it is the level of collective consciousness of an organization that is the prime mover of its behavior and development.[2]

A paradox exists for the leader. The leader can make people change their behavior when he is present, but he can't make people change. Typically, the person charged with changing an organization identifies the forces in the organization favoring change and those opposed to change. Change becomes framed as a political not a readiness issue. This way of framing change has historically been the source of problems for leaders. They soon discover that change is temporary in nearly all politically driven situations. Politically driven change temporarily modifies the behavior of the members of the organization, yet it never captures their soul. Members do what they are told to do because of the potential coercive power that may be used against them, all the while passively resisting the change. If the leader, in this context, is not vigilant, the members' behavior returns to the original pattern.

These types of leaders operate with a zero-sum paradigm. In this paradigm, there are only losers. Those who dominate lose the support of the minority. Those who resist the winning force find themselves subject to potential reprisal and operate as a distinct minority. There is a better way to lead and manage change. To discover this way, the leader must let go of outdated ways of thinking. He must be willing to shift from an archaic paradigm to one that answers the questions posed by the present context and provides hope for the future. The leader will have to construct new maps because he is walking in uncharted territory. His new map requires new thinking, different ways of behaving, and a new vision of change leadership. The effective leader knows when it is time to leave one paradigm and embrace a new paradigm shift.

PARADIGMS

Many well-intentioned leaders are stuck in outdated paradigms. Thomas Kuhn, in his seminal work, *The Structure of the Scientific Revolution,* tells us that paradigms have two common characteristics:

Their achievement was unprecedented to attract an enduring group of adherents away from competing modes of scientific activity. Simultaneously, it was sufficiently open-ended to leave all sorts of problems for the redefined group of practitioners to resolve. Achievements that share these two characteristics I shall henceforth refer to as paradigms.[3]

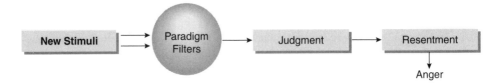

FIGURE 5.1   Paradigm and Behavior

Paradigms affect personal and collective behavior. As individuals, we use paradigms to interpret our environment. Our paradigms save us time from analyzing every situation. As new situations appear, our minds quickly process these situations against a myriad of paradigms that our minds maintain on active duty. When the new situation conflicts with the paradigm, a warning signal sounds and subconsciously a defensive reaction develops. In Figure 5.1 we see that the stimuli, processed through paradigm filters, cause instantaneous judgment that leads directly to anger with little cognitive processing. The greater the mismatch between the new situation and our existing set of paradigms, the greater the level of resistance. As resistance increases, our position becomes increasingly rigid. In this state, we no longer seek compromise, we seek to dominate and emerge victorious. Our emotional state becomes one of resentment for the intrusion and questioning of our paradigm. The resentment, if persistent, becomes one of anger.

On an organizational level, the rigidity of paradigms is directly proportional to the organization's age. New organizations are created without fixed paradigms; the genesis of paradigms occurs as the organization matures. The original creators of the organization have a higher degree of flexibility regarding work and the relationships within work. There are fewer rules and precedents to guide behavior.

It is through the development and application of paradigms that the organization survives the transition of people from one generation to another. People come and go, but the organization remains intact. In a school organization, the stabilizing force is generally the teachers and staff, whereas the administration is likely to turn over at a more rapid rate. In other organizations such as the federal government, career civil servants stabilize the government, whereas elected officials have a higher mobility rate.

Organizational paradigms, as well as personal paradigms, take on a sacred status; we seldom question these paradigms, even when they are the source of dysfunctional personal or organizational behavior. Radical, hate-filled organizations such as the Ku Klux Klan maintain and defend their irrational paradigms. The Klan's belief in racial separation, ethnic superiority, and its hatred of Catholics, Jews, and African Americans drive its dysfunctional behavior. Its people never stop to question their paradigm; they react defensively to any stimuli that threaten its examination.

Dysfunctional paradigms exist on all levels. They continue in existence until we become aware of the harm they are causing. Martin Luther King, Jr., for example, led a movement that forced a nation to consider how its racist-driven paradigm was destructive. King confronted the consciousness of the United States and challenged us to embrace a new paradigm, based on justice, equity, brotherhood, and love. The conflict that emerged was the conflict of two competing paradigms. King's movement, however, met both of Kuhn's conditions to be recognized as a paradigm: It was unprecedented and attracted a large number of adherents; it left a number of unresolved problems that needed addressing. The leader, in much the same manner as Martin Luther King, Jr., creates a readiness for change by heightening the awareness of members in his school community that is central to personal and organizational renewal.

REFLECTION IN ACTION

As you read the following case study, write down the principal's guarded thoughts and feelings that he hides from his faculty. Additionally, write the changes you think need to occur for the principal to be successful.

■ ■ ■ ■ ■ ▬▬▬▬▬▬▬▬▬▬▬▬▬▬▬▬▬▬▬▬▬▬▬▬▬▬▬

CASE STUDY

Malcolm Stephens is principal of Riverview High School, the oldest high school in the Sunset School District. The Sunset community has undergone a metamorphosis during the past decade. When Riverside was built, the community was a suburb of Stillman. Sunset was a getaway community for high-socioeconomic families. The mean income in Sunset was nearly triple that of Stillman. Sunset's population growth was slow in comparison to Stillman's. Before long, Stillman surrounded Sunset. Even though Stillman surrounded it, the Sunset community leaders fought hard to maintain their community's unique status as an enclave for the rich.

Bad political and economic news changed Stillman's destiny. The federal government announced the closure of military bases that were at the heart of the Stillman community. Stillman community leaders proactively sought to make Stillman a home to the high-tech industry. Stillman experienced high prosperity and rapid development. The new money in Stillman didn't move to Sunset; instead it went to the north side of Stillman well beyond the Sunset borders.

Sunset residents began to sell their homes and move into the new, more upscale developments in Stillman. Blue-collar workers began to move to Sunset. The mean income of the community rapidly dropped. Dramatic changes occurred in the school system. The demographics of the student body rapidly changed. Although the students at Riverside were significantly different in terms of culture, race, and ethnicity, the building and the teachers remained substantially the same. Mr. Stephens addressed this issue with his faculty at a faculty meeting.

Mr. Stephens began, "Riverside High School is not the same school many of you remember. We have a different student population with different needs. As a learning community, I believe we need to address this issue. These students respond differently from our former Riverside students. They are just as intelligent. They are just as quick to grasp new concepts. They simply come from cultural backgrounds significantly different from the population that many of you are used to teaching. What should we do? I am open to suggestions."

(continued)

CASE STUDY   CONTINUED

Joe Peterson, head of the teachers' union and a chemistry teacher, couldn't wait to speak. He was on his feet and with a loud voice stated: "Are you implying that the quality of our teaching is poor?"

"No, I'm not. I said we have to do things differently," responded Malcolm Stephens with a hint of irritation in his voice.

Rene DuCharme, an English teacher with more than twenty years' service at Riverside rose to speak, her arms akimbo: "If the quality of our teaching is not poor, then why do we have to do things differently? We've always had standards; these children need to meet those standards. Are you against standards?"

Rene DuCharme turned and smiled at her peers. Her comments were met with applause.

Malcolm Stephens's mind began racing; he wasn't ready for this strong reaction to his statement. He thought the faculty would understand the problem and want to cooperate. He tried to alleviate the concerns of the teachers by stating: "I didn't mention lowering standards. I just want you to consider alternative approaches to educating students from backgrounds quite dissimilar to those present in this room."

Jack Sloan, history teacher, stated: "What difference does that make? These kids will have to make it in the world and we don't do them any favors by coddling them."

The teachers erupted into applause. The faculty meeting continued along these lines for an hour with no resolution; many teachers left angry.

Malcolm Stephens returned to his office after the faculty meeting. He sat in his chair and stared out his window. He felt depressed. He asked himself why are they so blind? What's wrong with them? He felt strongly about this issue, but he had no support. When he walked down the hallways of his school he knew the demographics had changed just by observing the students. He felt that his teachers didn't care. All his teachers wanted to do, he believed, was to hold on to the past; they didn't care who got hurt.

Many leaders can identify with Malcolm Stephens. They find themselves in situations in which no one wants to recognize the reality of what is happening. No one wants to hear the truth. Everyone wants to continue operating as he or she always has, oblivious of the facts, into the future. Joseph Campbell, famed anthropologist, stated: "If we fix on the old, we get stuck. When we hang on to any form, we are in danger of putrefaction."[4]

These types of situations are the testing fields of those who desire to lead and manage change. The leader has an ethical imperative and stands nearly alone against overwhelming opposition. If the leader does nothing, then the leader is worse than the members of his organization, because he clearly understands what has to be done. It is the leader's responsibility to create readiness for change. James MacGregor Burns, in his seminal work, *Leadership*, states:

Leaders can also shape, alter, and elevate the motives, values, and goals of follow-ers through the vital teaching role of leadership. This is transforming leadership. The premise of this leadership is that, whatever the separate interests persons might hold, they are presently or potentially united in the pursuit of "higher" goals, the realization of which is tested by the achievement of significant change that rep-resents the collective or pooled interests of leaders and followers.[5]

When the leader prepares his organization for change, he applies his leader-ship role as teacher, challenger, and guide. He acts as a teacher when he provides new information regarding the paradigm shift and opens the organization to the possibility of change to address the shifting paradigm. He acts as challenger when he confronts the members' refusal to recognize the paradigm shift and requires them to confront the consequences of being in denial. He acts as guide when he prepares a map for the members to address the shifting paradigm. Chapter Five focuses on the principle that change leadership is proactive. The leader has an eth-ical imperative to make members aware of shifting paradigms and to change to meet the needs of the new, evolving paradigm.

ETHICAL IMPERATIVE FOR CHANGE

Contemporary leaders often act in transactional leadership roles. Their primary goal is to move the organization through a continuous series of negotiated steps. A crisis occurs; the leader intervenes and negotiates a settlement. The organization, temporarily stalled, again moves forward. Teachers complain about the schedule; the leader negotiates a compromise; the school again moves forward. Each day the leader negotiates a series of transactions with superordinates, peers, or subordi-nates to move the organization forward. There is little, if any, transforming leader-ship. The leader cannot create readiness for change as a transactional leader. The leader needs to act as a transformational leader to create conditions for change. James MacGregor Burns states:

> Transforming leadership is elevating. It is moral but not moralistic. Leaders engage with followers, but from higher levels of morality; in the enmeshing of goals and values, both leaders and followers are raised to more principled levels of judg-ment. . . . Much of this kind of elevating leadership asks sacrifices from followers rather than merely promising them goods.[6]

The transactional leader has no direction other than to move from point to point; the transforming leader has a moral compass and seeks to lift followers, rais-ing them to higher levels of purpose and achievement. In our case study, Malcolm Stephens has an opportunity to be a transformational leader. He is at a professional and personal crossroads. If he chooses to act as a transactional leader, the change process slows to a crawl. If change occurs, it will be externally driven. If he chooses to act as a transformational leader, he accelerates the change process; change becomes internally driven. If Mr. Stephens chooses to openly challenge existing practices, he will face severe opposition; he will know, however, that he stands on solid moral ground because he is doing the right thing.

ETHICS, CHANGE, AND PARADIGMS

A simple ethical heuristic is "to do the right thing, because it is the right thing to do." A person in a leadership position who does not have a well-founded set of values will never discover the right thing to do because the right thing to do changes with her context and is always self-serving. Leaders cannot operate from this sense of ethical relativism, whereby one path is as good as another path. The transforming leader is value driven. She understands that ignoring ethical principles degrades each member in the organization. For example, when one teacher abuses a student, all teachers suffer. When the leader ignores fairness in the application of discipline, the entire organization suffers. In effect, ignoring the ethical foundations inherent in all paradigms creates a transactional not a transformational organization. Many organizations, especially those in the business sector, are beginning to recognize that organizational ethical actions and success work synergistically. A paradigm that embraces this principle is the Japanese concept of *kyosei*.

Joseph Gorman, chairman of the U.S.–Japanese Business Council, states: "Kyosei, originally a biological term, translates literally as symbiosis, the living together of two dissimilar organisms in a mutually beneficial relationship."[7] We can adapt the *kyosei* philosophy to a dynamic, ethical-driven paradigm focused on continuous beneficial change by applying the following five stages:[8]

1. The educational organization focuses on academic achievement and establishes itself as a model for other schools.
2. The principal and teachers make a commitment to work together by recognizing that each other is vital to the school's success.
3. The principal and teachers extend their sense of cooperation to reach out to the school's constituents: the students and their parents.
4. The *kyosei*-driven school community reaches out to other schools in its district, serving as a model and mentor to elevate district-wide effectiveness.
5. The *kyosei*-driven school serves as a regional and national model for ethical-driven change.

Kyosei is a moral imperative that seeks to form a synergistic relationship first within the organization to develop a sense of internal harmony. It then seeks to act in harmony with the rest of its environment. This means that effective organizations change to act as a seamless web with their environment by embracing members as well as anyone affected by the organization's actions. Self-interest gives way to mutual interests. In the pursuit of mutual interests, the leader and teachers recognize that they have a social responsibility extending beyond the school's borders. It extends beyond the neighbor or community surrounding the school. It literally extends throughout the world. Each action of the leader and the teachers affects everyone. It is akin to chaos theory. When leaders use the concept of *kyosei* as a prerequisite for school change, we see the close relationship of change and ethics.

Change and Ethics

The whole notion of change is an ethical issue. Why change if the change does not better the organization? Why refrain from change if the change betters the organization? In each case, to change or not to change, the motivation is to bring benefit to the members of the organization and the community the organization serves. Stephen Carter, author of *Integrity,* states: "The first [step], and it's a hard one, is to do the difficult work of discerning what's really the right thing to do. The second step is to do that right thing even at some personal cost. And the third step is to be willing to be open about it—to say, I'm doing what I believe is right."[9]

The leader takes a series of actions to create a sense of readiness among the members of his organization. He chooses to be a transforming leader. He knows when change is necessary to bring benefit to all members of the school community. He is willing to act on his belief that the considered change is the right thing to do. Malcolm Stephens's desire for change is driven by changing demographics.

A starting point, and a model for Malcolm Stephens, is Martin Luther King, Jr. King challenged the existing paradigm of treating African Americans as less than equal to their white counterparts. The notion of separate but equal flew in the face of his definition of equality. He knew he had no other choice but to confront the existing unethical paradigm. King challenged America in August 1963 at his famous march on Washington, D.C. He named the existing paradigm and stated that it was no longer acceptable. He said:

> We have also come to this hallowed spot to remind America of the fierce urgency of now. This is no time to engage in the luxury of cooling off or to take the tranquilizing drug of gradualism. Now is the time to make real the promises of democracy. Now is the time to rise from the dark and desolate valley of segregation to the sunlit path of racial justice. Now is the time to lift our nation from the quicksand of racial injustice to the solid rock of brotherhood. Now is the time to make justice a reality for all of God's children.[10]

People choosing to be transforming leaders have no choice but to follow King's example. Fortunately, King provided a way to awaken people to their present condition. In this awakened condition they could grapple with the struggles associated with change. In King's *Letter from a Birmingham Jail,* he identified four basic steps that the transformational leader uses to create a readiness for change: collection of the facts to determine whether injustices exist, negotiation, self-purification, and direct action. We can adapt these four steps to assist leaders in creating a readiness state for change.

GENERATING A CHANGE ENVIRONMENT

Collection of Facts

Step One: Collect the Facts to Demonstrate That Change Is Essential.   The trans-formational leader changes her focus regarding facts. She focuses on a rationale for change and the benefits and consequences of change. On the one hand, she wants to maximize the benefits of change to affect all members of the school community pos-itively. On the other hand, she is cognizant of the consequences of change on each member of the school community. She asks if some members benefit more from the change than others. She asks if some members are hurt by the change. She asks if the change benefits the organization and the organization's stakeholders. The answers to these questions allow her to challenge her organization.

The data she collects form her ethical conscience. As the leader, she has a fidu-ciary responsibility to all members of the school community. She protects the rights of minority members of the organization by ensuring that the majority does not abuse its power. The facts lend support to her voice. She uses these facts to gain the cooperation of the members of the organization.

Malcolm Stephens, in his next faculty meeting, makes a PowerPoint presen-tation to demonstrate the shift in demographics to the faculty. He points out how minority males are disproportionately sent to the office. He shares the data that indicates the increased dropout rate. He indicates a significant drop in the college application rate. As he presents his facts, he speaks passionately about the need to address these issues. He clearly makes his case. As he looks at his faculty, he quickly reads their nonverbal defensive positions. He sees only a few faculty mem-bers whom he can count on for support. His meeting ends quickly and quietly with faculty murmuring to each other as they leave the meeting. Mr. Stephens, as a transformational leader, moves to step two, negotiations.

Negotiations

Step Two: Negotiate Changes to Create an Ethical Climate.   A transformational leader is unwilling to compromise on any ethical issue. He uses negotiations to provide reticent faculty the opportunity to reflect on the consequences of their obstruction to change. The negotiation's process allows the leader to bring the old paradigm from the shadows into the light of current conditions. He doesn't allow the old paradigm to exist on the glories associated with its past. He acknowledges its past, but asks how this paradigm addresses the current context. The negotiation process is cooperative in nature. Gerald Nierenberg, referred to as the father of contemporary negotiating, states:

> Think of negotiation as a cooperative enterprise. If both parties cooperate, there is a likelihood that they will be persuaded to strive for similar goals. This does not mean that every goal will be of the same value to the participants. But it does mean that there is greater possibility for each participant to reach successful coop-erative goals.[11]

At its best, negotiating is a cooperative venture wherein the negotiating process discovers the true interests of those opposed to the change. It takes patience to achieve this goal, but unless the leader achieves this goal, she will not reconcile the forces aligned with the old paradigm to her ethical imperative to change. The Harvard Negotiating Project provides a clear process to follow:[12]

- Separate people from the problem
- Focus on interests, not positions
- Invent options for mutual gain
- Insist on using objective criteria

Perhaps the biggest obstacle the leader faces when confronting people maintaining an outdated paradigm is their adherence to outdated behavioral scripts. He may find them rigid, unethical, or apathetic. If the leader focuses on the outdated scripts, he loses perspective to what he wants to accomplish. By focusing solely on the problem, he doesn't let their outdated scripts interfere with his change goals. Malcolm Stephens does not like some of the faculty members, especially those who seem to think that they are the interpreters of school history. He realizes that they are not the problem; he separates the problem from personal scripts.

There is a difference between position and interests. When Malcolm Stephens recognizes this difference, he liberates himself from being locked in a fixed position and opens himself to discovering common ground to integrate interests. At this point, Stephens and his faculty are locked into fixed positions. The faculty, operating out of the traditional paradigm, resist any efforts to change. He recognizes the changing demographic patterns and wants to embrace a new paradigm. In effect, Stephens and his faculty find themselves locked into a zero-sum contest.

By focusing on interests, the leader moves away from fixed positions. When the leader focuses on interests, he concentrates on individual needs, desires, apprehensions, and qualms. Each side has multiple interests. In our case study, for example, Mr. Stephens wants to address the issues caused by changing demographics. That is not his sole interest. He wants to prevent potential demonstrations by a vocal minority group. He wants to make sure that academic achievement scores improve. The issue that he refuses to bring to the table is that he wants to become superintendent of schools. Making these changes will provide him with the support he needs to make his move for the position. Conversely, the faculty worries about their professional evaluations. They fear that if they change, they will receive poor evaluations because they are on a learning curve. They fear that they will lose their elite status because teaching at Riverside will no longer be a prestigious job.

Malcolm Stephens now understands that the faculty position is different from their interests. By focusing on their interests, he can creatively generate options to produce mutual gain. A major obstacle in coming to an agreement supporting mutual interests is the misguided notion that there is only one solution. If both sides generate options that address mutual interests, a synergistic effect occurs. This process works best in a facilitated brainstorming environment. In this environment, neither group needs to be defensive, because there is nothing to defend; their positions are not being attacked. They seek ways to integrate interests. This requires the leader to be astute in reading between the lines to discover issues important to the faculty. The leader's sensitivity to nonverbal language or rephrasing statements by faculty members to include descriptions of the hidden issues may lead to issue discovery. New options, previously hidden, emerge. Malcolm Stephens likes this approach. He believes that its cooperative nature will build faculty morale and heal a growing rift between faculty and community.

In spite of his growing optimism, he knows that coming to a successful conclusion is easier said than done. Two of the three primary faculty leaders have no desire to compromise; they promised their colleagues they intend to obstruct and hinder the negotiations process. Malcolm Stephens understands the reality of his situation. He refuses to participate in their game. He wonders if there is another option open to him. Leaders, like Malcolm Stephens, frequently find themselves in this position. Many believe that their only option is to resort to manipulative political power to force the issue. This strategy has short-term gain and long-term disastrous effects.

Fisher, Ury, and Patton advocate using objective criteria. They state: "In short, the approach is to commit yourself to reaching a solution based on principle, not pressure. Concentrate on the merits of the problem, not the mettle of the parties. Be open to reason, but closed to threats."[13] The leader focuses on objective standards and makes a call to fairness, justice, and equity. By positioning himself on the side of objective standards, fairness, justice, and equity, the leader projects his reasonableness to the school community. He can stand his ground in the face of threats or intimidation because he has moral authority. Malcolm Stephens now has a way out. He is acting as a transformational leader. He researches for objective standards. He produces objective data. He frames his argument in terms of fairness, justice, and equity. His actions cause the faculty to stop and listen, yet the primary leaders still refuse to listen to reason. Malcolm Stephens has no options left but to proceed to steps three and four.

Self-Purification

Step Three: The Leader Prepares for Confrontation.   *Self-purification* was the term King used in the civil rights struggle. Self-purification takes place in reflective silence. Dag Hammarskjöld, former secretary-general of the United Nations, stated:

> Always here and now—in that freedom which is one with distance, in that stillness which is born of silence. But—this is a freedom in the midst of action, a stillness in the midst of other human beings. The mystery is a constant reality to him who, in this world, is free from self-concern, a reality that grows peaceful and mature before the receptive attention of assent.[14]

The leader adapts this notion as preparation for escalating the conflict. Personal silence allows the leader to discover true motivation through reflection. Moreover, out of this period of self-reflection, the leader prepares for direct action. The leader's choices, at this point, are significantly narrowed. She knows that in spite of her efforts to produce ethical-driven change, people opposed to reasonable and beneficial change still refuse to listen to reason. She does not rush into action; she takes time to reflect. She ensures her forthcoming actions are accurate and appropriate through reflection, personal review, and consultation.

Reflection.   The leader reflects on the situation. He uses reflection to assess his motives. He uncovers hidden motives that indicate any self-interest motivating his change plans. During this reflection, he examines the potential consequences of his actions if he pursues his change action. In the end, he knows that a transformational leader, one who is concerned about doing the right thing, will have no other choice but to pursue change. His reflective process assures him that the primary beneficiaries of the intended change are all members of the school community, including those opposed to change.

The leader understands more fully the words of John Gardner, expert on leadership, who stated: "We were designed for struggle, for survival. Only fatal and final injuries neutralize that irrepressible striving toward the light. . . . An older deeply rooted, biologically and spiritually stubborn part of us continues to say yes to hoping, yes to striving, yes to life."[15]

Malcolm Stephens spends his evening alone in his study. He wants no interruptions. He reflects on his situation. He wants to ensure that he is doing the right thing. He quickly realizes that he has some selfish motives. He wants to show the faculty who is boss. He wants to enhance his reputation in the community. He steps back; he knows that these are the wrong reasons for pursuing his change. He continues to reflect on the issues. In the end, he comes to one conclusion: The issue is bigger than the faculty and more important than his career. He understands that the course he is choosing has political risks. He pauses, becomes deeply silent as if in prayer, and decides to move forward.

Personal Review.   The next phase of self-purification is to review all that led up to this point, assess all that was done to resolve the issue, and ask if there is anything that can possibly be done to create the necessary changes before moving to direct action. The personal review is a preparation for direction. The leader thoroughly considers every detail left out of the previous steps. The leader responds immediately when she discovers what could have been done. She demonstrates leadership because her goal is to benefit everyone. She is not concerned about winning but with personal and organizational wholeness.

Malcolm Stephens took out a pad of legal paper and made three lists. The first list included the actions he took to prepare the groundwork for change. His second list included those in his organization opposed to his changes. His third list included each reason for his proposed change. He reviewed each item on his three lists. He wondered if there was anything different he could have done and if the groundwork for the change was inadequately prepared. He asked himself if he went the extra mile to engage those opposed to change. In each instance, he concluded that he was thoughtful, flexible, and above all, he listened. There was no more to do to move the faculty to embrace the proposed change. He knew that he had to take direct action. Before he moved to direct action, Malcolm Stephens took the final step of self-purification: He consulted with a trusted friend and mentor.

Consultation.   Consultation is the final phase of the self-purification process. The leader consults, not to discover the best course of direct action, but to bring the process to the eyes of a detached, unbiased observer. The leader consults with a person whom she trusts and yet this person must be willing to be truthful with the leader. The leader, if she is to fulfill her mission as a transformational change leader, needs objectivity. The consultant provides this objective advice. He uses questions to understand the leader's motives. He challenges the leader as to the expected outcomes. It is through the consultant's objectivity that the leader knows that she personally examined her motives and actions; she also opened herself to the scrutiny of another. At this point, the leader is prepared to act.

Direct Action

Step Four: Move to Direct Action.   Direct action is the leader's response to the change opponents' unwillingness to change constructively. The leader's response demonstrates patience, understanding, and a willingness to reconcile differences between those who want change and those who resist it. The leader moves to direct action because he has no other option. If he fails to move, he acts in complicity with those who resist the change. Martin Luther King, Jr., spoke of what it means to fail to act:

> At a small town along the way, some white passengers boarded the bus, and the white driver ordered us to get up and give the whites our seats. We didn't move quickly enough to suit him, so he began cursing us, calling us "black sons of bitches." I intended to stay right in that seat, but Mrs. Bradley finally urged me up, saying we had to obey the law. And so we stood up in the aisle for the ninety miles to Atlanta. That night will never leave my memory. It was the angriest I have ever been in my life.[16]

The leader is not afraid to act constructively. Direct action is not a massive attack on the enemy's positions. The transformational leader does not view those in opposition to the change as enemies. She understands their fear. She understands their inability to move from a fixed archaic paradigm. She understands their reluctance to give up something they have known for many years for something new. She knows her actions will provide hope to those desperately seeking change. The leader can gain inspiration from numerous historical examples whereby small acts of leadership changed organizations, countries, and the course of history.

It took the simple act of a woman, Rosa Parks, to spark the civil rights movement. It took Nelson Mandela's willingness to sit in jail to break the back of apartheid. It took a teacher, Anne Sullivan, to liberate Helen Keller from the tragedy of being blind, deaf, and mute into a brilliant author, speaker, and inspiration to the world. Anne Sullivan stated: "People seldom see the halting and painful steps by which the most insignificant success is achieved."[17] All great events are only great in retrospect. At their occurrence, they are simply a small act of direct action taken by a person who wants to change his or her context. Sometimes these acts of direct action spawn a national or global movement. Other times, they improve the condition of the person's context.

The transformational leader is decisive. His decisiveness comes from confidence and lack of fear and anxiety over potential consequences. The leader's courage to act transcends any crisis of confidence, fear, or anxiety. Often, his actions are taken alone with no visible support. His only support is an inner voice urging him to move forward. One way to break through the paralysis of action is to follow a simple four-step procedure:

1. Choose a straightforward, achievable goal.
2. Act in proportion to the context and people.
3. Sustain action.
4. Modify actions to sustain movement.

The transformational leader chooses a straightforward, achievable goal for action. This goal may be little more than a public announcement of intention to the faculty. It may be writing a memorandum to the superintendent requesting an item to be placed on the school board's agenda. It may be confronting a marginal teacher. The goal is the intention. It is something that the leader knows he or she can accomplish in a relatively short time.

The transformational leader acts in proportion to the context and people. The action has to have a sense of proportionality. The leader, for example, who chooses to confront the marginal teacher, acts with a sense of proportionality when she requests to meet with the teacher and initiates a discussion regarding the improvement of performance. The leader who acts disproportionately may immediately transfer the teacher, put a letter in the teacher's file, or announce that she is moving to terminate the teacher's contract.

The transformational leader uses the initial act as a catalyst for further action. Each act is part of a finely woven web. Malcolm Stephens takes direct action by calling a faculty meeting and announcing that he is directing department chairpersons to work with their faculty to conduct a self-study on how effectively their departments address academic issues related to minority students. This direct action sends a message to the school community that he wants the school to meet the academic needs of minority students. Malcolm Stephens's next direct act is to form a steering committee comprised of faculty and community members. The steering committee's charge is to develop recommendations, based on input of the academic departments, community members, and students, for improved academic achievement among minority students. Each of Malcolm Stephens's actions is part of his web of direct action. Each direct action creates more lines to his web and moves his school toward his visualized change.

The transformational leader modifies action to sustain movement. She has one eye to the future, one eye to the past, and two feet in the present moment. This leader understands that any action needs monitoring. From an ethical perspective, she knows that she cannot justify the continuation of an action that brings direct harm to the organization and its members, or an action that produces few beneficial results.

She modifies her actions as the process unfolds. In the case of the principal who confronts the marginal teacher, the principal discovers that the initial session with the teacher did not produce any results. The principal recognizes that her intervention needs to be more than a discussion to raise the awareness level of the teacher. She now works with the teacher to videotape the teacher's classes as a means of helping the teacher gain awareness of the teacher's marginal performance.

Direct action unexpectedly catches those who adamantly resist change off-guard by forcing resisters to respond. They may more actively resist the direct action, they may grudgingly give in to the change, or they may have an enlightening experience and embrace the change. The leader cannot ignore resistance to the change. He must act to confront faculty resistance. His actions are directed at the problem and never at the person. He knows, in the end, he must govern the school. He knows that eventually he will lead a healing process. As long as he focuses on the problem and not on the person, he increases the opportunity for healing rifts that occurred during the direct action stage. The leader, however, does not worry about hurting someone's feelings during direct action. He knows that he has tried to work with them, but was unable to make progress. One school principal explained how a faculty member threatened him with a grievance if he forced the faculty member to conform to his required actions. The principal told the faculty member to file the grievance stating that the grievance process identifies and remedies contractual conflicts. The faculty member left and never filed a grievance.

CHANGING CULTURE

According to Edgar Schein,

> The term culture should be reserved for the deeper level of basic assumptions and beliefs that are shared by members of an organization, that operate unconsciously, and that define in a basic taken-for-granted fashion an organization's view of itself and its environment. These assumptions and beliefs are learned responses to a group's problems of survival in its external environment and its problems of internal integration.[18]

The group responds to survival problems through a series of strategies adapted to interact successfully with its environment. Understanding the synergistic interaction between an organization's culture and its dominant paradigm is one way of explaining how difficult it is for the leader to win majority support for change. The difficulty is exacerbated because values and beliefs embedded in the culture and made manifest in its operational paradigms become stratified over time. In Figure 5.2, the organization's degree of flexibility is directly proportional to the organization's age. Stratification occurs as the organization matures and leads members to believe that the organization's values and actions are above questioning. As the organization becomes increasingly inflexible, it develops a type of organizational paranoia because of the group's attitudes and behaviors.

Whoever questions its actions or values is an enemy. Thus, members commit themselves more firmly to the organization and its culture, values, beliefs, and paradigms. The greater the number of people committed to the culture, the more

Maturity

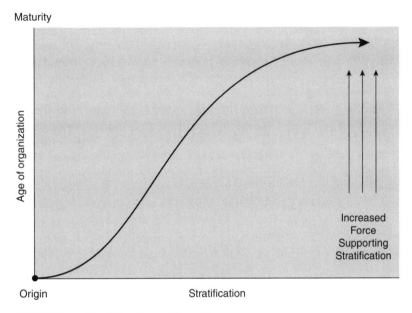

FIGURE 5.2   **Stratification of Paradigms**

difficult it becomes to challenge, let alone create, an environment for constructive change. This is evidenced every day in monolithic organizations. Sometimes
the cultures of these organizations go awry, and the organizations act in self-serving
ways that bring harm to their constituencies. We see, for example, the harm
brought about by Nazi Germany, the Inquisition, and the American conquest of
Native Americans. Well-intentioned people act in opposition to their espoused values as the organizational culture and its values and beliefs override personal values and beliefs.

   If we assume that people are innately good and will cooperate to get along,
then we have to wonder why they resist change, even when it is in their best interests. Part of the answer rests in the nature of the organization's paradigm. For
example, you and a friend decide to go to a movie. Neither you nor your friend has
a fixed idea of the movie that you want to see. Prior to going to the theater, you and
your friend go out for dinner. You have a wonderful meal. The food, service, and
conversation make the experience delightful. You both are in wonderful moods.
When you get to the theater, both of you decide to risk and see a new movie. You
have no idea as to the movie's plot and themes. The movie is as intense as it is
excellent. Both of you lose your sense of being together in the theater; instead, you
seemingly move into the screen taking on the strong emotions of the characters
with whom you identify. The tragic ending leaves you, as well as the other theater
patrons, sitting in your seats wanting a different ending; however, that is not going
to happen. You and your friend leave the theater silently and walk to your car
without saying a word. Now, you both feel depressed, angry, and filled with anxiety. You adopted the emotions of the actors in the movie.

You and your friend moved between paradigms. You moved from the paradigm of the restaurant to the paradigm of the theater. Each venue presented you with a set of beliefs and values. Each venue presented an environment that supported these beliefs and values. Assume that you and your friend desired to have a romantic evening. The restaurant you selected had soft lights, romantic music, and discrete seating. The restaurant's environment supports the beliefs and values of its paradigm: Patrons experience quality food in a romantic atmosphere. Conversely, the theater provides an entirely different environment. It is not designed for romance. Its design links you to the movie. You identify with the characters, plot, and story lines. The theater provides stereo sound that seems to come from all parts of the room. The screen is so large that it mesmerizes you. The theater's environment supports the beliefs and values of its paradigm: Patrons will enjoy the movie and live out their fantasies vicariously by identifying with the actors and actresses on the screen.

The description of your experience of attending a restaurant and movie with your friend is exactly the same as what happens to each of the members of your organization when he or she comes to work each day. Embedded in the organizational paradigm is a set of beliefs and values that determines how teachers and administrators interact, work together, relate to students and parents, and value their work. This environment, like that of the restaurant and theater, creates a paradigm that determines reality. Moreover, like the restaurant and theater, the reality it creates may be only an illusion. Martin Luther King, Jr., knew that the phrase "separate but equal" was an oxymoron. He knew that living that illusion was wrong for African Americans as well as for every U.S. citizen. Similarly, we have teachers, counselors, and administrators who wake up each morning in a wonderful mood. They are ready to change the world. They walk into the school and within minutes their attitudes change and they move to a survival mode. Kurt Lewin said that a reeducation process was the only way to alter this environment. Lewin stated:

> It [the reeducation process] changes his cognitive structure, the way he sees the physical and social worlds, including all his facts, concepts, beliefs, and expectations. It modifies his valences and values, and these embrace both his attractions and aversions to groups and group standards, his feelings in regard to status differences, and his reactions to sources of approval or disapproval.[19]

The transformational leader realizes that change resisters are not the enemy. She realizes that they are caught in a paradigm they did not create. She also knows that each day they unwittingly contribute to the sustenance of that paradigm. Consider, for example, walking into the faculty lounge in which the dominant conversation relates to put-downs of students. If the person is a teacher, the teacher can participate, ignore the conversation, confront the participants, or leave. If the teacher chooses to confront, she takes on the culture of the organization and risks the wrath of her colleagues. If she chooses to leave, she isolates herself from her colleagues. If she chooses to remain and not participate, she risks being drawn into the conversation or being a silent coconspirator. In the end, if she stays, she slowly takes on the beliefs and values of the group. These beliefs and values drive the organizational paradigm creating a world of reality for its members during their workdays. It is through the lens of this overriding paradigm that members interpret all experience. David Zatz, organizational development expert, states:

> The underlying causes of many companies' problems are not in the structure, CEO, or staff; they are in the social structure and culture. Because people working in different cultures act and perform differently, changing the culture can allow everyone to perform more effectively and constructively. This applies to colleges and schools as much as it applies to businesses.[20]

Lewin informs us that people cannot change unless their structure and social support system change (see Learning from Lewin, Chapter Two). Thus, the leader who demands change in the face of a hostile, nonsupportive environment will not achieve lasting change. Lewin's lesson, then, is to focus on the organization and determine the degree that the organization supports change and the degree of nonsupport that exists. Organizations, like individuals, have an espoused theory. In most cases, leaders will declare that they are change agents and that they support those who desire to change. In reality, their policies, rules, and sanctions provide different answers. One principal, for example, claimed to be a change leader. The principal, however, refused to allow teachers to travel to specialized workshops. He claimed that the loss of instructional time for students didn't offset the knowledge gained by teachers. Teachers in this school soon stopped asking to attend workshops. They taught as they had always taught. Ironically, this principal complained about the quality of teaching when achievement scores declined. Transformational leaders operate differently by providing an environment that encourages and sustains personal growth and organizational renewal.

CONCLUDING POINT

Malcolm Stephens learned how he has to prepare his organization to change. He knows that he has to make choices. He has to choose between being a transformational and a transactional leader. He understands that at times being a transactional leader is in the organization's best interests; however, he realizes that transformational leadership elevates the moral discourse within the organization. He feels organizations can change, but organizations committed to a higher cause change in the right direction.

Malcolm Stephens didn't realize the personal investment involved in becoming a transformational leader. This will take personal and emotional investment; he, however, knew that this was his path. The first step he chose to take was a personal and an organizational examination. He wanted to discover the ways that he discouraged change. He knew that if he wanted the members to change, he first must change. He wanted to be sure there would be no excuses when he challenged the faculty to examine their attitudes toward changing demographics. He wanted to be sure that he led by example and that those who wanted to change received support and encouragement.

One path to creating a supportive, change-nurturing environment is to embrace the concept of *kyosei.* This Japanese term embodies the philosophy that Malcolm Stephens wanted to bring to Riverside. On the one hand, he wanted his school to be quality driven. On the other hand, he knew that quality without a cooperative, synergistic relationship within the school community and between the school community and its external constituents is an illusion. His first step was to assess the stage of *kyosei* of his school. He concluded he and his faculty had yet to enter stage one. He was excited; he had a vision. He knew where he wanted to lead his school and community.

By embracing the concept of *kyosei*, Malcolm Stephens moved toward transformational leadership. Malcolm Stephens reflected on the lives of transformational heroes. He began to read books about Martin Luther King, Jr., Gandhi, Madame Curie, Winston Churchill, Joan of Arc, and John F. Kennedy. He recognized that they, like all transformational leaders, elevated their followers to a higher plane. He believed that teaching is a great cause and he wanted his faculty to rekindle their fire for teaching. He became determined to challenge them, no matter the cost. He internalized King's four steps to prepare the organization for change. Malcolm Stephens knew he was ready to lead and manage change.

SUGGESTIONS FOR ACTION

- What rules, polices, and regulations in your school or organization discourage members from changing?

- What is the prevailing paradigm in your school? Does it support inclusion? Is it supportive of exclusion?

- At what stage of *kyosei* do you find your school? What is the first action you need to take to move your school to the next level of *kyosei*?

- To what extent does your school or organization incorporate the concept of *kyosei*? Do members work in harmony? If the school is clique driven, how does this impact the school's relationship with the community?

- What needs to change in your school? How can you frame that change as an ethical imperative? Will this change benefit all people or just special interests?

- Take time for personal reflection to delve into your innermost being and discover your core values. In this quiet time, renew your sense of resolve to complete your current mission.

- Do you understand your faculty? Alternatively, do you see them as allies and enemies? How can you move away from this reference point and seek to unite and not divide?

CHANGE FACTORS

TERM	HOW TO USE IT	WHAT IT MEANS
Collective consciousness	The leader seeks to promote continuous learning until the number of people who have learned the new skill achieves a critical mass and the new skill is automatically incorporated into the organization's consciousness.	Collective consciousness refers to the critical mass of people required to have an idea, concept, or skill become a part of the entire organization.
Direct action	The leader confronts change resistance after following the steps recommended by Martin Luther King, Jr., in this chapter. Direct action by the leader focuses on the moral reasons for change.	Direct action is a moral activist stage in the change process. It is an active confrontation of change resistance based on moral issues.
Kyosei	The leader seeks to assist the faculty in understanding that whatever happens in the school affects the entire community. Also, whatever happens in the community affects the school.	A Japanese term that refers to the development of a symbiotic relationship that one has with one's environment.
Paradigms	The leader seeks to have faculty continually review existing organizational paradigms to ensure that the paradigms are current and applicable to current contexts.	*Paradigm* is a term coined by Thomas Kuhn. It refers to a model of thinking, behaving, or inquiry that guides behavior.
Transactional leader	The leader uses transactional leadership only when it is in the organization's best interests. At times, the leader will have to negotiate with other people or agencies to promote the school's interests.	Transactional leadership refers to the action of the leader who exchanges one action in return for another. It can be summarized with the Latin term *quid pro quo*.
Transformational leader	The leader seeks to raise the aspirations, ideals, and hopes of the members of his or her organization.	Transformational leadership is seen as elevating the moral and aspiration levels of members of the organization.

N O T E S

1. Keyes, K., Jr. The Hundredth Monkey. Retrieved August 14, 2001, from the World Wide Web: http://www.worldtrans.org/pos/monkey.html.

2. Gustavsson, B. and Harung, H. (1994). Organizational Learning Based on Transforming Collective Consciousness. *The Learning Organization* 1, no. 1: 33–40, 34.

3. Kuhn, T. (1962/1996). *The structure of scientific revolutions* (3rd ed.). Chicago: University of Chicago Press, p. 10.

4. Osbon, D. K. (1991). *The Joseph Campbell Companion.* New York: HarperCollins, p. 18.

5. Burns, J. M. (1978). *Leadership.* New York: Harper & Row, pp. 425–426.

6. Ibid., p. 455.

7. Gorman, J. T. (April 5, 1993). The Road to Kyosei: Government and Industry Must Work Together. *Industry Week* 242, no. 7: 66f.

8. Adapted from Kaku, R. (July–August 1997). Thinking about the Path of Kyosei. *Harvard Business Review*, p. 55.

9. Carter, S. (1996). Winning Isn't Everything. *Across the Board* 33, no. 4: 40.

10. King, M. L. (August 28, 1963). I Have a Dream. *A Call to Conscience: The Landmark Speeches of Dr. Martin Luther King, Jr.* The Martin Luther King, Jr. Papers Project at Stanford University. Retrieved August 14, 2001, from the World Wide Web: http://www.stanford.edu/group/King/.

11. Nierenberg, G. (1968/1995). *The Art of Negotiating.* New York: Barnes & Noble, p. 21.

12. Fisher, R., Ury, W. and Patton, B. (1981/1991). *Getting to Yes: Negotiating Agreement without Giving In.* New York: Penguin.

13. Ibid., p. 83.

14. Hammarskjöld, D. (1963/1987). *Markings.* New York: Ballantine Books, p. 103.

15. Gardner, J. (1970). *Recovery of Confidence.* New York: W. W. Norton, p. 117.

16. Washington, J. M. (Ed.) (1986). *A Testament of Hope: The Essential Writings of Martin Luther King, Jr.* San Francisco: Harper & Row, p. 343.

17. On teaching Helen Keller, Letter, October 10, 1887; in "Helen Keller, The Story of My Life," 1903. Retrieved August 14, 2001, from the World Wide Web: http://www.bemorecreative.com/one/548.htm.

18. Schein, E. (1985). *Organizational Culture and Leadership.* San Francisco: Jossey-Bass, p. 6.

19. Lewin, K. (1948). *Resolving Social Conflicts: Selected Papers on Group Dynamics.* New York: Harper & Row, p. 59.

20. Zatz, D. (2000). Organizational Development: A Tool Pack for Enhanced Organizational Effectiveness. Retrieved August 14, 2001, from the World Wide Web: http://www.toolpack.com/culture.html.

ACCELERATE THE CHANGE PROCESS

Strategy ▪ *Control the Driving and Restraining Forces*

STARTING POINT

Imagine you are a strong swimmer with the ability to swim easily from one side of a bay to a cottage on the other side. You have confidence in your ability; the conditions are perfect. You enter the water and begin your swim. About one-third of the way across the bay, you feel cramps in your stomach and begin to think about your large lunch. You have had cramps before and know how to handle yourself in the water if they occur; you continue to swim. Midway through the swim, you glance toward the sky and notice a large thunderstorm approaching. It doesn't matter if you turn around or continue on the present course, the thunderstorm is going to pass right over you within the next ten minutes. As if the thunderstorm were not trouble enough, you become seized with apprehension when you detect a dorsal fin thirty yards in front of you. Is it a shark or a dolphin? Your circumstances have changed; you have become caught in the swirl of events in a dynamic context. Do you have the skills to survive? You have no choice but to call upon your experience and knowledge to survive.

Fortunately, this is a fantasy; but it contains striking parallels to events that occur in our lives. Moreover, the story provides two lessons for the leader who desires to lead or manage change. The first lesson is that things do change. The future will always be uncertain. With careful planning, we can minimize the impact of many unforeseen events. Yet, even with meticulous planning, catastrophic events occur. Our response to change determines our leadership effectiveness. Unfortunately, even if we have all the skills and attributes of an excellent leader, we can fail. We fail, unwittingly, because we never had a chance to succeed. We are like the swimmer in our story. The swimmer was full of confidence to perform the given task; however, the swimmer was unaware that circumstances were about to change. The swimmer was unprepared. The effective leader prepares for change and plans accordingly.

A second lesson is that hidden forces often conspire against successful change. Chris Argyris calls these resistance forces defensive routines. He states: "Organizational defensive routines are policies and actions that prevent individuals, parts, or the whole organization from experiencing threat or embarrassment and simultaneously prevent them from identifying and reducing the causes of the potential embarrassment or threat."[1] Defensive routines inhibit organizational learning. When an organization and its members fail to learn, they are condemned to repeat past mistakes. These defensive routines are also constraining forces.

A constraining force is any external or internal source that intervenes against the successful completion of an action. Constraining forces can be internal in the sense that their sources are suppressed beliefs and values, personal rules, personal and professional scripts, cognitive processes, and learning capacity. Constraining forces are external in the sense that each person with whom we come into contact consciously or subconsciously brings his or her constraining forces to the interaction. They are also external in the sense that the organization has rules, expectations, policies, and customs that diminish successful and constructive change. Identifying personal and organizational constraining forces is an important part of change leadership. Once the leader identifies these constraining forces, she can replace the constraining forces with change catalysts. In other words, the leader can reconstruct her professional approach to change to increase her effectiveness as a change agent. She can also reconstruct the school environment so that it promotes change.

We can increase our chances for success if we replace organizational constraining forces with driving forces that act as catalysts. Ralph Larsen, chairman and CEO of Johnson & Johnson, states:

> How, then, were we to go about informing our operating management worldwide about the increasingly serious, company-wide challenges we faced? How could we inspire our leaders to embrace a more unified perspective? How could we establish an environment in which we could break down organizational, functional, and geographic barriers and act in concert on challenges best met through a cooperative approach?[2]

The leader, like his organizational counterparts, must identify and replace organizational constraining forces to create a change-enhancing environment.

REFLECTION IN ACTION

As you read the following case study, write down the principal's guarded thoughts and feelings that he hides from his faculty. Additionally, write the changes you think need to occur for the principal to be successful.

CASE STUDY

The superintendent of schools personally recruited Jeremiah Costanza to be the principal of Aver High School. Mr. Costanza's reputation as a strong disciplinarian preceded him. Mr. Costanza's predecessor was forced to resign after ten years as principal. The superintendent, in a private meeting with Jerry Costanza, pulled no punches:

"Jerry, you've got a mess on your hands. The parents are outraged; they don't think their kids are safe. Teacher morale is the lowest I've seen in twenty years in this district. The hotheads are all in your school and I have a contract to negotiate with them. It's going to be tough enough without having them angry over the situation in your school. You have a great reputation. You get things done. That's why I personally recruited you. I'll stay out of your way; do what you need to do; just keep me informed."

"It is a challenge. Thanks for the vote of confidence. I'll get the job done," replied Mr. Costanza while he wondered about the meaning of the superintendent's words.

Jeremiah Costanza's experience prepared him for this job. He had learned from his previous mistakes. He knew there were changes he could make within twenty-four hours to stabilize the situation. He knew as he drove up to the school that he would easily recognize the small things that could be done differently. He wondered if this was a gift or if the other principals he replaced were blind. As he walked into the main office, he noticed a large wooden board attached to the wall. The board was covered with little hooks and on each hook was a key. He had never seen anything like this before. He asked Larry O'Reilly, one of his assistant principals, to tell him about the board.

"We've had that board for five years. It was my idea and all of us think it has worked great. It allows us to keep tabs on teachers," stated O'Reilly.

"What do you mean keep tabs?" replied Costanza.

"Before we had that board we never knew when teachers were in the building. Now we require them to hang their keys on the board in the evening when they leave and pick them up when they come to school in the morning. No one sneaks in late anymore. We've got it covered."

"Larry, take the board down and put the keys in the teachers' mailboxes. We are going to treat them like adults."

"You can't do that. It's policy," argued O'Reilly.

"I am doing it. I want it down today."

O'Reilly turned red. It was clear he was trying to control himself. "Is that all?"

"Yes; let's plan to meet a little later."

O'Reilly turned around without shaking hands; he stormed off to his office and slammed the door behind him. Costanza later saw O'Reilly meeting with the other assistant principals. He guessed at the topic of their discussion. He wondered about the existence of other rules and policies that might be a cause of the toxic atmosphere at Aver High School.

Jeremiah Costanza wasn't about to allow his assistant principals to start a rebellion. He called them to join him in his office for a meeting.

(continued)

CASE STUDY CONTINUED

"Together we're going to turn this school around. The teachers, students, and parents are not your enemies. We are going to be uncompromising in uncovering every policy, rule, custom, belief, value, script, and collective cognitive process that stands in the way of making the beneficial changes. I want this to be a team effort. I want you to be part of that team. It will mean that we are going to question everything. Don't take it personally. Any questioning is not directed at you and your past performance. All questioning has the goal of making Aver High School the top high school in the state. Are you with me?"

He asked each assistant principal for a personal commitment. One by one, the assistant principals made the commitment. He looked at O'Reilly. O'Reilly shuffled his feet; he looked down at his papers. After what seemed an eternity, O'Reilly stated:

"The board wasn't my idea in the first place. I was new and put in charge of the board. You have my commitment. Let's get to work."

Jeremiah Costanza smiled and said, "Thank you. We have a lot of work to do and very little time before the start of the school year. We are going to go over every rule, overt and covert, discarding or upgrading those that are outdated. We're going to review the scripts that people follow and change the scripts where necessary. We're going to check our beliefs and values to make sure they're valid and aligned. We're going to examine our organizational purpose as well as our individual purposes. We have to know what we're about as professionals. Finally, we're going to check to see how well we learn as an administrative group and as an organization. If we can't learn, we can't change."

The room became charged with excitement. For the first time in years, O'Reilly later reflected, "We had hope. We all knew at the same time that we had bottomed out and started to turn the corner. It was the start of the greatest educational experience of my life."

Chapter Six focuses on the change principle that leaders must be aware of and control both the driving and constraining forces that influence change. Ignorance of these forces leads to organizational disaster.

THE RULES OF THE GAME

The Purpose of Rules

Rules are a personal and organizational necessity. They simplify life on a personal or organizational level. In the most basic sense, rules provide two common guidelines: I should do this; I should not do that. Most of the time, these rules evolve with practice. They are part of a family or organizational legacy. Rules drive our assumptions about how we act and expect each other to act. Some people, for example, have a rule as to the time they go to church services. It is painful for them to break this rule, so they design their lives around maintaining this rule. Other people have a rule about dinner. One family may have a rule that no one eats until everyone is ready to eat, whereas another family may have a rule that people come and go, taking what they need to eat to the television room, study, or deck. You may want to consider some of the rules that govern your life. Do you have a rule that dictates which section of the Sunday paper you read first? Do you have a rule about working late at the office? What is the rule about doing dishes at your home? Who makes the coffee? Do you call home, send an e-mail, or assume that people know you are working late? You will find that you have hundreds of unwritten rules that tell you what you should and should not do.

On an organizational level, rules are essential to govern how members relate to and work with each other. In one sense, rules are restrictive. They limit freedom. They place a fence around what we can and cannot do. In another sense, rules are liberating once we understand that we are free to roam within their restricted boundaries. Many parents who set rules report that their children, once grown, thank them because the rules gave the children the personal authority to tell peers that they had to refrain from harmful behavior because of potential parental sanctions. Rules, in any event, serve a function.

The function that rules serve can be functional or dysfunctional. Psychologist Virginia Satir provides four guidelines to determine if rules are functional or dysfunctional. These guidelines apply to personal as well as organizational settings. I added a fifth guideline regarding the importance of rules being ethical.

1. Are the rules overt?
2. Are the rules discussable?
3. Are the rules current?
4. Are the rules humane?
5. Are the rules ethical?

Effective Rules Are Overt.   When rules are overt, every member of the organization knows what the rules are and the purpose for each rule's existence. Overt rules have meaning. Teachers understand the necessity of the rule for beginning instruction at the start of class rather than wasting time with noninstructional issues. Covert rules, however, are sources of power that some people use as a means of control. Mr. Costanza and his team uncovered a series of covert rules in Aver High School. These covert rules, instituted by the previous principal, included the principal's requirement of having coffee each morning at 9 A.M. with two department chairpersons. The three of them determined policy for the school without consulting anyone else. Another covert rule they discovered was the requirement of teachers to return phone calls to parents from high socioeconomic backgrounds and to ignore phone calls from parents of low socioeconomic backgrounds. The team uncovered a third covert rule: Teachers supporting the former principal received more privileges and resources than did teachers who were neutral or outwardly opposed to the former principal. Covert rules disrupt and demoralize an organization. All rules need to be overt. Mr. Costanza and his team eliminated covert rules and together with the faculty began to discuss the types of rules that are important to an effective school.

Effective Rules Are Discussable.   One of the clearest signs of a dysfunctional organization is the inability of members to discuss openly what is happening in the organization. These organizations have an unwritten rule that no one openly talks about important issues. As Argyris points out, there is little discussion about issues that cause potential threat or embarrassment. However, effective rules are discussable. This means that any member of the organization can question the rule and have it explained. In effect, the rule must make sense. A person may disagree with the rule. If the rule is openly discussed and agreed upon by the majority, then there is fairness to the rule. Mr. Costanza and his team quickly discovered that the culture of the school prevented people from discussing anything that appeared to be a threat or proved to be embarrassing. It was little wonder, Mr. Costanza reflected, that rules were covert and undiscussable. Mr. Costanza and his team made plans to change this dysfunctional pattern. During the two planning days prior to the start of school, Mr. Costanza and his team were going to lead the faculty in identifying the rules that were to govern them during the year. Mr. Costanza told his team that he had two rules for this meeting: Rule one, every rule would be overt. Rule two, every rule would be discussable.

When asked by one of his administrators if he would feel threatened by the power given to teachers, Mr. Costanza replied, "The biggest threat to leadership is silence. When we're afraid to talk about any issue, we are afraid to grow. If we are afraid to grow, how can we change?"

Effective Rules Are Current.   Rules, once made, take on a separate life. They tend to exist long after the need for the rule ceased to exist. Because we become used to living by these rules, we fail to question the need for their existence and assume that these rules must continue to exist. The organization remains the same; yet the people within the organization change. The organization, to maintain stability, adheres to consistency in rules. As a result, outdated rules exist and act as constraining forces to change. Examples of outdated rules abound in all areas of life. Copernicus challenged the outdated rule that the earth was the center of the universe. Women challenged public and private organizational rules that excluded them from leadership positions. Outdated rules generally have one common purpose—they serve as a means of control. The outdated rule becomes a point of authority when people want to change. The outdated rule, because it has a history, acts as the standard and eliminates the challenge. It is only when people challenge the rule and not the person in authority that change has a chance to succeed.

Mr. Costanza and his team discovered a series of outdated rules. The rule regarding the board for teachers' keys was outdated. The requirement for teachers to submit lesson plans each Friday to the principal was outdated. The requirement for teachers to sit at desks in the hallways during their planning periods was outdated. Mr. Costanza and his team decided that each year the faculty would examine all rules and determine which ones were current and which were outdated. The outdated rules will be updated, made current, or discarded.

Effective Rules Are Humane.   Rules are made for the benefit of people, not people for the benefit of rules. This heuristic makes common sense, yet it is frequently violated. In rigid, closed systems, people exist to serve rules. These rules seldom benefit the members of the organization. In an open system, rules exist to facilitate the work and interaction of the members of the organization. Virginia Satir states: "The human–inhuman sequence means that you ask yourself to live by a rule that is nearly impossible to keep: 'No matter what happens, look happy.' "[3] When rules are impossible to keep we set people up for failure. We put them in a position of knowingly violating a rule. Simultaneously, the leader finds that he or she is in a position of enforcing a rule that puts an undue burden on members of the organization. These rules exist all around us. Have you ever traveled on a highway on which everyone exceeded the posted speed limit? If you were to obey the posted speed limit you would place yourself in jeopardy, so you, too, exceed the speed limit. The library at my university at one time had a rule that prohibited patrons from taking any beverage into the library. It was common to see students smuggling cans of soda into the library. The library supervisors constantly confiscated soda cans. Finally, someone had the insight to change the rule. The new rule allows patrons to take drinks into the library provided they are in approved containers. Students no longer violate the rule and supervisors no longer feel the pressure to enforce an inhumane rule.

Mr. Costanza's team identified inhumane rules. An assistant principal pointed out that teachers assigned to bus duty supervision also had to remain in their classrooms until the last student left the room. Mr. Costanza and his team had an "aha" experience. They understood the concept about outdated rules. They knew that following both rules was impossible for the teacher. Another inhumane rule was the requirement for teachers to stand in the lunch line with students. Because teachers stayed in the classroom until the last student left, teachers were always last in line. How could they eat lunch and be ready for their afternoon classes? Inhumane rules need to be replaced with rules that are more humane.

Effective Rules Are Ethical.   According to the Institute of Management Accountants,

> Ethics, in its broader sense, deals with human conduct in relation to what is morally good and bad, right and wrong. To determine whether a decision is good or bad, the decision maker must compare his/her options with some standard of perfection. This standard of perfection is not a statement of static position but requires the decision maker to assess the situation and the values of the parties affected by the decision. The decision maker must then estimate the outcome of the decision and be responsible for its results. Two good questions to ask when faced with an ethical dilemma are, "Will my actions be fair and just to all parties affected?" and "Would I be pleased to have my closest friends learn of my actions?"[4]

Effective rules are ethical when they guide people to do what is morally right and inhibit them from doing what is morally wrong. For example, even though rules may have legal and organizational sanction, they may still be unethical. Rules upholding segregation in the United States were ethically wrong; rules requiring soldiers to murder innocent people during war are ethically wrong; and unspoken rules requiring principals to support teachers who emotionally abuse students are ethically wrong. Effective ethical rules guide relational behavior ensuring that no harm comes to any party.

Ethical rules, because they are relational in nature, operate to bring benefit to as many people as possible. When an organization's rules are ethical, members assume that the rules are fair, just, and equitable. These rules provide a sense of fair play and elevate the standards by which the organization operates.

Mr. Costanza and his team uncovered many rules. The following are two examples, one overt and the other covert, that compromised the integrity of the staff and administration at Aver High School. The first rule required guidance counselors not to allow students to drop out of school. Seemingly, this overt rule was positive. The rule, however, turned out to be questionable. When a student would go to the counselor's office and inform the counselor that she was going to drop out of school, the counselor, at the conclusion of the conversation, told the student that dropping out was not permissible. The student stopped attending school. The school did not have to register a dropout statistic for state review. The student became an attendance statistic. The purpose of the rule was not to help students; it was to disguise the high dropout rate at Aver High School.

The second rule was covert. The former principal required every teacher to come into his office on Friday afternoon and wish him a good weekend. All the faculty knew the reason: The principal wanted to make sure that no one left school before the posted time of one hour after the close of school. If a teacher failed to obey the rule, the principal called the teacher's house and left a "have a good weekend message." The teacher followed the rule the next week. The principal's covert rule was unethical because the rule had no practical benefit for the principal or for the teachers. It was an imposition designed to maintain the principal's control. When unethical rules operate as covert rules, everyone in the organization knows that he or she must follow the rules or receive some type of sanction.

Mr. Costanza's work to update rules and to create an open, ethical organization paved the way for the establishment of a learning environment. The faculty, however, had experienced a decade of repressive leadership. The rules changed, but their attitudes remained frozen. Mr. Costanza realized that changing the rules was only the first step in creating a change-empowering environment. He knew that the teachers and his administrators were operating with poorly written scripts, scripts that each person memorized and played back as though he or she were constantly on cue. These scripts, when rewritten, provide a chance for sustained change.

UNDERSTANDING SCRIPTS

We normally associate a script with a text of a play or movie. In another sense, we can learn much about organizational change and what inhibits organizational change from occurring if we consider the notion of scripts and apply it to the roles and relationships between and among roles as they evolve in the organizational setting. According to Gioia, "Scripts are dynamic event sequenced oriented webs of structured knowledge held in memory."[5] That is, they represent a specific, rational way of responding to circumstances or events.

Scripts can be personal or occur in a group-culture context. Scripts operate on a personal level through the roles that we play. Imagine applying for a position as a school principal. No one sends you a script to memorize, but you have already memorized a script that was passed on to you via word of mouth and through observation. On the one hand, you understand what the community, teachers, and students expect of the principal. If you get the position and understand your script in the same way that everyone else interprets it, you will be successful. On the other hand, if you misread the script or play the role of principal differently from the one the audience expected you to play, your part may not last. The organization will get a new player for the role of principal.

Scripts operate on group-culture context when the group takes on a collective consciousness. This collective consciousness is systemic behavior that overrides individual behavior. Have you ever walked into a faculty lounge in a wonderful mood? What happened to your mood if the group's consciousness centered on negative attitudes toward parents, students, or administrators? Most likely, your good mood transformed into a negative mood. You left the lounge feeling depressed, angry, and perhaps upset for going into the lounge. It was no single person's fault. A collective, systemic consciousness guided the discussion. This consciousness had its genesis long before the current participants entered the room; it determined the group-culture scripts (see Figure 6.1). The consciousness is the sum of the combined historical collection of the interactions between and among members of the school community in general. The collection of interactions carries a history of interactions so that past interactions impact current and future interactions. The statistically overwhelming number of possible interactions forms the collective consciousness of the group.

The collective consciousness evolves into scripts. These scripts, like the script being played out in the lounge, can be a detriment to growth and change and create a lethal environment, destroying any attempt at creating a learning organization. Mr. Costanza's focus must be on the group's collective consciousness, not an individual's script. He knows that the starting place in changing scripts, whether personal or driven by group culture, is the role expectations driven by the collective consciousness of the group.

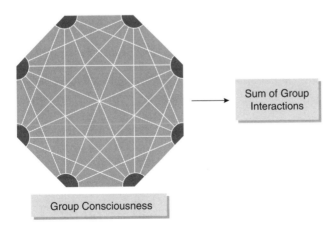

FIGURE 6.1 **Group Consciousness**

Role Expectations

Each role in the organization has role expectations. The person playing the role, like the actor on stage, wants to interpret the role to fit his personality and acting skills. According to Richard and Lawrence Goodman:

> Organizations are not revolutionary; they are evolutionary. Be they for profit or not, they need stakeholder acceptance to locate a viable space within which to pursue their existence. A sharp break with current practice and stakeholders cannot follow, cannot appreciate, cannot strongly support continued existence. Eventually, the sharp break becomes more common and the zone of legitimacy expands. This is because the stakeholders have learned a new language and like what they hear and see.[6]

The roles that members play are learned through training, experience, or induction. A teacher, for example, begins to learn to be a teacher the moment that he goes to school. In front of him, guiding his learning and shaping his behavior, is a teacher. The teacher models to the young student dreaming of becoming a teacher what it means to be a teacher. This informal training continues through high school and college. Finally, the apprentice gets a chance to practice his trade. He becomes a student teacher. Here, his induction is more formal. He is rewarded or punished, in terms of a grade, for his performance as a teacher.

The script that he must follow is written by his supervising teacher and reinforced by the teachers in the culture in which he begins to practice. After graduation, he takes his first formal position as a teacher. He is idealistic and eager to teach. At first, he meets with great success. The students love his new ideas and fresh approach to teaching. He finds, however, that his peers are not happy. They begin to make comments regarding the noise level and disorder that seems apparent as they walk by his classroom. His colleagues' complaints lead to a conference and classroom observation by the principal. The principal reinforces the script as written by the new teacher's colleagues. He is told to change. Over the next month, the new teacher teaches more traditionally; he is less enthusiastic, but his evaluations improve as well as his standing among his colleagues. He is an accepted member of the fraternity of teachers. He learned his script. Over time, he becomes a master performer. Some years later, a new student teacher comes to him eager with a different teaching script. The now veteran teacher smiles and says, "You'll learn."

Identifying Scripts

Operating with a script is normal. Some researchers refer to scripts as schemas. According to Duane Lyon, Mental Health Net,

> Schemas are the unspoken but common understanding of what behavior is suitable for a given social situation, like going to school, the theater, a church service, a symphony concert, or ball game. We may also have restaurant scripts, traffic scripts, and family scripts. The public sharing of such concepts of good, social behavior helps avoid confusion, embarrassment and ill will. Schemas may take the form of scripts, scenes, scores, roles, and ritual.[7]

We can identify scripts by identifying patterns of behavior. Each of us falls into a pattern that we repeat whenever the stimuli call for a learned script. For the most part, these scripts help us to be successful at our work and in our relationships. As we grow and mature, we discard old scripts and acquire different scripts based on the wisdom we acquire throughout life. There are scripts with which we become comfortable; we never question these scripts; they operate constantly in the background much like a computer operating system. If we are unaware of these scripts and they are destructive, we may continually sabotage our best interests. Maria Contera, a social studies teacher at Aver High School, has such a script. In a stress-free environment, Ms. Contera normally is an excellent teacher; she plays her idealized teacher script to perfection. When Ms. Contera is under stress or engaged in a conflict situation, she reverts to different scripts. When a male student challenges her in class, Ms. Contera becomes combative. She escalates the conflict and eventually sends the student to the office. At first, the school administration supported her script, which reinforced her behavior. Eventually, the school administration stopped supporting her and sent the student back to her class. Ms. Contera then played another script; she confronted the former principal of the Aver High School. She went into a tirade. When this failed, she broke into tears. The tears always worked for her, and the student was transferred out of her class. Her dysfunctional scripts, when reinforced, have wide ramifications. Her behavior impacts the students, peers, and the administration.

Mapping Scripts

Becoming aware of our dysfunctional scripts and understanding their consequences are important parts of rewriting scripts so that they become a catalyst for change rather than a constraining force. These maps, although individual in nature, contribute to the group-culture map. The National Institute for Mental Health (NIMH) reports:

> During the past 15 years, research exploring "social cognition" has . . . shown that people consciously and unconsciously process their experiences in accord with pre-existing views (or filters) of reality. Because these views are unique to individual social histories, each person interprets reality in a distinct way and responds differently to events. Moreover, a person's reactions to a given event may differ over time, depending on which views are elicited and become dominant in response to that event. Thus, understanding a person's behavior requires knowing which specific event(s) may have elicited it and how that person interpreted what happened. To understand someone's psychological distress, one must consider not only the person's social context but also those mental frameworks and interpretations that might provoke and maintain psychological difficulties.[8]

An effective way for individuals and groups to determine the effects of their scripts is to map the script beginning at its origin to the consequences that occur as the script plays itself out. Mapping requires honesty and objectivity. If done in a group setting, it requires that the group's focus is on the issue and not on any single person.

TABLE 6.1   Identifying Values and Beliefs

RECONSTRUCTION OF PAST ACTIONS	ASSOCIATED VALUES AND BELIEFS
May 8 I got to the high school at 7:45 A.M.	Values: Punctuality is not a value. All other administrators are on duty by 7 A.M. This is typical behavior. Belief: I don't believe it's important for me to be on duty before 7:45. That's when the first bus arrives.
I wandered through the halls speaking to students and teachers. I made sure I checked all lavatories for smokers.	Values: Interpersonal relations are important to me. I like human involvement. I also carry out assigned tasks. Beliefs: People are at the heart of being successful in my job. If students misbehave, it is in areas where there is little observation.
Mrs. Rostino called me about her daughter's suspension. I told her to stop babying her daughter and making excuses for her. Mrs. Rostino hung up.	Values: I don't like Mrs. Rostino. I don't act this way with other parents. I wonder if I am prejudiced because Mrs. Rostino is a single mother. I like telling people what to do—especially parents and children who are having problems. Beliefs: I think that single mothers make poor parents. I also believe that I don't have a clue as to how they raise their children.

Mapping begins by identifying values and beliefs. The most accurate way to determine values is to identify actions. In Table 6.1, Joe, an assistant principal at Aver High School, identified his values and beliefs by reconstructing his past actions.

The assistant principal reviewed and reflected on his reconstruction of a previous day's activities.

"I would not believe that I am so callous about getting to school on time. I never think about it; I justify being late. That must impact my other assistant principals. I'll bet you've been covering for me all the time," he said to the administrative team.

They smiled and nodded. He was now aware of his behavior and his rationalizing script. He made a mental note to rewrite his script about arriving to school on time.

"My treatment of Mrs. Rostino bothers me. I'm a people person; my reconstructed diary indicates that much. Don't you agree?" as he glanced up toward to the administrative team.

"Joe, you may be a people person, but do you count single moms in that group?" said Eileen, another assistant principal and single mom.

Joe felt his face getting red. He realized that Eileen was right on target. He took a deep breath, nodded affirmatively to her, and made a note to call Mrs. Rostino and apologize for his behavior. Joe's mapping of his behavior included his reconstruction of events; the identification of values and beliefs associated with his actions; and the acknowledgment of the negative impact of the consequences of his behavior on other people. By working through this process, Joe rewrote his script.

Writing the New Script

Joe learned that his practicing beliefs and values were not the same as his espoused beliefs and values. He didn't like admitting this, but he knew it was true. Joe's task is to write a new script aligning his beliefs and values with his actions. Metaphorically, Joe is rewiring his house to provide updated lighting. He has three choices: He can change his beliefs and values to align with his current actions. He can change his actions to align with his espoused beliefs. He can adopt new beliefs and values consistent with his image of himself and allow these new beliefs and values to dictate different behaviors.

Change Beliefs and Values That Align with Current Actions.   When we want to change our actions, we need to change the beliefs and values that drive those actions. Change is difficult when we focus only on the action. Imagine Joe accepting his primary belief that single moms cannot be good parents. This belief inhibits Joe from effectively interacting with 30 percent of parents in his school community. Even if Joe wants to change his actions toward single moms, his belief system will prevent him from effectively making the change. When people operate this way, they become isolated from the mainstream. They operate on the fringe in small close-knit groups of similar believers. Their primary task is to block out disconfirming information and to build a case of half-truths bolstering their untenable positions. Focus on identifying constraining beliefs and values and replace them with empowering beliefs and values.

Change Actions to Align with Espoused Beliefs.   Most people, once made aware of their dysfunctional behavior, choose to change their behavior to align with their beliefs and values. This is a good choice, if their beliefs and values are personally and communally beneficial. One way for Joe to be successful in changing his behavior is to reconstruct his daily activities for a month. Each day Joe has to review each event, determine his actions, and identify the beliefs and values that he expresses through his actions. This effort forces Joe to maintain the alignment of espoused beliefs and values with his actions. Joe will discover that he is memorizing a new script that provides personal growth and satisfaction with communal benefit.

According to neurolinguistic psychologists Dilts, Allbom, and Smith, "Beliefs represent one of the larger frameworks for behaviors. When you really believe something, you will behave congruently with that belief."[9] Because Joe assumes his beliefs help define his personal and professional identity, he will, through focused attention, gradually alter his behavior to correspond with these beliefs.

Adopt New Beliefs and Values Consistent with a Self-Image to Dictate Different Behavior.   Joe can adopt new beliefs and values consistent with his self-image and allow these new beliefs and values to dictate different behavior. This is the most demanding option, yet it has the potential to be the most efficient and effective. We learned or acquired all of our beliefs and values. Richard Bandler, one of the founders of neurolinguistic programming, contends that you can help people change if you can change their belief systems. The medical field takes advantage of this concept by using placebos—substances containing no medication. The patients, however, believe they are taking medicine that will make them well, so, in effect, they heal themselves. Our brains form beliefs by doing things quickly and simply, over time, and making patterns. The brain learns through rapid repetition.[10] These patterns become the paths that the mind follows. The patterns that the brain creates become the scripts that we follow.

Scripts and Beliefs

We have to replace beliefs taught at a formative stage to change our belief system. If we simply discard our current beliefs and do not replace them, other beliefs, not chosen by us, will take their place. These beliefs may be worse than the beliefs we originally held. There are three stages to follow to change a belief system.

1. Identify a new belief system and discard the previously held belief system.
2. Separate from people and groups espousing the discarded belief system.
3. Join a group espousing the new belief system.

Identify a New Belief System and Discard the Previously Held Belief System. The first stage is to identify the new belief system and discard the previously held belief system. As new, disconfirming, and discrediting information filters into the mind, the open mind realizes that currently held beliefs and values conflict with the new data. The flexible person investigates to see if the new data supports different beliefs and values that make personal and communal sense. These new beliefs and values make personal and communal sense if we can see that they contribute to constructive personal and communal growth. Once Joe determines his new beliefs and values, he learns to reference his behavior to these governing structures. If Joe returns to social groups that still hold his old values, he must challenge them to change and embrace his values. If they fail to change, they will challenge Joe's continued membership in the group. Joe can choose to remain a member by forsaking his newly acquired beliefs and values or he can leave the group.

Separate from People and Groups Espousing the Discarded Belief System.   The second stage is to separate from the group that supports the old belief system. Joe has little choice but to leave the group if he is a person of integrity. If he maintains his new beliefs and values, he will find that he compromises them each time he is with his group. Gradually, they will wear down his resistance. As he compromises his beliefs and values, he will feel a sense of guilt because he is violating his conscience. Joe's only option is to leave the group.

Leaving a group is emotionally difficult. The group may be family, colleagues, or long-time friends. Joe's actions to break away are possible, necessary, and courageous. Viktor Frankl, author of *Man's Search for Meaning,* stated: "Man simply does not exist but always decides what his existence will be, what he will become in the next moment. By the same token, every human being has the freedom to change at any instant. . . . man is capable of changing the world for the better if possible and of changing himself for the better if necessary."[11] Joe's departure from the group is a death symbol. Joe will feel all the symptoms of loss (see Chapter Four). If he continues to the next stage, Joe will experience a rebirth.

Join a Group Espousing the New Belief System.   The third stage requires Joe to join others who espouse his new belief system if he is to sustain his change. To embrace the third way, Joe has to be open to incoming data and allow the data to interact with what he already knows. The incoming information may support Joe's existing beliefs and values; it may question his existing beliefs and values, or it may discredit his existing beliefs and values. If Joe is willing to observe, listen, and reflect, he will discern the appropriateness of his beliefs and values. Psychologist Abraham Maslow stated:

> One finds what is right for one by listening in order to let oneself be molded, guided, directed. . . . One finds out what is right to do with the world by the same kind of listening to its nature and voices, by being sensitive to its requiredness and suggestions, by hushing so that its voices may be heard; by being receptive, noninterfering, nondemanding, and letting be.[12]

It is the foundation behind all major change programs and originates with the twelve-step program. Once we leave our social group and their espoused values, we have to find a new home. The selection of this new home is critical if we are to sustain our newly acquired beliefs and values. In the case study, the new group must simultaneously espouse similar values and be willing to embrace Joe. If Joe enters the group and does not feel welcomed, he will seek affiliation elsewhere. It is through meeting Joe's affiliation need that the group sustains his new set of beliefs and values. This is the practice of all formal organizations inducting new members. The new member quickly learns that the people who surround him are friendly, kind, supportive, and caring. The actions of these people confirm the validity of his switch in values.

Identifying Inhibiting Scripts

Mr. Costanza and his team realized the enormity of the task before them. They needed to identify Aver High School's inhibiting scripts in a collective sense; yet they also had to facilitate the discovery of inhibiting scripts within each member of school staff. He knew that discovery was personal; as a result, it had to be an internal experience. He had witnessed, as an assistant principal, a new principal describing the faculty's shortcomings to the faculty at the first faculty meeting. The faculty immediately turned against the new principal without giving him a chance. Mr. Costanza was not going to make that mistake. His process would take more time, but, in the end, he knew he was going to generate a strong sense of community at Aver. He read a story in the *New York Times* of a similar conflict between a new baseball manager and the star ballplayer on the team.

> [Sammy] Sosa [the star], the biggest name in Chicago baseball, has spoken out the past two days about what he sees as unfair criticism that [Don] Baylor [the manager] leveled at him indirectly when he was named manager of the Cubs last November. Baylor said at the time he wanted to see Sosa be more than a home run hitter. He said he should try to become a more complete player, playing better defense in the outfield and stealing bases more frequently [Baylor names Sosa's script without consulting Sosa]. "You don't criticize a player who comes here every day and plays hard," Sosa said yesterday. . . . He added that Baylor "has got no class."[13]

Mr. Costanza knew that the issue of identifying inhibiting scripts was necessary and fraught with danger. His experience and experiences that he had read about in other organizations made him caution his team to refrain from acting self-righteously by identifying everyone's inhibiting script. "Change," he said, "is less about telling and more about personal discovery and growth."

CHANGE CATALYSTS

Actions of Change Agents

His administrative team seemed overwhelmed with the task. Its focus to this point had been diagnostic and analytical. Mr. Costanza knew this was the right time for a transition. He had to move the team from viewing themselves as diagnosticians to seeing themselves as change agents. As change agents, he envisioned his administrative team as the primary source of energy for change. They were to be catalysts for the school community in the school's transformation into a learning organization. He knew from personal experience that the rhetoric of change had minimal motivating power. He had seen too many leaders use charismatic speaking power to motivate faculty to aspire to lofty challenges. He had seen these faculty members applaud the leader and leave the meeting room with great enthusiasm only to feel deflated, frustrated, and depressed because their efforts seemed futile. His administrative team members were going to be model change agents with a never-ending supply of energy, enthusiasm, and ideas for the faculty.

Effective change agents follow a different model. They ply their craft, like all quality artists, from their individuality. They embrace the seven characteristics of effective change agents.

1. They are catalysts for change.
2. They see things differently.
3. They have an attitude of optimism.
4. They are tenacious.
5. They are self-motivated.
6. They believe in people and in life.
7. They are real people.

Change Agents Are Catalysts for Change.   You can't have a cookout without a fire. If you want a fire for your cookout, you need to strike a match and apply the match to the fuel. Otherwise, you can sit and look at the food on the grill and you will only see the food gradually spoil. Likewise, someone has to be the match applied to the fuel so that the organization starts to move. Someone in the organization has to be the catalyst for change. This analogy tells us two things: (1) The leader, as change agent, must be the spark to ignite the dormant fuel. (2) The energy resources to sustain the change rest with the members. In other words, the leader and the members work collaboratively to sustain change.

The leader as catalyst intuitively identifies those members who have the readiness to change. She knows that readiness means a receptivity to change, the aptitude to acquire new skills, and the motivation to work at the change process until it succeeds. She does not consume the organization with massive change. Instead, she begins at the grassroots level, nurtures the organization's success, and gradually brings about the genesis of a team of catalysts for change. She no longer has to be the sole catalyst; she allows members to share in her role. In effect, the leader's role as a catalyst for change is to foster the formation of other catalysts for change.

Change Agents See Things Differently.   Much of the research on leadership speaks to vision and how leaders have a vision of where the organization should be heading. Having a vision is important for leadership. Equally important is the leader's ability to see things differently. A leader may have a clear vision; yet the vision may be disastrous for the organization. If the leader's thinking is rubricized, then the leader thinks in familiar patterns and sees only what he has always seen. Abraham Maslow states:

> In this area rubricizing consists of: (1) having only stereotyped problems, or in failing to perceive new ones, or in reshaping them, in a Procrustean fashion, so that they may be classified as familiar rather than novel, and/or (2) using only stereotyped and rote habits and techniques for solving these problems, and/or (3) having, in advance of all life's problems, sets of ready-made, cut and dried solutions and answers. These three tendencies add up to an almost complete guarantee against creativeness or inventiveness.[14]

In effect, the leader as change agent cultivates the ability to see things differently. He must see the glass half full as opposed to half empty. He must see the possibilities of what may be, not the stultifying existence of what seems to be. This is the stuff of leaders, change agents, and people regardless of gender, race, age, ethnicity, or creed that transcend the ordinary. *Time* magazine cited President John F. Kennedy as making one of the twentieth century's greatest speeches. In his speech, Kennedy saw things differently. President Kennedy's ability to communicate a new paradigm rallied people to a greater cause. He stated:

> I do not believe that any of us would exchange places with any other people or any other generation. . . . And, so, my fellow Americans, ask not what your country can do for you—ask what you can do for your country. My fellow citizens of the world, ask not what America will do for you, but what together we can do for the freedom of man.[15]

President Kennedy saw things differently and acted on his vision. He saw what was hidden from the collective consciousness and through his leadership ability created well-lit paths for others to travel. What he saw became the collective consciousness while the old reference points gradually diminished and disappeared.

Change Agents Have an Attitude of Optimism.   John W. Gardner, leadership expert, defines the optimistic actions of change agents when he says, "There is no seeking when you already found; no problem solving when you have the answers; no joy of the climb when you're sitting at the summit. No thrill of cultivation when it's always harvest time."[16] We can add to Gardner's statement by claiming that there is no constructive, long-term sustained change without the optimistic energy provided by the leader. The leader's optimistic attitude is not a Pollyanna type of attitude whereby the sun shines even when it rains. The leader's optimistic attitude is realistic and filled with hope. In the midst of problems, there is no denial. Instead, the leader's optimism projects a hope that current problems provide lessons on the way to achieving hard-won goals. Harold Bloomfield and Robert Cooper, authors of *The Power of 5*, state: "Overall, the mental attitude or outlook that pays the greatest dividends is characterized by flexible, real-life optimism—what some researchers simply call hopefulness—that prompts you to be contemplative and sensitive to the world's needs on the one hand and active on the other."[17]

The words *can't, won't,* and *impossible,* or the phrases "it's never been done before" or "we need to take a wait and see attitude" are not part of the optimist's vocabulary. The optimist is full of the possible and possibility thinking—one who continually reframes the current context from a problem to a challenge. She knows that pessimism, like optimism, is contagious, so she opts for optimism and does not tolerate negative thinking. A large number of medical doctors agree that patients who are optimistic about the outcome of their treatment fair far better than those who are pessimistic. According to Herbert Benson, Harvard Medical School physician, and Eileen Stuart, staff member of the Mind/Body Medical Institute of New England Deaconess Hospital and Harvard Medical School,

> Drs. Seligman, Vaillant, and Peterson have been tracking the lives and health of ninety-nine male Harvard graduates from 1945 to the present. One of the most interesting findings is that men who were generally optimistic in college are healthier in later life than those who were pessimists. By age forty-five, the pessimists began to have more health problems than their more positive-thinking classmates.[18]

The route to change is paved one brick at a time by optimistic bricklayers. They know that carrying and laying bricks is a difficult task. They also know that through consistency and diligence they will complete their task.

Change Agents Are Tenacious.   Effective leaders maintain a fierce tenacity. When the leader knows he is right, there is no force that can cause him to move. This leader does not have the rigidity of the inflexible person. He arrives at his fixed position after careful study, consultation with all members of the school community and other experts, and detailed analysis; he measures this data against his belief and value system. He knows where he wants to lead his school. He knows the direction of change. He also knows that circumstances dictate strategy and tactics and these may change; however, he is clear about the final destination. Tenacity is a result of belief in oneself and a sense of personal meaning.

Change Agents Are Self-Motivated.   The effective change agent has a different source of motivation than most people do. Her source of motivation is a deep-rooted need to grow, expand, and utilize her full potential for personal and communal benefit. She has a well-honed balance between personal and communal interests. She knows that if her motivation is directed solely inward, all that she attains—although personally satisfying—is communally meaningless. She knows that if all of her motivation is externally focused, she loses sight of who she is and what it is that she contributes to the greater good. Abraham Maslow, when speaking of self-actualized people, stated:

> They attempt to grow to perfection and to develop more and more fully in their own style. The motivation of ordinary men is a striving for the basic need gratifications that they lack. But self-actualizing people in fact lack none of these gratifications; and yet they have impulses. They work, they try, and they are ambitious, even though in an unusual sense. For them motivation is just character growth, character expression, maturation, and development; in a word self-actualization.[19]

Motivation of effective change agents emerges from within the person. In leaders, it is impossible to repress. The leader as change agent uses this deep source of motivation to stay focused on the challenge. There is no room for chaotic and random wandering. Full attention is given to challenge. As a result, the leader's single focus and intense motivation serve as a catalyst to inspire and motivate members of her staff.

Change Agents Believe in People and in Life.   The effective change agent believes in people and in life. His belief centers on the capacity of people to collaboratively solve their problems. He knows, from observing nature, that there is tremendous life energy present on Earth. He recognizes that in disasters, people come together to rebuild their communities. He recognizes that even after devastating forest fires, the forest, if left alone, is self-renewing. In effect, the process of renewal overcomes the process of decay. It is the leader's positive constructive action that sustains growth and promotes renewal.

The leader, as change agent, communicates his belief in people by the way he respects their ideas, efforts, beliefs, and values. He sees each member of his community as complementary to himself. He does not try to remake them; instead, he prepares his administration and organization to be inclusive; he expands his tent.

Change Agents Are Real People.   The effective leader is a real person. It is because she is a real person that members of her organization trust her. A real person is one who does not have guile. She is honest, forthright, and trustworthy. Her life experiences have sensitized her to the pain and joys felt by members of her organization. They recognize her as a person who not only understands their anxiety but also has experienced something similar. The real person does not hide behind masks, but has a deep sense of who she is and the meaning associated with her life. Organizational members recognize the leader's integrity and have confidence in her. They may not always agree with her vision, strategy, or tactics, but they believe she is working in their best interests. This is learned through personal reflection on experiences. Her experiences did not harden or anger her; she grew and learned from each of her experiences. She was grateful that these experiences provided her with lessons of life.

These seven traits of change agents are crucial to lead faculty through a systematic change process. They counterbalance the constraining forces that each member brings to the context. When leaders focus on applying the seven traits, they become change catalysts. They ignite the dormant resources within their organization. Without the application of these traits, the resources remain dormant, eventually decay and rot, and the organization dies. With their application, the resources become self-generating and the organization learns how to learn, grow, regenerate, and renew.

CONCLUDING POINT

Jeremiah Costanza understands the two primary lessons embedded in this chapter: Things change and constraining forces to change exist within every organization. He knows that constraining forces are not permanent; their cause is a result of misguided beliefs and poorly written scripts. He felt comfortable with the way he guided his administrative team through the process of learning to identify constraining forces and scripts. He felt they were conscious of his caution that script identification was personal and that they were to act as guides and facilitators in this process. He felt that he possessed the seven characteristics essential for a change agent to be a catalyst. He did not have, however, the same assurance that his administrative team members possessed these characteristics. He pondered this thought and then started laughing at himself. Perhaps one of his personal scripts was an overinflated sense of self-confidence bought at the expense of others. He knew he had to review his own scripts. He did not want to be a constraining force of change in his school. He also realized that if he had all seven characteristics, he had faith in people and their ability to regenerate and renew the organization. His course was clear. He was going to create an atmosphere in which these characteristics would naturally grow. He was ready to follow his own admonition: He was going to be a facilitator and guide for his team members and the faculty. He trusted the process.

SUGGESTIONS FOR ACTION

- Identify the rules in your school. What are your written rules for the staff? What are your unwritten rules for your staff?

- Examine each rule to determine if it is overt, discussable, up-to-date, humane, and ethical.

- What are your personal scripts? Can you identify the scripts that you use when you are under stress? Are they different from those when you are not under stress?

- Examine how your scripts differ as related to context. What does this teach you about yourself? Should some of these scripts be rewritten?

- Determine, with faculty, the group consciousness of your school. What is the attitude in the faculty lounge? What is the consciousness regarding faculty meetings, parents, students, and testing? Begin to rewrite scripts that inhibit constructive growth with faculty assistance in the process.

- Map your actions for a full day. At the end of the day, isolate each action and determine the beliefs and values expressed by each action. Reflect on what this activity taught you about your scripts.

- Identify the beliefs and values of your friends and others in your support network. You can identify their beliefs and values by listening to them and observing their behavior. Decide whether each person in your support network advances or retards your personal growth and development based on an alignment of their goals with your goals.

- Identify the seven elements essential for a change agent to act as a change catalyst. Create a plan to strengthen each of these seven elements.

CHANGE FACTORS

TERM	HOW TO USE IT	WHAT IT MEANS
Change catalyst	The leader encourages members of his or her organization to become change catalysts: people responsible for providing the necessary energy to start and sustain change.	Change catalyst refers to the energy needed to start and sustain the change process until it acquires its own self-sustaining energy.
Constraining force	The leader identifies constraining forces to change in the organization and replaces them with growth forces.	A constraining force refers to rules, beliefs, values, policies, or personal scripts that prohibit constructive change.
Role expectations	The leader understands the role he or she is expected to play and operates to meet that role so stakeholders do not become confused.	Role expectations refer to the probable behaviors that people external to the role expect from the person in the role.
Rules	The leader identifies all rules, overt and covert, and ensures that they are open to discussion, up-to-date, humane, and ethical.	Rules are guidelines, written and unwritten, designed to direct behavior.
Script	The leader helps to facilitate the understanding of personal scripts as a means to identifying behaviors that prohibit personal and organizational growth.	A script refers to sequenced events that we store in memory and use to guide behavior when presented with appropriate stimuli to engage the script.

NOTES

1. Argyris, C. (1992/1999). *On Organizational Learning*. Malden, MA: Blackwell Business Publishers, p. 336.

2. Larsen, R. (May 1999). Frameworks: Turning the Challenges of Change into Opportunities for Growth. *Chief Executive*, p. 11.

3. Satir, V. (1988). *The New Peoplemaking*. Mountain View, CA: Science and Behavior Books, p. 128.

4. Institute of Management Accountants. *Ethical Behavior for Practitioners of Management Accounting and Financial Management*. Retrieved August 14, 2001, from the World Wide Web: http://www.rutgers.edu/Accounting/raw/ima/imaethic.htm.

5. Gioia, D. (1986). Symbols, Scripts, and Sensemaking. (49–74). In H. Sims and D. Gioia (Eds.), *The thinking organization.* San Francisco: Jossey-Bass, p. 50.

6. Goodman, R. and Goodman, L. (July 1997). The Empty Space. *A paper presented at the Fifteenth Standing Conference on Organizational Symbolism,* Warsaw, Poland, p. 3.

7. Lyon, D. (1995–2000). Quick-Response Memories: Icons, Schemas and Expectancies. Mental Health Net. Retrieved August 14, 2001, from the World Wide Web: http://mentalhelp.net/articles/consc36.htm.

8. National Institute of Mental Health. Social Influence and Social Cognition. In *Basic Behavioral Science Research for Mental Health.* (1995). A Report of the National Advisory Mental Health Council. NIH Publication No. 96–3682. Retrieved August 14, 2001, from the World Wide Web: http://www.nimh.nih.gov/publicat/baschap5.cfm.

9. Dilts, R., Allbom, T., and Smith, S. (1990). *Beliefs: Pathways to Health and Well-being.* Portland, OR: Metamorphous Press, p. 12.

10. Bandler, R. (1993). *Time for a Change.* Cupertino, CA: Meta Publications.

11. Frankl, V. (1984). *Man's Search for Meaning.* New York: Washington Square, p. 154.

12. Maslow, A. (1971/1993). *The Farther Reaches of Human Nature.* New York: Penguin Arkana Group, p. 119.

13. Chass, M. (June 8, 2000). The Sosa–Baylor Dispute Is No Big Deal, Cubs Say. *The New York Times Sports.* 159, no. 51, 423: p. A26.

14. Maslow, A. (1970). *Motivation and personality* (2nd ed.). New York: Harper & Row, p. 218.

15. Kennedy, J. F. (January 20, 1961). Inaugural Address. Retrieved August 14, 2001, from the World Wide Web: http://www.hpol.org/jfk/inaugural/.

16. Gardner, J. (1970). *Recovery of Confidence.* New York: Norton, p. 139.

17. Bloomfield, H. and Cooper, R. (1995). *The Power of 5.* Emmaus, PA: Rodale Press, pp. 447–448.

18. Benson, H. and Stuart, E. (1992/1993). *The Wellness Book.* New York: Fireside, pp. 223–224.

19. Maslow, A. *Motivation and Personality,* p. 159.

CHAPTER SEVEN

MANAGE STRESS AND PROMOTE ACCEPTANCE OF CHANGE

Strategy ■ *Plan to Effectively Manage Personal and Organizational Stress*

STARTING POINT

The principal just returned from an emergency district-wide administrators' meeting. She asked her assistant principals to join her in her office. Her normally smiling face had a stern look. Those in the office knew she was serious. "I've just returned from a meeting with the superintendent. Whatever I say in this office stays in this office. Does everyone understand?" Those in attendance nodded and fidgeted. An eerie silence enveloped the room.

The principal continued, "The superintendent told me that the varsity girls' basketball coach was caught last night with an underage player down on Lovers Lane. I am to inform the coach that he is suspended until the resolution of his case. I know the state finals are this week, but we have to act."

All change produces stress. This is true on a personal as well as an organizational level. The greater the change we experience, the greater the stress we feel. According to Steven Burns, M.D., "To your body, stress is synonymous with change. Anything that causes a change in your life causes stress. It doesn't matter if it is a 'good' change or a 'bad' change they are both stress. . . . Even imagined change is stress. . . . Whether the imagined change is good or bad, imagining changes in your life is stressful."[1] Understanding stress is important to the leader on a personal and a professional level; therefore, the leader needs to know how to manage stress. Stress levels increase proportionately with the demands associated with the role.

When the leader fails to manage stress successfully, she makes poor decisions, disrupts relationships, and is a primary cause of poor morale. Moreover, the leader who fails to manage stress sucessfully creates organizational conditions for a series of health and psychologically related problems related to workplace stress. Workplace stress is the primary source of stress in most people's lives. According to the American Psychological Association, "A study by the Northwestern National Life Insurance Company found that 53 percent of supervisors and 34 percent of non-supervisors consider their jobs highly stressful. . . . Some national studies suggest that, on average, corporations lose about 16 days annually in productivity per worker due to stress, anxiety and depression."[2] Administrators, teachers, and students also face similarly high levels of stress.

The leader knows that change generates stress. The greater the pressure from external and internal sources on the leader to make change happen, the more stress the leader feels. As soon as the leader announces change plans to the faculty, the faculty feels stress. Their stress, whether real or imaginary, causes an emotional and psychological response. The stress that they feel at work with the impending changes proposed by the principal is added to the stress they feel in their private life. Stress is impossible to compartmentalize.

Imagine filling a balloon with air. Before you exhaled into the balloon, the empty balloon rested in your hand. You began to fill the balloon with air; as you exhaled into the balloon, the sides of the balloon expanded, stretching it well beyond its original state. Your actions stretched and stressed the balloon. Although you knew the balloon could be stretched beyond its initial shape, without your actions the balloon would not achieve its potential. The balloon was not alone in feeling stress. You also felt stress. You had to fill your lungs. You had to blow into the balloon. As the balloon came closer to achieving its potential, it became more difficult for you to blow into a balloon that was nearing capacity. You also felt a little emotional stress. You did not want the balloon to explode, yet you wanted the balloon to appear full. This metaphor represents the stress the change initiator and the change recipient feel.

The balloon metaphor represents the stress dynamics associated with change. Even localized change influences the entire organization. Imagine that the school board decides to reduce the district's budget. The superintendent requires each principal to submit recommendations for budget reductions. One principal decides that she does not want to impact instructional programs; as a result, she recommends the elimination of a secretarial position. Is the secretary the only one affected in the school? The other secretaries must assume the extra work. They feel stress. When teachers ask for assistance from the remaining secretaries, they meet angry, overworked people. The teachers feel more stress because they are now doing work once done by secretaries. The stressed teachers put more pressure on their students. They no longer overlook small things, but begin to make an issue out of minor annoyances. More students are referred to the office for disciplinary reasons. The administration feels the stress of having to support teachers. Is this hyperbole? Unfortunately, it is close to reality in many school districts.

Ironically, the discussion of stress and its impact on change is lacking in the literature regarding organizational change. One reason why we ignore stress is that we are culturally conditioned to be "tough" in the face of increased stress. Cultural pressures encourage people to repress sharing feelings or expressing emotions. It is a learned response in our Western culture to ignore stress and continue to work. If we keep adding stress without a suitable release, such as regular exercise, participation in a support group, or meditation, a stress-driven explosion occurs. We are all familiar with the stories of workplace violence. Workplace violence can occur in potentially every organization. It is not only to prevent workplace violence that the leader needs to understand and manage stress; it is because the effective management of stress creates a healthy work environment in which members of the organization see stress associated with change as positive, constructive, and adding value to their personal and professional lives.

REFLECTION IN ACTION

As you read the following case study, write down the principal's guarded thoughts and feelings that she hides from her faculty. Additionally, write the changes you think need to occur for the principal to be successful.

■ ■ ■ ■ ■

CASE STUDY

The school year is nearly half over. Dr. Susan Jackson, principal of Jefferson Elementary School, sat in her office and examined the practice achievement test scores. She wrinkled her brow; there was no smile on her face. Her anger grew; she saw no improvement from the previous practice test. She asked herself, "Just what are these teachers doing? Don't they know we have the state-mandated tests in one month?"

Although it was 2:30 P.M. with only an hour left to the school day, Dr. Jackson called an emergency faculty meeting. She made it clear in her memo, carried by student courier to every teacher, that everyone would attend the meeting; she would not accept excuses.

The meeting room gradually filled with teachers; some openly angry, others sullen, and others were talking about anything other than school. Dr. Jackson, arms filled with papers and overheads, entered the room five minutes late. She attached the portable microphone to her collar, turned to the faculty, and stated: "I've spent the entire day reviewing the practice achievement scores. They are terrible. There is no single bright spot. This is unacceptable to me and to the community. Just what is happening in your classrooms? Don't you realize that the state-mandated exams begin in one month? I want results. My assistant principals and I will be observing your classrooms on a regular basis during the next four weeks. Everyone is to focus solely on the achievement test. If anyone fails to do this, I personally will sign the transfer papers to the worst place in the district. I hope I'm making myself clear."

The faculty sat quietly; some stared at Dr. Jackson in anger and others looked down at their laps. Finally, one teacher raised her hand to speak.

Dr. Jackson saw the raised hand and said, "I'm not discussing the issue. Anyone with questions can see me in my office."

The teacher kept her hand in the air. Dr. Jackson picked up her papers and left the room. The teachers sat silently and then began to get up and slowly leave. No one said a word. Morale was the lowest it had ever been.

Dr. Jackson and her assistant principals returned to her office. She looked at both assistant principals and said, "I guess I made them sit up and take notice."

The assistant principals remained silent. Jackson continued, "I want to make plans for us to observe classrooms every day for the next four weeks. We're going have to increase the pressure on the teachers to improve the achievement scores."

"Did you think this out before the meeting?" asked Harry Jones, an assistant principal.

"What do you mean, did I think this out?" she snarled as she stared at Jones with anger blazing in her eyes.

"How can the three of us observe eighty teachers on a regular basis over the next four weeks? How can we observe and do the other work we need to do?" Harry responded as he tried to avert her intense stare.

"You'll just have to do it!"

Harry grew red; he had never challenged Dr. Jackson, but he felt it was now or never. He cared about his school, its faculty, and the students. He looked directly at Dr. Jackson and in a soft but strong voice replied, "There is no way it can be done. You have to know that in five minutes you've ruined the morale in the entire school. You never asked for faculty input. You never asked them to be part of the solution."

The meeting ended. Dr. Jackson sat stunned in her office and wondered how the situation had gotten out of hand. For the first time, she noticed that her eye was twitching; she ignored the twitching eye because her headache was making her miserable. She needed aspirin. Chapter Seven focuses on the change principle of managing stress and promoting acceptance of change.

The leader who recognizes this relationship works to create a balance between stress levels and change. She knows that sustained change efforts require the cooperation of members; the cooperation of members is directly related to their level of morale, and their morale is greatly influence by felt stress.

UNDERSTANDING STRESS

The Symptoms of Personal and Organizational Stress

People comprise organizations. The gestalt of the actions of the members comprises organizational activity. To the degree that the members operate efficiently, the organization flourishes. To the degree that members' efficiency is less than optimal, the organization deteriorates. Their efficiency is less determined by specific procedures than by their state of wellness. They operate efficiently when they are physically, psychologically, and emotionally healthy. This is a state of wellness. Dianne Dyck, a senior management consultant, states:

> In its simplest form, workplace wellness can be viewed as having two components—organizational wellness and personal wellness. Organizational wellness involves managing both business functions and employee well-being in a manner that allows the organization to be more resilient to environmental pressures. On the other hand, personal wellness involves managing both psychological and physical issues in response to environmental stress, including one's work environment.[3]

Wellness is what we want to achieve. When an organization is in a state of wellness, it functions efficiently. Not paying attention to the organization's wellness contributes to the deterioration of a manageable situation. Consider, for a moment, a severely overweight person. He seemingly works efficiently and contributes to the organization; he does not believe his weight is a problem. He continues to gain weight and does not monitor his health. His work circumstances become stressful and he suddenly experiences a heart attack. His feelings of productivity did not reflect the vulnerability of his potential health risk.

If we return to our balloon metaphor, the leader can imagine that each member of her organization is a unique balloon in a balloon bouquet. Some balloons are extremely strong; these are difficult to inflate, but once these balloons give way to inflation, they fully inflate. Other balloons pop as soon as inflation begins. They never achieve their full potential. Most balloons fall somewhere between these two extremes. The way that these balloons respond to inflation is similar to the way members of the school organization respond to stress. The leader has an organization filled with people who respond differently to stress. The leader cannot assume that because she handles great amounts of stress in a nearly tireless fashion, all members react similarly. The leader has to be aware of the stress symptoms in each member and in the organization.

Personal Stress Symptoms.   Personal stress symptoms are warning signs that members feel overwhelmed. Members respond in one of two ways to the perceived stress from their changing environment: They employ a fight-or-flight response. Dr. Herbert Benson, Harvard Medical School, and his co-author, Eileen Stuart, member of the staff of the Mind/Body Institute of New England Deaconess Hospital and Harvard Medical School, state:

> The flight-or-fight response, also called the stress response . . . is a profound set of involuntary physiological changes that occur whenever we are faced with a stressful or threatening situation. This response, critical to the survival of primitive humankind, prepares the body for a physical reaction to a real threat—to fight or to flee. Today, however, we do not often face the life-threatening situations that primitive people responded to frequently, and flight-or-fight response cannot distinguish between a serious threat and the everyday stresses of modern life.[4]

Each prospective change causes stress; yet each of us responds differently to the change. For example, one person is fearful of marriage whereas another embraces marriage. One person refuses a job opportunity in an urban environment whereas another embraces the opportunity to live in an urban environment. Our personality and experience contribute to how we consider each change. In effect, for some people a prospective change is catastrophic; for others, it is a challenge. So much of our response depends on the way we frame the prospective change. When we view change as disruptive, we automatically initiate a fight-or-flight response.

The fight-or-flight response is the first set of symptoms that the leader seeks to identify as a stress-driven reaction. Dr. Jackson's decision to confront and aggressively challenge the faculty was a fight response. If Dr. Jackson reviewed her history, she would probably find that she learned to cope with stressful situations by being strong. She has learned to be resolute in tough situations. She responded to the faculty in the only way she knew how to respond. She did not consider the consequences of her actions. Her faculty responded both predictably and unpredictably. Although Dr. Jackson allowed no questions, one faculty member raised her hand. She wasn't afraid of Dr. Jackson. She was responding to the imposed change by fighting. Other faculty members silently resisted; they folded their arms across their chests in a nonverbal declaration of war. Others tried to find a place to hide; they felt terribly uncomfortable. Their primary response was flight by openly agreeing with Dr. Jackson, yet, without monitoring, they plan to return to their comfortable ways of acting.

People who respond to prospective change vis-à-vis fight or flight are not angry with the person initiating the change. The members are fearful that they are going to be hurt. Their psychological scanning systems discovered a threat. The threat may have been Dr. Jackson's warning that teachers who did not improve scores would be transferred, or it may have been a perceived attack on the teachers' professional identities. The perceived threat evokes a personal alarm to sound, causing the teacher to react with a fight-or-flight response.

The fight-or-flight response also causes a chemical chain reaction in the body. According to the Mayo Clinic,

> "Our response to stress is not only mental. Under stress, our bodies behave as if under attack—whether the threat to our physical or emotional well-being is actual or imagined. Chemical messengers are released, producing physical changes that prepare the body for fight or flight. In the modern workplace, our stressors are numerous. . . . If the chemical reaction to stress continues over a long period of time, it may contribute to physical or emotional illness."[5]

The chemical reaction in our bodies is real. However, many members of the organization undergoing change may not link their stress symptoms with the organizational change. They view their symptoms in isolation from the primary cause. The Mayo Clinic categorized stress symptoms into three broad categories: physical, psychological, and behavioral (see Table 7.1).

TABLE 7.1 Stress Symptoms

PHYSICAL	PSYCHOLOGICAL	BEHAVIORAL
Headaches	Anxiety	Overeating or loss of appetite
Grinding teeth	Irritability	Impatience
Tight and dry throat	Sadness	Quickness to argue
Shortness of breath	Defensiveness	Procrastination
Pounding heart	Anger	Increased use of alcohol
High blood pressure	Hypersensitivity	or drugs
Muscle aches	Apathy	Increased smoking
Indigestion	Depression	Withdrawal or isolation
Constipation or	Slowed thinking or	from others
diarrhea	racing thoughts	Neglect of responsibility
Increased	Feelings of helplessness	Poor job performance
perspiration	Hopelessness	Poor personal hygiene
Fatigue	Worthlessness	Change in religious practices
Insomnia	Lack of direction	Change in close family
Frequent illness	Insecurity	relationships

Use Table 7.1 to check for personal symptoms of stress. Have you experienced any of these symptoms during the past year? Review the list and indicate the frequency with which you experienced each symptom. Effective symbols are F for frequently, O for often, and R for rarely. Dr. Jackson, for example, put an (F) next to headaches. The leader, concerned about the stress level among her staff, should ask staff members to complete this table and then use it as a basis for a faculty discussion regarding organizational-generated stress. The greater the amount of symptoms with an F or O, the greater the stress level.

These symptoms signal that the change is producing a negative stress reaction. Because the leader seldom has the opportunity to enter into close relationships with all members of his staff, he may fail to detect these symptoms. Instead, the first vestiges of stress overload appear in the form of increased absenteeism or increased requests for personal days. In high-stress school environments, one frequently hears teachers speak of "taking a mental health day." Unless the leader is sensitive to the high-stress environment and his staff's reaction to the stress overload, he may view increased absenteeism as faculty retribution directed toward him. This increases the leader's defensive posture and level of stress.

In Dr. Jackson's case, the faculty reacted immediately: Absenteeism increased by 25 percent. Dr. Jackson now faced a new stress-filled problem; substitute teachers were preparing students for examination. Not only was instruction suffering, but discipline problems associated with substitute teachers brought about a significant increase in student referrals to the office. Her assistant principals reduced their classroom observations. Dr. Jackson's plans were falling apart. Dr. Jackson reacted in the only way she knew to react; she chose to fight. She demanded the absent teachers present signed notes from their doctors.

In looking at this situation from a systems viewpoint, we begin to understand the part that stress plays in restricting or diverting the flow of change. We also see that those opposed to change and those in favor of change don't see the entire picture. If they did, they would alter their behavior. In effect, both sides contribute to an escalating cycle of increased stress in the workplace (see Figure 7.1).

In Figure 7.1, the speed associated with each cycle increases with each action. Each action provides a renewed source of energy to the latent and active anger that exists on both sides of the issue. As both sides continue to react, the stress level in the organization approaches a critical mass. If left unchecked, the stress level will cycle out of control. Essentially, both sides are in an arms race in which each action is met with a counteraction. Neither side considers a compromise. In the end, no one is aware of the cycle or how it started. The principal and the teachers become aware of what is happening when their situation becomes intolerable. They then focus on the symptoms, never giving thought to the cause.

This negative cycle frequently occurs in schools. Dr. Jackson's situation leaves the superintendent with few choices. The superintendent can find a mediator to resolve the issue. This approach simply slows down the escalation; it does not bring peace. The superintendent can replace the "troublemakers." More likely, the superintendent replaces the principal with another principal. This is a case of eliminating symptoms and ignoring causes.

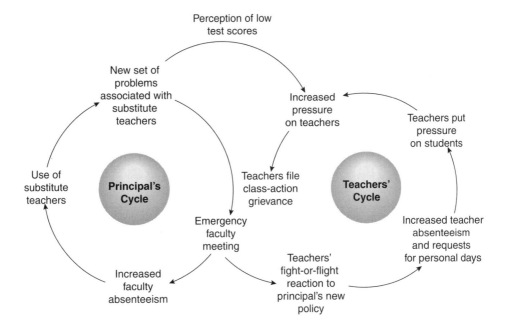

FIGURE 7.1 Escalating Cycle of Increased Stress

Symptoms, Causes, Sources. The tragedy of this situation is that everyone suffers. There are no winners. There is plenty of blame for the principal and teachers to share. The principal, however, must take primary responsibility for creating this stress-filled environment. The principal, Dr. Jackson, was under stress. She attributed her stress to the teachers and what she considered their lack of effective teaching. Dr. Jackson chose to fight. If Dr. Jackson were aware of her stress symptoms, she could have chosen a more effective response to her faculty.

Dr. Jackson, at any time, could have deescalated the stress environment by using the medical model for diagnosing disease. The medical model of diagnosis has three separate stages: symptoms, causes, and sources. According to William Long, the principal research associate at the MIT Laboratory for Computer Science,

> The physician needs to determine what diseases the patient has and the causal mechanisms by which they are producing the observed symptoms in order to determine whether there are treatable causes and what therapies might limit or correct the undesirable effects of the other causes. Thus, the goal of diagnosis is to determine the pathophysiological state of the patient in enough detail to guide therapy.[6]

Leaders, like physicians, must move beyond symptoms if they are to lead and manage change successfully.

Dr. Jackson recognized symptoms of potential poor performance on the forthcoming achievement test. The students' performance on the practice test alerted her that something was drastically wrong. Dr. Jackson jumped to conclusions regarding the cause of the symptoms. A proper diagnosis requires more information. It also requires the cooperation of the patient. Imagine a person going to a doctor for his annual physical checkup. The doctor's first question may be, "How do you feel?" The patient responds, "Absolutely terrific." As the doctor conducts her examination, she asks questions related to the patient's history during the past year. The patient mentions that he got dizzy twice during exercise during the past two months, but the dizziness left almost as soon as it appeared. The doctor takes notes and continues her examination. The doctor's examination reveals that the patient has elevated blood pressure, a possible cause for the dizziness. The patient forgot about the symptom. The patient only reported his health on the day of his examination. The doctor's examination discovers the patient's elevated blood pressure. The doctor could immediately prescribe medication for the patient's elevated blood pressure. The doctor, however, realizes that the medication takes care of only the patient's symptoms; it does not cure the problem. The doctor continues to probe the patient with questions.

"Your weight seems fine. Do you have a family history of hypertension?"

"No, I don't. I've never had a problem before now."

"Have you had a change of lifestyle in the past year?"

"I was divorced about a year ago—it was amicable. I didn't feel too much stress. I did feel stress when my mother died last December. I feel that I've dealt well with that."

"Do you have any other stress in your life?"

"My work is nearly intolerable. I'm a school principal in an urban environment. I feel under pressure to ensure that the students increase their test scores."

"I've read a lot about that. Do you have any help?"

"At times I feel that I am all alone—I think that I'm the only one who cares."

"Have you asked for help from the teachers or the superintendent?"

"No, that is a sign of weakness."

"Who told you that asking for help is a sign of weakness?"

"That's the way I was raised. My father taught us to be strong and independent. I never ask for help."

The doctor discovered the source of the patient's hypertension. The real source of the patient's symptoms was the patient's misguided belief system he had inherited from his father. If this patient wants to be healthy, he has to change his belief system. If the patient changes positions in order to seek a less stress-filled principalship, the patient carries his misguided belief system with him. It is the source of his stress and related health problems. It is also the source of his problems with his teachers.

The Sources of Stress.   There is no single source of stress. Stress is a complex phenomenon caused by internal or external stimuli. It originates internally, for example, when we set an expectation for ourselves that we can't achieve. We may blame others for our inability to achieve our goal; yet, the real source of our anguish is the unattainable standard that we set for ourselves. Psychologist Karen Horney spoke of this phenomenon as the idealized image. She stated:

The idealized image might be called a fictitious or illusory self. . . . It usually contains traces of the person's genuine ideals. While the grandiose achievements are illusory, the potentialities underlying them are often real. . . . The more firmly it is established the more he is his idealized image, while his real self is proportionately dimmed out.[7]

To the extent that we are attached to this unattainable goal, we become frustrated in our attempts to achieve its end. As we continue to work through our frustration and find new ways of attaining the goal, we become increasingly stressed. In effect, we find ourselves caught in a vicious circle of increasing frustration and stress that often results in anger projected onto the person who is in closest proximity.

Stress is also externally driven. We operate simultaneously at various cultural levels. Each of the cultures we interact with operates with a set of assumptions. These assumptions act as filters to tell us what is relevant and irrelevant regarding our immediate environment to provide stability in a turbulent world. According to Edgar Schein, management consultant and MIT professor, "One reason why we resist culture change is that it is inherently anxiety producing to give up the assumptions that stabilize our world, even though different assumptions might be more functional."[8] We have a need to predict our environment. When our environment is predictable, we feel safe. When our environment becomes unstable and unpredictable, our anxiety increases and produces increased stress. We naturally resist change to our cultural environments. Any change to these environments, whether at work, at home, or in our public culture, is met with resistance. When our resistance proves futile, our stress increases.

Internal or external stimuli leading to personal stress is a function of how the person views the stimuli. Some people, for example, find rush hour to be exasperating while others find it a place to listen to instructional media. Each of us responds differently based on our constitution and cultural conditioning. Regardless of how we respond to stress-generating stimuli, we do know that some environments are more conducive to producing stress stimuli. Environments that elevate stress levels have specific characteristics as seen in Table 7.2.[9,10] Examine

TABLE 7.2   Workplace Stressors

Recent promotion beyond capacity	Conflicts due to multiple responsibilities
Increased time demands	Lack of worker involvement in decision-making
New technology requirements	
A new or unreasonable supervisor	Too little or boring work
Sexual harassment or bullying	Increased productivity targets
High sickness or absence among colleagues	Threat of redundancy
	Poorly organized work
Poor working relationships with peers and supervisors	Changes at work
	Lack of personal control over work
Threat of violence	Poor communications regarding role responsibilities
Threats against job security	
Unrealistic deadlines	Low levels of support from supervisors
Poorly defined roles or duties	

your school environment and place a check mark next to any characteristic that you have observed in the last six months. The greater the number of checks you have, the higher the probability that your environment is a significant contributor to the stress experienced by members of your organization.

Even though these characteristics are present in the work environment, the stress level experienced by the members of the organizations depends greatly on their personality makeup. The individual characteristics we bring to our environments help determine our belief systems. Our belief systems are our maps of the world. We experience little stress when there is a clear match between our belief system and the world, as we perceive it to exist. We experience high levels of stress when there is a mismatch between our belief systems and the world, as we perceive it to exist. This is especially true when we discover that, in spite of our efforts, we cannot force the world to conform to the patterns demanded by our personalities.

There are many personality identification models accounting for human behavior. Hidden within these models are specific personality characteristics that contribute more to stress than others do. Six primary personality characteristics are found among members in most organizations: perfectionist, helper, achiever, power acquirer, loyalist, and loner. Although, at times, we may share each of these characteristics to a degree, each person has one characteristic that dictates the primary way he or she perceives the world.

The perfectionist seeks to organize everything; she wants everything to work as it is supposed to work. Her model includes people as well as organizations. The principal who is a perfectionist feels stress when things do not work as planned. She feels alienated from her environment when faculty and staff do not care about her penchant for order and perfection. Her stress level increases, for example, when her instructional plans are thwarted by a fire drill or other announced event. She does not realize that the majority of faculty and staff are not perfectionists who share similar values.

The helping person has a primary characteristic of desiring to nurture and care for others. As long as she can help, she overrides the time-induced stress by her desire to collaborate and cooperate with others. The social experience of work adds to her job satisfaction. When work demands prevent collaboration and opportunities to connect with colleagues, her stress level increases. It also increases when her helping commitments erode her time, leaving little or no time to care for herself. A second-grade teacher, for example, volunteers to be the lead teacher on her team; she accepts the principal's request to chair the curriculum committee, and she volunteers to be president of the teacher's association. Her desire to help overrides the time available to her. Her life becomes unbalanced.

The achiever enjoys challenges. This person wants others to view him as successful. He is highly competitive. When he loses, he takes it personally and his stress level increases. When he wins, he experiences positive stress and feels exhilarated. When supervisors reward him, he sees it as a public sign that he is successful. When a supervisor directly or indirectly suggests that his work can improve, he takes it personally and his stress level rises. A department chairperson, for example, assumes personal responsibility for his department's performance. When student achievement scores rise, the department chairperson feels successful; when test scores drop, the department chairperson sees it as a personal leadership failure.

The power-driven person seeks to control others and events. He can use his power beneficially or he may use it destructively. He experiences high levels of stress when he feels that he is not in control. He will fight to regain control. When he feels assurance that he is in control, his stress level disappears. A teacher, for example, who is power driven feels increased stress when he learns that he cannot teach the same grade level the next year. His response may be to file a grievance. He uses the grievance as a means of asserting power and regaining control.

The loyalist commits herself to the organization, its members, and its leadership. Her commitment transcends the needs of people as she staunchly stands by the organization, regardless of the issue. When the organization suffers, she suffers. The assistant principal, as a loyalist, feels that when people attack her school they are attacking her because she so closely identifies herself with the school. When her school is not under attack, she appears to be in control and does not suffer stress. When the school is under attack, her stress level increases as she rises to defend the school. The loyalist can also commit to individuals. If the loyalist commits to the leader, she faces similar fluctuations of stress determined by the status of the person to whom she committed herself.

The loner prefers isolation and quiet. He doesn't like committee work. He enjoys the sanctity of his classroom or office. His stress level increases when people intrude on his space. He may interpret his space as a physical location, time, money, or some other resource that he does not want to share. The more he protects his isolation and perceived resources, the less stress he feels. Imagine the stress that he feels when the principal informs him that he will share an office or classroom. His reaction is immediate: He seeks to defend his territory. His stress level rapidly escalates. As soon as he regains his privacy, he withdraws. His stress level returns to normal.

Even in a perfect world, each of these six types will find stress. The mere fact that they have to interact with each other is a significant source of stress, regardless of the stressors that emanate from the organization. Each person, to some degree, attempts to control his or her environment. When people have similar outlooks, it appears that harmony exists. What may really exist is the fact that each holds a similar worldview; then they develop a common language sustained by comparable group values. Imagine the internal confusion of a person who does not share the same worldview and is a minority within the group. This person's worldview may be ignored or disparaged and given no legitimate hearing within the group context. What does this mean to the person who holds the minority worldview? It means that this person, because of the way she views the world, is isolated or alienated from the group unless she adopts the prevailing worldview of the group. What may appear to be a harmonious relationship within the group is an illusion. Trying to maintain this illusion creates enormous stress on the person who suppresses her worldview for the sake of harmony.

Resilience.   When a person is unable to control his environment, his stress level rises. He has a series of choices: to continue to fight until he regains control, to remove himself from the context, or to adapt to the context. Healthy people adapt.

Learning to adapt to a constantly changing environment is known as resilience. According to Kimberly Gordon-Rouse,

> Resilience is a multi-faceted phenomenon that encompasses personal and environmental factors that interact in a synergistic fashion to produce competence despite adversity. . . . Resilience is the ability to thrive, mature, and increase competence in the face of adverse circumstances. These circumstances may include biological abnormalities or environmental obstacles. Further, the adverse circumstances may be chronic and consistent or severe and infrequent. To thrive, mature, and increase competence, a person must draw upon all of his or her resources: biological, psychological, and environmental.[11]

People who demonstrate resilience, regardless of personality characteristics, have a higher internal locus of control than do those who lack resilience. People who have a high internal locus of control see themselves as having the ability to manage events. People with a low internal locus of control see external events and people as controlling their lives. Two principals in the same district, for example, receive new state-directed mandates. One principal has a high internal locus of control. He studies the mandates and feels confident in his ability to lead his school in meeting and possibly exceeding the new state standards. The other principal has a low internal locus of control. She becomes angry. She calls a faculty meeting and laments the requirements imposed by the state. The same mandates, the same district, two different principals; one has high resilience, the other low resilience. Who do you believe will have the lower level of stress?

CHANGING THE DYNAMICS

The situation in the case study occurs in all organizations. Teachers as well as leaders experience it. Dr. Jackson doesn't want to create a stress-filled situation. Her bottom line is that she wants the students in her school to succeed. Dr. Jackson is not alone. In a reflective moment, Dr. Jackson realized what was happening at her school. She knew if she could keep up the pressure scores might improve. She now wondered if the cost would be worth the victory. What could she do? Dr. Jackson made an appointment to speak with her mentor at the university. The following is part of the conversation that took place between Dr. Jackson and her mentor, Dr. Salese.

"Susan, what is the problem?"

"It's my faculty, Dr. Salese. They don't want to cooperate with me in raising the achievement scores. Our last practice test was a disaster. They don't understand that my job is on the line. They don't want to change their teaching styles. I have to watch them to make sure they are teaching the skills the children need to pass the exam. Do you want me to continue?"

"You're angry."

"I'm very angry. The superintendent personally picked me for this job. He had confidence in me. If I fail, I will let him down, the students down, and myself down."

"From what you've told me, I bet you laid down the law to the faculty. This would be consistent with your personality."

"You know me. I don't know any other way other than to confront these people. I'm not going to let them stand in the way of improving instruction."

"I've always admired your courage, Susan. Let's slow down and examine the situation. First, move away from a 'them and me' situation. I don't believe that the teachers are against you. These teachers gave you a surprise party at Christmas for your outstanding leadership. Second, move away from framing this situation as success or failure. You're not letting the superintendent, students, or yourself down if you give it your best. You have enough pressure on you without your trying to please everyone. Third, I believe there is a way out of this quagmire if you are willing to try a different approach. You are going to have to act counterintuitively; that is, you are going to have to go against your natural urge to fight and confront your staff."

"What is it Dr. Salese? I am willing to try anything that's going to work."

Reducing Stress by Understanding Anxiety 1 and Anxiety 2

Edgar Schein provides the path for Dr. Jackson. Schein speaks of two types of anxiety associated with change: anxiety 1 and anxiety 2. Schein states:

> Anxiety 1 is the fear of learning something new. Adaptive learning individuals, groups, and organizations tend toward stability. . . . Instability or unpredictability or meaninglessness is uncomfortable and arouses anxiety, what I have called anxiety 1 or the fear of changing, based on a fear of the unknown. . . . If I don't change and learn how to learn things will go badly for me. That brings us to anxiety 2, the uncomfortable realization that in order to survive and thrive I must change, and that unless I change and learn how to learn I will fail.[12]

Anxiety 1 and anxiety 2 exist in individuals and organizations undergoing change. To the extent that the leader is aware of these types of anxiety experienced by members of her organization, she can manage their anxiety levels and create an environment more conducive to change.

On a practical level, information regarding the health hazards associated with smoking has been widespread; yet millions of people smoke, oblivious to the warnings. For these people, the pleasure they receive from smoking is too great to give up. They continue to smoke until forced to confront a serious health-related issue. Their doctors may tell them to give up smoking or die. At this point, anxiety 2 becomes greater than anxiety 1. They are ready to change. Try this experiment. Are you right-handed or left-handed? Imagine that I ask you to do everything with your nondominant hand. If you are right-handed, write with your left hand, brush your teeth with your left hand, eat with your left hand, and comb your hair left-handed. Most people will refuse to do this task for a day, let alone a lifetime. The pain associated with learning how to do something new is too great an effort. Now imagine that you lost your dominant hand in an accident. You quickly set your mind to learning how to use your nondominant hand. You have to survive, so you change.

Everyone experiences both types of anxiety to some degree when faced with change. For most people, the fear of having to change (anxiety 1) is far greater than the consequences of not changing (anxiety 2). There are many factors why we become fearful of changing. These factors include fears of

- The new learning involved in the change
- Failure
- Rejection
- Losing the familiar
- Losing one's cherished values or beliefs

Fear of the New Learning Involved in Change. For most people, especially those involved in education, it seems strange that there is fear associated with new learning. Learning should be exciting, motivating, and pleasurable. Yet this is not always the case. Remember the last time you loaded a new and unfamiliar piece of software on your computer. Do you remember your learning curve? If your experience was similar to mine, it was painful. I wanted to get started as soon as possible because of the advantages offered by the new software, yet I frequently felt frustrated because I was not familiar with the program's language. If the program was user-friendly, I patiently learned and my skill level grew each time I used the program. If I found the program user-unfriendly, I tried to learn, but the experience became too painful and I no longer used the program. I even removed the program from my computer. Many people share these experiences.

The fear of learning among faculty in school organizations may be driven by the fact that the staff development and trainers who deliver these resource programs fail to consider that adult learner needs are different from those of other age groups. According to William Graves, founder of the Academic Institute for Technology,

> Where once faculty resistance could be characterized by plain old fear—This is a fad; it may go away; I'd like to retire before I have to confront it, today the resistance can be characterized by a lack of faith that institutions are supporting faculty in their efforts to transform learning through information technology. I find a lot of faculty members who say, "Yes, I take this seriously. I can see the value of using this with my students, and I'd really like to do so. However, I'm not ready to commit, because I don't think my institution will support me." . . . Institutions are not removing the barriers to the fair consideration of this type of work in advancing the careers of faculty.[13]

Adult learners have special considerations regarding personal needs and the ways in which they process information. The leader understands these needs and ensures that they are incorporated into staff development that addresses learning. By applying adult learning precepts to staff development, the leader acts to reduce the level of anxiety 1 and the stress associated with it.

Fear of Failure. Contemporary American culture places a high importance on success. It is a highly competitive culture in which competition surrounds each person. People root for the favorite teams. People compete on the golf course, on the racquetball court, on the tennis court, in beauty contests, and alone with computer games. The desire to win and be successful is a culturally taught and embraced value. The positive side of the value is that it causes people continually to seek to surpass their previous performances. This results in many personal and societal benefits. The space race between the United States and the Soviet Union produced technical and medical benefits for all of society. The negative side to intense competition is the paralysis of failure. Some people won't try if they believe that they will fail. Others will try to cheat to succeed. When success is the only value and the leader views failure as bad, the members of the organization will not try anything new unless they are sure of its success. Management expert Tom Peters states: "The goal is to be more than tolerant of slip-ups. You must . . . actively encourage failure. Talk it up. Laugh about it. Go around the table at a project group meeting or morning staff meeting: Start with your own interesting foul-up. Then have everyone follow suit."[14] Failure is the learning laboratory of life. People need encouragement to risk even when failure is a distinct possibility. When the leader encourages people to risk without having to fear failure, the leader takes a step in the creation and maintenance of the school as a learning organization.

Fear of Rejection.   It is natural for us to seek the approval of others as a primary means of affirmation. When the approval of others controls our behavior, we have to rethink our relationships with these people. Some people continually seek approval from friends, peers, supervisors, and others in their support network. The approval they gain is a type of personal validation. When the need for approval is too strong, then the person needing the approval fears trying anything that leads to disapproval. A teacher, for example, may need his principal's validation. He knows that his principal likes to see a sense of order in the classroom. This teacher continually makes sure his classroom matches up to the principal's expectations. At a recent workshop, the teacher learned some exciting teaching strategies. These new teaching strategies, however, did not present the type of order the teacher believed the principal desired. The teacher never tried the new strategies. Many leaders use approval and the withholding of approval as a behavior modification strategy in dealing with their staffs. This approach is misguided because it limits the growth potential of staff members.

Fear of rejection is also associated with the threat of embarrassment that each of us may feel when we have to admit to ourselves and others that our current performance is lacking. Our embarrassment may turn to defensiveness as we attempt to hide our deficiencies. This is especially true in low trust environments in which threat of punishment is prevalent.

Fear of Losing the Familiar.   It is natural to fear losing the familiar. Unknowingly, the familiar can become addictive. Addiction, according to Gerald May, author of *Addiction and Grace,* "is a state of compulsion, obsession, or preoccupation that enslaves a person's will and desire. Addiction sidetracks and eclipses the energy of our deepest, truest desire. . . . We succumb because the energy of our desire becomes attached to specific behaviors, objects, or people."[15] These addictions come from our habits. In many ways, they make life easier for us. We go to work the same way each day. We go to the same restaurants each weekend. We go to the same places for vacation. We treat problems with procedures that solved similar problems in the past. Our habitual practices become so engrained in our being that we can actually do them subconsciously. When we find that we can't live without our habit, we have an addiction.

Normally, we think of addiction as related to drugs or alcohol or some other substance. In reality, we can be addicted to anything. Do you enjoy your cup of coffee each morning? Just stop drinking coffee for one month. You will feel the physical and psychological pains of withdrawal. Our ways of acting can be just as addictive. Imagine a teacher who has taught the same way for ten years. When this teacher is asked to change, she will rebel. Her familiar way of teaching is all that she knows. She understands it so well she could do it in her sleep. The effective leader understands the tenacity with which people hold on to behavioral patterns. He knows that change, taken a step at a time with continuous support, can lead a person away from one behavior and toward a more constructive way of behaving.

Fear of Losing One's Cherished Values or Beliefs.   Each of us espouses a set of values. These values guide our lives. Our values determine our behavior and tell us what is important and unimportant. We select our work based on our values. We decide how to work within our workplace, in a great part, based on our values. Psychologist Gordon Allport stated:

> The most important categories a man has are his own personal set of values. He lives by and for his values. Seldom does he think about them or weigh them; rather he feels, affirms, and defends them. So important are the value categories that evidence and reason are ordinarily forced to conform to them.[16]

When the leader understands the power that values hold over each of us, she realizes that any change has to embrace the values held by the member needing to change. The leader accomplishes this by framing the change to embrace the values held by the member. If the teacher, for example, places a strong value on student discipline and respect, the principal shows the teacher how the prospective change embraces the same value and makes it occur more easily. In some instances there is no congruence between the values espoused by the member and those held within the needed change. The member, for example, may harbor a prejudice against minority members. The leader needs to disconfirm the member's attachment to this value and replace it with another value (see Chapter Two). Disconfirming occurs through the application of credible information that is accepted by sources important to the member. The greater the number of people who embrace this information and change, the more pressure the member feels to discard his disconfirmed value and embrace the values of the group. The leader knows that the human being's desire for acceptance is a strong motivator.

Each of these fears adds to the power held by anxiety 1. To the extent that these fears are real to a person, her anxiety 1 level increases and correspondingly her stress level increases. The leader also needs to be aware of anxiety 2, the fear we have of not changing. It is related to our primal need to survive. Whenever this fear is greater than anxiety 1, our change rate accelerates.

Society teaches us to focus on anxiety 2 if we want to change or lead others to change. We warn people about the dangers of smoking. We warn people about the risks associated with overeating. We warn people that we have to maintain a large military force if the nation is to survive. We warn people that the state department of education may sanction us if we don't improve. The primary method for getting people to change is to focus on anxiety 2: fear of survival. Figure 7.2 illustrates this pattern. The problem with this pattern, and usually unseen by the leader, is that anxiety 2 is significantly less than anxiety 1. This means that regardless of the rhetoric, the members of the organization seldom feel compelled to change. As a

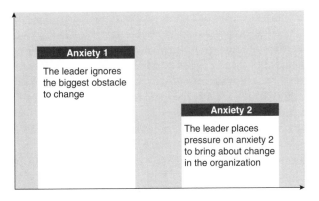

FIGURE 7.2   Anxiety 1 and Anxiety 2 in Traditional Organizations

result, leaders use the tactics employed by Dr. Jackson: They threaten people with job survival. By focusing on job survival, Dr. Jackson temporarily moves anxiety 2 to a higher level than anxiety 1.

A Counterintuitive Way to Approach Change.   Dr. Salese mentioned a counterintuitive way to approach change. Dr. Jackson needs to focus on anxiety 1 rather than anxiety 2. If Dr. Jackson works to reduce anxiety 2, she may create an illusory state that nothing needs to change. She knows that the pressures for success are real. She also knows that increasing anxiety 2 has brought her faculty to a state of near revolt. She is aware that continued focus on anxiety 2 is a poor leadership decision. Switching focus to the staff's anxiety 1 level will help Dr. Jackson determine the fears her faculty associates with making prospective changes. To ease faculty anxiety associated with new learning, Dr. Jackson must become familiar with how adults learn.

All new learning requires a learning curve. Learning is not instantaneous. It is a process of taking in information, processing the information, integrating the information, and practicing with the new information. There is a distinct difference between learning and performance. Thomas Good and Jere Brophy, experts on classroom learning, state: "Learning refers to the information processing, sense making, and advances in comprehension or mastery that occur while one is acquiring knowledge or skill; performance refers to the demonstration of such knowledge or skill after it has been acquired."[17]

Neither learning nor excellence in performance is instantaneous. Both require patience. Unless sufficient time and resources for training, learning, and practicing of performance exists, anxiety 1 will remain at abnormally high levels. The leader can create and sustain an environment that accelerates learning. As learning accelerates, change naturally happens. Simultaneously, stress loses its hold on the organization. People cooperate because their fears no longer exist. A leader creates this type of environment by ensuring psychological safety.

Psychological Safety.   Psychological safety requires an environment in which people can participate in learning without the fear of having their identities destroyed or losing their senses of personal efficacy. Safety is such an important issue that Maslow placed it only above physiological needs in priority. Maslow states: "If the physiological needs are relatively well gratified, there then emerges a new set of needs, which we may categorize roughly as the safety needs (security; stability; dependency; protection; freedom from fear, from anxiety and chaos; need for structure, order, law, limits; strength in the protector; and so on)."[18] Refer to Chapter Two, the section Learning from Maslow.

Members of the organization need to be free of actual or perceived threats to their physical safety. A member who goes to work each day and wonders if the supervisor will make an unkind and untrue remark has high anxiety before he enters his building. The anticipation of the event produces stress, whether the event ever occurs. A teacher, for example, who tries a new teaching methodology and does not have psychological safety acts with great courage. He understands that he must succeed or receive some type of sanction. In our case study, unless Dr. Jackson provides psychological safety, teachers will not dare to risk trying new methodology. They will continue to rely on what they have already done. Their methods may be outdated, but they believe they have no other choice but to work harder using only their present skills. Imagine the stress felt by the teacher whose skills are outdated. The teacher works harder using a teaching methodology that ultimately ends in failure. The teacher, fearful of failure, will attribute blame to parents, students, the system, or the principal. She will not examine her performance. If she did examine her performance, she would conclude that she is at fault. She cannot do this, because she has no alternative but to continue to teach as she has always taught.

Psychologically safe environments have distinct characteristics. Schein provides eight criteria essential for establishing and maintaining this environment.[19] For further insights, see Chapter Two, the section Learning from Schein.

1. The leader and other supervisors must be friendly and supportive.
2. The leader provides a vision of a better future, even though achieving it demands sacrifice.
3. The leader provides the staff with chances to practice and make mistakes without penalty.
4. The leader provides a map as to what needs to be done and how it is to be done.
5. The leader initiates the learning process as a group activity.
6. The leader ensures that appropriate coaching and feedback occur over time for all staff.
7. The leader finds ways to reward even the smallest change in the positive direction.
8. The leader encourages people to see mistakes as essential to learning.

There are other guidelines to create psychological safety to reduce the stress associated with change. The noted author on community building, M. Scott Peck, stated: "But put a human being in a truly safe place, where these defenses and resistances are no longer necessary, and the thrust toward health is liberated. When we are safe, there is a natural tendency for us to heal and convert ourselves."[20] The leader focuses on the cultural assumptions that govern interactions among members of the school organization and prevent an organization from becoming, in

Peck's words, a truly safe place. Organizations that are authoritarian in nature have a difficult time creating psychological safety. In these types of organizations, people fear offending supervisors because the supervisors have authority to punish. In many cases, the culture dictates that the supervisor must punish anyone who steps out of line.

Three Guidelines for Creating a Psychologically Safe Environment. The first guideline is that workers must not fear their supervisor. If they fear their supervisor, they will try to predict what their supervisor wants them to do. Supervisors who need to employ fear as a motivating tactic harbor an internal fear of their ability to motivate people to perform essential tasks. They do not have confidence in people because they do not first have confidence in themselves. Confidence in others is a leadership mandate. When the leader expresses confidence in her faculty, she taps into the faculty's innate sense of self-efficacy. As a result, the faculty feel an inner drive compelling them to succeed.

A second guideline is to have open and honest communication. Members need to learn how to communicate with one another. According to David Sobel and Robert Ornstein, authors of *The Health Mind Healthy Body Handbook,* "New evidence suggests that communicating effectively enhances our health and self-esteem, nurtures our relationships, and helps us cope with stress. Healthy communication is the life-blood of relationships, and relationships are a lifeline to health."[21] Many people come from backgrounds in which communication was not a value. They never learned to communicate their needs effectively. Others may have had effective communications skills, but saw these skills atrophy in a repressive environment. Effective communication is a learned skill. It is at the heart of a psychologically safe environment. Trust is at the heart of all effective communication. When people trust each other, they believe that they will not be hurt.

A third guideline is to have civility as a central workplace component. Effective leaders practice civility. Frances Hesselbein, CEO of the Drucker Foundation, states:

> Civility has to do with respect for other people. [It is] indispensable in building effective organizations. We acknowledge the humanity of the other person when we communicate at many levels that person's worth and dignity. Our behavior as well as our words build a climate of trust, a climate of respect, and a climate where mission, values, and equal access permeate the organization.[22]

When people operate in an environment driven by civility, they intuitively know how to communicate and how to work with each other. They are patient and allow the process to unfold. They know there is a way to disagree without condemning those who oppose them. Civility provides the foundation for basic mutual human respect. A safe environment is impossible without the presence of mutual respect. We not only respect each other because we are human beings but also respect our histories, experience, and efforts to be competent.

Creating a psychologically safe environment reduces the stress associated with change. Ironically, as stress is reduced, the organizational environment generates the conditions for constructive change and renewal of the organization. The change that occurs in a safe environment is natural and facilitates member cooperation.

CONCLUDING POINT

Dr. Jackson gained personal and professional understanding of the stress associated with the change process. She realized that her personal methods implying "my way or the highway" needed to change. For the first time, she understood that everyone in her school felt stress to succeed on the achievement tests. She also understood that the stress that the staff felt was compounded by stress in their personal lives; therefore, she needed to be more sensitive to the whole person. One of her first tasks was to request a half day from the superintendent of schools for faculty formation. She was going to start to create a psychologically safe environment for her staff. She knew that she had to start with herself. She was going to apologize to the faculty for the blunder of the previous faculty meeting and ask them to be partners in addressing the problem of raising achievement scores. Her rule of never apologizing was outdated; her faculty needed her apology and she was going to give it to them. Her goal was to focus on reducing anxiety 1. She trusted that the staff knew the importance of student performance on the achievement tests. Now she had to learn how to reduce their anxiety 1. The only way to understand their anxiety 1 was to ask them. She was going to conduct a series of small focus groups with the faculty to develop a clear understanding of their fears. After she understood their fears, she would develop her change strategies. She and her staff are learning ways to manage stress associated with change. Dr. Jackson is well on her way to creating a psychologically safe, healthy learning organization.

SUGGESTIONS FOR ACTION

- What is the level of stress in your school? Organize a faculty meeting that focuses on levels of stress and suggestions for reducing the stress levels.

- What personal stress symptoms have you experienced? Do you ignore these symptoms or have you taken action to reduce your stress level?

- What is the primary way that you deal with stress: Is it fight or flight? Can you identify the primary ways that each member of your staff deals with stress: Is it fight or flight?

- Provide your staff with a copy of Table 7.1. Ask them for feedback about their level of stress. Develop a series of support groups that helps each member cope more effectively with the stress level normally associated with teaching school.

- Identify an area of stress in your school. Use the symptoms, causes, sources model to discover the sources of the stress. Take action to eliminate the sources of the stress.

- How many workplace stressors occur regularly at your school (see Table 7.2)? Match your assessment to that of other members of your staff to ensure accuracy.

- What is your primary personality characteristic and how does it contribute to your stress level? How does it contribute to the stress levels of other people in your organization? Can you identify the primary personality characteristics of the other members of your organization?

TERM	HOW TO USE IT	WHAT IT MEANS
Anxiety 1	The leader seeks to manage the anxiety 1 level of faculty by reducing faculty fear of learning. The leader does this, in part, by creating a safe, nurturing environment.	Anxiety 1 is a phrase coined by Edgar Schein to explain the fear that organizational members have to acquiring the learning associated with new change.
Anxiety 2	The leader seeks to reduce the faculty member's fear of losing job security because of demanded changes by encouraging and facilitating appropriate professional development.	Anxiety 2 is a phrase coined by Edgar Schein to explain the fear that organizational members have with mandated change tied to job survival.
Fight or flight	The leader seeks to intervene in situations in which members respond through fight or flight. The leader knows that such behavior is an avoidance maneuver designed to bypass confrontation of the cause of stress.	Fight or flight refers to the psychological explanation for behavior describing how people act when under high levels of stress.
Personal stress symptoms	The leader pays close attention to the stress symptoms exhibited by members of the organization as well as personal awareness to his or her own symptoms. He or she then acts to manage the stress stimuli provoking the symptom.	Personal stress symptoms refer to the warning signals that people feel when under increasing stress. The louder the signal, the greater the danger to the person or organization.
Symptoms, causes, sources	The leader observes the symptoms of change-resistant behavior and seeks to identify their causes. Once the leader has identified the causes of the behavior, the leader is better able to search for the originating source.	This tripart medical model identifies the three phases to effective diagnosis. Only by discovering the three components of the problem can a permanent solution be found.
Wellness	The leader works to create and sustain an ongoing state of wellness in his or her organization by paying attention to the whole person.	Wellness refers to the inclusiveness of human and organizational health. It balances all components into a synergistic whole in which each component contributes to the well-being of the whole.
Workplace stressors	The leader seeks to identify, with the help of faculty and students, all workplace stressors. In a collaborative effort, workplace stressors are eliminated or more effectively managed.	Workplace stressors refer to organizational stimuli, overt or covert, that produce unnecessary stress on members.

N O T E S

1. Burns, S. L. (1989/1990). The Medical Basis of Stress, Depression, Anxiety, Sleep Problems, and Drug Use. Retrieved August 14, 2001, from the World Wide Web: http://www.teachhealth.com.

2. American Psychological Association. (1996). Doing More and More with Less and Less. *Psychology at Work*. Retrieved May 29, 2000, from the World Wide Web: http://helping.apa.org/work/less&less.htm.

3. Dyck, D. (January 1999). Wellness Package. *Benefits Canada*. Retrieved August 16, 2001, from the World Wide Web: http://www.benefitscanada.com/Content/1999/01-99/ben019901.html.

4. Benson, H. and Stuart, E. (1992/1993). *The Wellness Book: The Comprehensive Guide to Maintaining Health and Treating Stress-Related Illness*. New York: Fireside, p. 33.

5. Mayo Clinic. (2000). Workplace Stress: Can You Control It? *Mayo Clinic Health Oasis*. Retrieved August 16, 2001, from the World Wide Web: http://www.mayohealth.org/home?id=ST00001.

6. Long, W. (1989). Medical Diagnosis Using a Probabilistic Causal Network. *Applied Artificial Intelligence* 3: 367–383. Retrieved August 16, 2001, from the World Wide Web: http://www.medg.lcs.mit.edu/people/wjl/aaij88/aaij88.html.

7. Horney, K. (1945/1992). *Our Inner Conflicts: A Constructive Theory of Neurosis*. New York: W. W. Norton, pp. 108–109.

8. Schein, E. (1985). *Organizational Culture and Leadership*. San Francisco: Jossey-Bass, p. 83.

9. Health, Environment and Work Web Site. Stress and Work. Retrieved August 16, 2001, from the World Wide Web: http://www.agius.com/hew/resource/stress.htm.

10. National Institute for Occupational Safety and Health (NIOSH). (1999). Stress at Work. Retreived August 16, 2001, from the World Wide Web: http://www.cdc.gov/niosh/stresswk.html.

11. Gordon-Rouse, K. (Spring 1998). Resilience from Poverty and Stress. *Human Development and Family Life Bulletin* 4, no.1. Retrieved August 16, 2001, from the World Wide Web: http://www.hec.ohio-state.edu/famlife/bulletin/volume.4/bull41f.htm.

12. Schein, E. (1994/1997). Organizational and Managerial Culture as a Facilitator or Inhibitor of Organizational Learning. MIT: *The Society for Organizational Learning*. Retrieved April 21, 1999, from the World Wide Web: http://learning.mit.edu/res/wp/10004.html.

13. Rickard, W. (January–February 1999). Technology, Education, and the Changing Nature of Resistance: Observations from the Educom Medal Award winners. *Edcom Review* 34, no.1. Quoting William Graves. Retrieved August 16, 2001, from the World Wide Web: http://www.educause.edu/ir/library/html/erm9915.html.

14. Peters, T. (1988). *Thriving on Chaos: Handbook for a Management Revolution*. New York: Harper & Row, p. 317.

15. May, G. (1988/1991). *Addiction and Grace*. New York: HarperCollins, p. 14.

16. Allport, G. (1954). *The Nature of Prejudice*. Reading, MA: Addison-Wesley, pp. 25–26.

17. Good, T. and Brophy, J. (1997). *Looking in Classrooms* (7th ed.). New York: Longman, p. 232.

18. Maslow, A. (1954/1970). *Motivation and Personality* (2nd ed.). New York: Harper & Row, p. 39.

19. Schein, E. Organizational and Managerial Culture as a Facilitator or Inhibitor of Organizational Learning.

20. Peck, M. S. (1987). *The Different Drum*. New York: Simon & Schuster, p. 68.

21. Sobel, D. and Ornstein, R. (1996). *The Healthy Mind Healthy Body Handbook*. New York: Patient Education Media, p. 124.

22. Hesselbein, F. (Summer 1997). The Power of Civility. *Leader to Leader* 5. Retrieved August 16, 2001, from the World Wide Web: http://www.pfdf.org/leaderbooks/L2L/summer97/fh.html.

CHAPTER EIGHT

ORGANIZATIONAL RENEWAL IS PERPETUAL CHANGE

Strategy ■ *Follow the Seven Lessons to Institute Organizational Renewal*

STARTING POINT

The president of the school board looked directly at the superintendent of schools and said, "Why do we always have to change? Can't we just grow and continuously evolve? In my business, we think in terms of renewal; that way we are constantly changing—changing with a purpose."

Real change is an ongoing process of renewal. Renewal has two major organizational functions: It connects the organization to its roots, and it links the present to the future without forgetting the past. These two related functions interact to sustain organizational survival and maintain organizational health. Change can exist without renewal, but renewal cannot exist without change. Effective leaders represent both change and renewal. It is through leadership committed to change and renewal that people and their organizations thrive. John Gardner states:

> A society whose maturing consists simply of acquiring more firmly established ways of doing things is headed for the graveyard—even if it learns to do these things with greater and greater skill. In the ever-renewing society, what matures is a system or framework within which continuous innovation, renewal and rebirth can occur.[1]

Renewal is at the heart of all constructive change. It is a purpose of leadership. In it lies the hope of people committed to each other and to the meaning that drives their social unit, organization, community, or country. Renewal is the underpinning of an organization's basic founding principles. It is renewed dedication to those principles and a generative application of them to evolving contexts. Renewal in healthy organizations is a continuous activity. Because it is a continuous activity, it represents constant, progressive, and constructive change that unites members in a common purpose.

When people are committed to each other and a common purpose, they commit themselves to continuous renewal, provide energy to their current aspirations, and give hope to those who succeed them. According to John Gardner, "Civilizations rise and fall—and sometimes if they are lucky—they renew themselves. One striking sign of renewal is a wave of innovation in grassroots problem-solving that covers virtually every relevant topic. . . . It represents an astonishing burst of vitality."[2]

Renewing organizations are healthy organizations. They maintain their vibrancy and vitality. These organizations recognize continuous renewal as existing at the heart of survival. They know that living species learn to renew by adapting to their environments or they become extinct. This is true for animal, human, and organizational species. On one hand, primitive species such as the cockroach befuddle pest control experts by adapting to the latest insecticides and therefore continuing to flourish as a species. On the other hand, some species are so fragile that they need legislative protection and international cooperation to survive.

Human beings, unlike insects or animals, do not have an automatic behavior-driven program that tells them how to survive. Instead, human beings have a complex cognitive capacity that places the responsibility for survival on the ability to work collaboratively in the context of a social group to solve survival-related problems. This problem-solving capacity is a renewal mechanism that accelerates the adaptation process. Human beings use this capacity to continue to thrive as a species. The capacity to identify problems, develop solutions, and permanently resolve problems is evident in all human endeavors such as medicine, government, engineering, or space exploration. This renewing capacity is unlimited and engrained in the human DNA. As Gardner stated: "But in the spirit of renewal it could be an exhilarating climb. Failure and frustration are not reason to doubt ourselves, but reason to strengthen resolve. Americans are sick and tired of being sick and tired. We are happiest when we are taking charge of our future and working together."[3]

The leaders' task is to maintain the spirit of continuous renewal. They cannot satisfy their constituents by maintaining the status quo. Maintaining the status quo is an abrogation of leadership and a sign of fear. Effective leaders recognize the need for renewal and openly reject complacency. They realize that renewal is associated with risk. They also realize, however, that all aspects of life represent degrees of risk. These leaders recognize that there is no safety net; any thought of creating a safety net is an attempt to live in an illusion. They recognize that renewal and change are inextricably linked to benefit the organization, its stakeholders, and the community within which the organization exists. Organizational renewal requires the commitment of each person within the organization to continuously renew him or herself.

The leader who integrates change into a continuous renewal process sets in motion a human and organizational capacity to sustain growth, successfully meet challenges, and maintain confidence in the future. Change, channeled into renewal, becomes a dynamic leadership tool for the leader. This leader views change as a necessary and integrated part of the capacity to lead and renew any organization.

A REFLECTIVE CONVERSATION WITH A PRINCIPAL

Jo Ann Brimfield is principal of Jordan Middle School. Although offered the opportunity for a central office position that promised promotion to superintendent in five years, she chose to remain a school principal. She has a commitment to students and the community. Her work as a principal gives her a great deal of fulfillment. Educators throughout the district recognize her as a special leader—one who has transformed problem school after problem school. In each case, the problem school became an exceptional school and remained an exceptional school long after she moved on to her next challenge. What is her secret? Ms. Brimfield retires next month. She agreed to an interview with a colleague and friend, Dr. Bob Jenkins, from the state university.

"Jo Ann, what is your secret to leadership? I've marveled at what you have achieved. I must be missing something, because I don't seem to be creating any more Jo Ann Brimfields."

"Dr. Jenkins, your comments are flattering—but I am just a principal. I've only done what I have been asked to do by the superintendent."

"Jo Ann, you make things happen. Each school is a better place after you've left."

"Dr. Jenkins, I believe in the capacity of people to renew themselves and their school. I think it is just that simple."

"What do you mean by 'the capacity of people to renew themselves and their school'?"

"That's simple; either people will choose to grow or they will choose to decay. There are no other choices. If they choose to remain complacent, they choose to decay. If they choose to resist change, they choose to decay. The rate of decay varies with the environment, but decay is inevitable. Now let me ask you some questions, Dr. Jenkins."

"Sure, go right ahead."

"You prepare leaders and have for some time, right?"

"Yes, I've had you come and speak to my classes about leadership."

"Do you teach your students how to create a renewing system? Do you teach your students how to empower people so that they can run their school? Do you teach your students about healthy organizations and how to create a healthy organization? Do you teach your students how to form and make lasting commitments to each other and to their organization? Do you teach your students how to be optimistic and rid themselves of negativism?"

"I confess that I don't. I might teach about some of these things, but I don't teach them how to do all of these things."

"I don't want to sound preachy, ungrateful, or dogmatic, but it's about time you started, Dr. Jenkins. If we are going to pass a worthwhile legacy on to our children and grandchildren we have to renew our commitments to each other; we have to renew our institutions; we have to renew ourselves. I've got no secrets. I just believe that people have the answers for their problems. The problem is that we've created leaders who believe that they have to supply all the answers. All the leader has to do is to empower, encourage, and stay out of the way; it does work."

"Jo Ann, you make a good case and your work history supports your claims. I want to know how you did it. I think there is more to it than just words. What exactly did you do?"

"If you've got the time, Dr. Jenkins, I believe I can describe what I do in seven lessons."

"I am waiting; let's begin."

SEVEN LESSONS TO CONTINUOUS RENEWAL

Intuitively, Jo Ann Brimfield knew how to create continuous renewal of people and organizations. Perhaps she had a magic chemistry that many people lack; however, she did not believe in magic for a second. She learned each lesson the hard way. She learned from mentors, through trial and error, from criticism, and by maintaining a constant desire to learn. Chapter Eight focuses on the change principle that organizational renewal is perpetual change. In this chapter, we look at the seven principles of organizational change and renewal. These seven lessons are the secret ingredients that sustain change and lead to a continuously renewing organization.

Lesson One: People Are the Secret to Success

"Dr. Jenkins, my first lesson is that people are the secret to success. Sustained change and renewal are impossible without the application of this lesson. Each person in the organization is critical to the organization's success. There is no replaceable person as far as people are concerned. Each person holds an essential piece to the puzzle for sustaining organizational change and renewal."

Dr. Jenkins poured himself a cup of coffee, moved over to his favorite soft chair in his office, smiled, and said, "I'm going to enjoy this. Jo Ann, I understand that people comprise an organization, but what do you mean by saying that each person holds a piece to the puzzle for sustaining organizational change and renewal?"

"Dr. Jenkins, it is a truth that organizations left alone whither and die. They are nothing more than an illusion, a figment of one's imagination. The organization is a social construct to organize people to fulfill a common purpose. An organization takes on a sense of life when people fill roles that cause the organization to function. To the extent that each person in the organization functions effectively, the organization functions effectively."

"Imagine the organization as a long-running Broadway play. Each day there is a new performance. For the most part, the actors and actresses remain constant. Occasionally, a substitute player enters, or a player leaves and needs a permanent replacement. In this play, some players have starring roles and others have supporting roles. Even though the audience sees only the players on stage, there is a crew working behind the scene to make sure that the sets are in place, costumes are ready, and props are available to support the actors and actresses on stage."

"The director needs to understand the roles of the players. The director does not look at one actress and her role and assume that all other actresses will play the same role. On the contrary, each actress has a different and specific role. She brings her unique personality to her role. Even though the script may be the same, no two actresses play the same role in the same way. In effect, the director understands the script and the personality of each actor and actress."

"The performance of the lead characters is crucially important; it constitutes the focus of the audience. The lead character's performance, however, is supported by everyone associated with the performance. One person, regardless of role, either acts to make the performance a memorable one or detracts from the performance's potential. Just listen to this review in the *New York Times* about a production of Macbeth:

> To tell the truth, though, this was the only scene in the entire production that made me sit up straight and prick up my ears. The rest of the evening holds no surprises. No one else in the cast stands out, particularly, as being horribly embarrassing or wonderfully inspiring. As a result, a work that traditionally gallops off the page here does indeed creep in a petty pace from scene to scene.[4]

"It seems that everyone did his or her job; however, that is all anyone did. They did just enough to get by and the play suffered because of their marginal performances. The audience did not get the performance they deserved; the players let the audience as well as themselves down."

"The metaphor of a long-running Broadway play has significant applications to how I view a school organization. I am not the star player. I am the producer and director. I want the spotlight to shine on my teachers, students, and support staff. They are the stars of the show. If my show is to be successful, I need to understand the scripts and the people. It is the same way with any organization. The responsibility is on the leader to bring the scripts and people together into a coherent role. The leader cannot assume that a person understands the script or how the script plays in the interaction with other people. This brings me to the central tenet of my philosophy. I believe that in any successful organization, people understand their roles and how their roles interact with those of other people."

Dr. Jenkins stared at Ms. Brimfield. He felt mesmerized by her use of the Broadway play as a metaphor for school organizations. Her comments raised a question. "Are you saying that teamwork is the most important part of running a successful school?"

Jo Ann Brimfield smiled and responded: "Teamwork is an important part; it is not the central part. The leader's role is to help each person understand that he or she is part of a larger team. An organization suffers when a member of the organization chooses to act in isolation. Isolated, disconnected actions subvert the constructive actions of all other members."

"Teamwork is an interesting concept; it is, however, not for everyone. Some people function more effectively on teams and others work more effectively alone. I believe that you allow people to work in an environment in which they flourish. When people work alone, if they properly understand their role, they do not work in isolation. They discover that their actions influence other people. Teaching is a good example. In many ways, teaching is isolating. Once the teacher closes the door to his classroom, he is separated from other teachers and isolated with his students. It is easy for the teacher to disconnect from other teachers and to focus solely on the immediate needs within his personal classroom space."

"I move teachers away from this isolationist mentality. One way that I do this is to use a media presentation that demonstrates the impact of a single action. I show a videotape of a variety of nature scenes. The videotape includes an avalanche started by one hiker who accidentally knocked a rock loose and started an avalanche that devastated a village. The video shows how a single mosquito spreads a virus through an entire village. A village member transported the virus to another village when he infected members of his visiting extended family. Eventually the virus became a national health issue for this African community. Teachers relate to this videotape because they realize that one child with a cold can spread the cold to students and teacher alike. In essence, as a learning community we discover that everything we do impacts everything every other person does."

The Renewal Process.   Jo Ann Brimfield understands the importance of people within her organization. It is not only people who make the difference but also the interactions between and among people. Russell Ackoff, management expert, states: "The performance of any system, therefore of a company, is never equal to the sum of the performances of its parts taken separately. It is the product of their interactions."[5] Continuous renewal requires the leader to examine and strengthen the interactions that occur within the school and those occurring between school members and the school community. This renewal process has three components:

1. Identification of formal and informal relationship paths
2. Identification of obstructions to paths
3. Renewal of paths

Identification of Formal and Informal Relationship Paths.   Each organizational role has a set of formal and informal paths. In Figure 8.1, the teacher formally interacts with her immediate colleagues. She interacts with her grade level, department, and team members within the constraints of school policy. These formal interactions

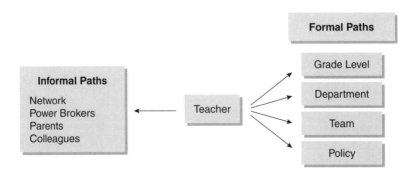

FIGURE 8.1   Informal and Formal Interaction Paths

are limited. Her informal interactions are more numerous. The set of informal interactions include the teacher's interactions with students who are not part of her normal teaching assignment, teachers not assigned to her team, administrators, counselors, secretaries, custodians, parents, and community members.

In some instances, the teacher's interactions may dynamically move between formal and informal depending on the circumstances. A department chairperson, for example, has coffee with the principal. This is an informal interaction. During the course of the informal interaction, the department chairperson briefed the principal on new department plans and sought approval for continued planning. Here, the department chairperson bridged the gap from informal to formal interactions. Many interactions depend on organizational policy. The policy may require a teacher to speak directly to her department chairperson or team leader regarding an issue before taking the issue to the principal. Her interactions with the principal may be informal or formal depending on policy or contract.

Formal and informal paths are important to organizational vitality. In a formal sense, the interactions represent how effectively organizational subunits work together. If these interactions are broken, the subunit loses effectiveness. In an informal sense, the dysfunctional interactions subvert the organization's process, yet because they are informal they may not be immediately visible. For example, a dysfunctional interaction exists between a teacher and a custodian. The custodian does not wash the boards one evening, a subtle action that causes minor turmoil. The teacher publicly berates the custodian. The custodian then acts to punish the entire team. This causes greater turmoil. The first step toward renewal is to become aware of these interactions. The second step is become aware of the obstructions to the paths of these interactions.

Identification of Obstructions to Paths.   Obstructions to paths can be overt or covert. The motivation for creating an obstruction is often obscure. Unless the leader discovers the underlying causes for the obstruction, significant personal and organizational harm is frequently the consequence. Edgar Schein states: "Even the familiar daily problems of organizational life—the unproductive meeting, the difficulty of getting a point across to a subordinate during performance appraisal, the difficulty of communicating instructions clearly enough to ensure correct implementation, and so on—may be productively analyzed from the cultural perspective."[6] Schein believes that obstructions to healthy interaction are the result of miscommunication between and among three separate organizational cultures. He identifies these cultures as the executive, engineer, and operator cultures (see Chapter Two).[7]

The three organizational cultures work efficiently as long as they stay within their defined roles. Once they move beyond their defined roles and penetrate the world of a different culture, problems occur. The problems are the result of misalignment. Each culture has its own mission, values, and goals. The mission, values, and goals of each culture may not be aligned with those of the organization or with the other cultures within the organization.

Figure 8.2 identifies misaligned cultures. When misalignment occurs, it is impossible for members of any organizational culture to communicate effectively

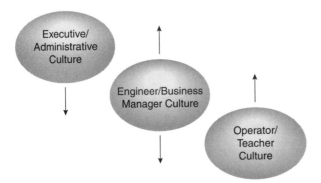

FIGURE 8.2   Misaligned Cultures

with members representing a different culture. Each culture sees its view of the world as valid. As a result, cultural defensive reactions occur. For example, school administrators (executive culture) receive a mandate from the school board to reduce the budget significantly. They make plans to reduce staff and restructure the operation of the school. The teachers (operator culture) rally their students and the students' parents to oppose staff cuts. They refuse to cooperate with administrators on any issue until the administration resolves the budget crisis. The business managers, department chairpersons, and other staff (engineer culture) find themselves caught between two warring cultures. Their roles are to make sure the school functions efficiently on a day-to-day basis. As far as they are concerned, the executive and operator cultures are both ignorant of organizational needs. In effect, no culture makes an effort to understand the other cultures' needs; the outcome becomes a zero-sum contest in which the most powerful culture wins.

The dysfunction associated with misaligned cultures is exacerbated when the relationship paths within each culture disintegrate. When these paths disintegrate, it is impossible for the collective culture to consensually agree to a mission, values, or other purpose. The members are in continual conflict. One principal, assigned to an inner-city barrio elementary school, stated that her biggest problem was not the children in school, but teachers, divided by long-established cliques actively opposing each other. This principal needed outside extended intervention to bring teachers to where they could meet and hold a civil conversation related to instructional issues.

Relationship building between and within cultures is a central tenet to personal and organizational renewal. Dean Ornish, author of numerous books related to personal health, states: "An important reason why early family relationships are so predictive of later illness is that these patterns of relating do not change very much in most people over time. These patterns of relating do not change very much in most people over time because our culture does not often encourage us to examine these issues."[8] Ornish's advice related to personal health extends to organizational health. If an organization is to renew, then the members must remove the obstructions that sever relationship construction within and between organizational cultures.

Renewal of Paths. Organizational renewal begins through the renewal of paths. The leader renews these paths by promoting three essential renewal components:

1. Civility
2. Respect
3. Dialogue

RENEWAL THROUGH CIVILITY. Civility is at the heart of the renewal of relationship paths because people have different opinions and strong feelings about their opinions. In a democracy, it is not healthy for people to attack each other, prevent others from being heard, or refuse to listen to opinions that represent an alternative voice. Frances Hesselbein, editor-in-chief of *Leader-to-Leader,* president and CEO of the Drucker Foundation, and former chief executive of the Girl Scouts of the USA, states:

> In the rush to "reinvent" our organizations, or our communities, or ourselves, we sometimes overlook the time-tested principles that helped early great leaders succeed. We forget that long before "relationship marketing" or "unit of one" became buzzwords, leaders built genuine and felicitous relationships in work life, public life, and family life. The organization of the future will be relationship-centered, mission-focused, values-based, and demographics-driven. Good manners and civility are essential to the success of relationships across the organization, and will move to the front of the effective leader's portfolio.[9]

Civility speaks to the way that we choose to relate to each other. It does not occur in an environment in which threats and accusations are the norm. It occurs in safe environments, in which each person feels respected. In safe environments, civility leads to discussion; discussion leads to respect for different ideas, values, and opinions; respect leads to dialogue; dialogue leads to deeper understanding; and deeper understanding leads to agreement on fundamental issues without sacrificing one's identity or one's beliefs.

RENEWAL THROUGH RESPECT. Respect is an internal feeling that one has for oneself and an external expression for another person, institution, or symbol. It is impossible for a person to respect someone who does not respect him or herself. Respect for others originates with a healthy self-respect. As a person, I appreciate who I am, where I have come from, and where I desire to go. I do not loathe, belittle, or berate myself. I am who I am. When I have this type of positive self-regard, which is the same as self-respect, I am no longer threatened by others and I am free to offer my respect to them. The respect that we owe ourselves is also owed to others in a renewing organization. Maslow states:

> Respect for another person acknowledges him as an independent entity and as a separate and autonomous individual. The self-actualizing person will not casually use another, control him, or disregard his wishes. He will allow the respected person a fundamental irreducible dignity, and will not humiliate him. This is true not only for interadult relationships but also in a self-actualizing person's relationship to children.[10]

In the renewing organization, respect requires that members let go of control. They no longer attempt to control each other's ideas, values, concepts, or behavior. In a respectful environment, it is possible to eliminate obstructions to relationship paths and create new relationship paths between and within cultures.

RENEWAL THROUGH DIALOGUE.   Once the leader establishes a climate in which respect becomes a mutually reciprocal value, members can enter into dialogue. Dialogue ensues from an environment based in civility and driven by respect. Dialogue means letting go of one's perceived notions, concepts, and ideas and entering into another's space to understand and allow the synergy of conflicting thoughts and opinions to take on new meaning. David Bohm, the English physicist, believes that dialogue is essential to global survival. He states:

> . . . a form of free dialogue may well be one of the most effective ways of investigating the crisis which faces society, and indeed the whole of human nature and consciousness today. Moreover, it may turn out that such a form of free exchange of ideas and information is of fundamental relevance for transforming culture and freeing it of destructive misinformation, so that creativity can be liberated.[11]

If this is true for global society, how much more appropriate is it for an organization or a school? Leaders and teachers lead primarily through example; it is incumbent that they demonstrate to the school community and larger community that dialogue is possible.

Dialogue requires people, committed to each other, to explore the meaning hidden in each other's words and the ideas that emerge from the dialogue. It is a generative process that leads to creative solutions. In effect, dialogue cultivates personal and organizational renewal because it stimulates the growth of mutual respect; it is a collaborative process whereby people work together creatively to resolve challenges to the relationship paths, organizational problems, and cultural-driven issues. Although dialogue is time intensive, it is central to a permanent solution to many problems that confront school organizations. When leaders and members of the school organization bypass dialogue for the sake of efficiency, they quickly find short-term solutions. Predictably, they return to the problem context, never fully resolving it. In the end, they spend more time on short-term solutions than they would have spent in dialogue aimed at a permanent solution.

Lesson Two: Create Healthy Organizations

Dr. Jenkins got up, stretched, and went to his desk. He retrieved a note pad and pen. He looked at Jo Ann and smiled, "I need to take notes, if you don't mind. I believe you're right when you say people are crucial to organizational success. The type of involvement you require entails trust and a sense of personal and professional identity. Why not focus on policy, vision, or mission instead of people?"

Jo Ann Brimfield laughed, "You've been reading too many books, Dr. Jenkins. In the real world leaders understand that healthy people comprise a healthy, effective organization. Without people filling necessary roles, there is no organization. Without people to serve, there is no purpose for the organization's existence; they work in the organizational context. The leader works best with people when she understands that the people in her organization and community have countless needs and pressures that they work through each day. The effective leader works successfully with people when she develops a holistic approach to managing a change environment. For example, let us suppose one of your children is having problems at college. Do you forget about it when you go to the university to teach?"

Dr. Jenkins responded, "Of course not. I love my children. It bothers me when any of my children struggle. What's your point?"

"Your response is precisely the point. No one compartmentalizes his or her life. We may try to separate work from our private life; however, we end up suppressing what bothers us. If our problems are significant, we project our emotions onto others. The teacher, who is angry with his wife, hollers at his students. The teacher, whose child is on drugs, thinks more about her child than she does her lesson plans. Each staff member takes his or her whole person to work. If I am concerned about organizational health, the staff member's personal problems are my problems. I work to optimize organizational health. This means that I work to construct and maintain an environment in which people feel welcomed, challenged, motivated to grow, supported, and understand the responsibility they have to their stakeholders. Each day we become healthier or we move toward dysfunction and disease; there is no gray area."

Focusing on Creating and Sustaining Healthy Organizations. Continuous renewal focuses on creating and sustaining healthy organizations. Healthy organizations provide an environment that enhances employee growth, sustains high levels of productivity, and provides benefit to its stakeholders. Organizational health, like personal health, is a complex issue. On a personal level, some people define health as the absence of disease. The body functions efficiently and without pain. A healthy person has the energy to perform the functions central to his or her survival. It is possible to maintain health by practicing health-producing behaviors. Henry Dreher, author of *The Immune Power Personality,* identified seven traits associated with healthy people:[12]

1. Being in touch with our psychological and bodily needs
2. Being able to meet those needs by assertive action
3. Coping skills, including a sense of control, that enable us to ward off depression
4. Expressing emotions, including sadness and anger
5. The willingness to ask for and accept support from loved ones
6. A sense of meaning and purpose in our work, daily activities, and relationships
7. The capacity for pleasure and play

It is easy to spot unhealthy people or organizations; the symptoms abound. Reflect for a moment on the different organizations that you interact with each week. These organizations may be schools, churches, hospitals, supermarkets, malls, universities, or a military base. Intuitively, you know when you are in an effective, healthy organization and when you are in a disorganized, unhealthy organization. Have you stood in a long line at the post office and wondered why only one clerk was working at the counter? At the same time, you may have seen two clerks in the background ignoring the line. How did you feel as a consumer? Have you been present when the person serving you was complaining about her work, coworkers, or supervisor? All of us have had these or similar experiences. We have also had experiences in which we felt welcomed, our needs were met, and going to work seemed more fun than not working. These are symptoms of unhealthy and healthy organizations. Review Table 8.1 to rate the health of your school. The more Xs you place next to the symptoms, the more symptoms that exist indicating that the health of your school is deteriorating.[13]

Organizational Health.   We understand what health is by examining nonhealth. We seldom pay attention to our condition when we are healthy. We don't worry about our waist size, for example, until we need to buy larger clothes. It is the same with organizations. Members of a school organization know when the organization is sick. Teachers speak of low morale and infighting. Teachers complain about

TABLE 8.1   Symptoms of Unhealthy Organizations

Place an X in the column to the right for each of the symptoms that you have observed in your organization during the past month. In parentheses next to the X, estimate the number of times you observed the symptom, for example, X (5).

Judgment and criticism are major events instead of a learning environment.	
Stress and tension are prevalent rather than an open and relaxed atmosphere.	
Confusion reigns without order or structure.	
Fear and paranoia are rampant instead of trust and faith in others.	
Leadership is erratic and unpredictable instead of stable.	
"Yes" people are subservient instead of independent forces who can interact.	
Expectations and disappointment are prevalent.	
Goals are unrealistic.	
Rules are abundant, but rebellion is popular.	
Loyalty is demanded instead of earned.	
Communication is covert rather than open and encouraged.	
Workaholism is progressive without a prioritization of tasks.	
Written memos and e-mails exceed oral communication.	
Responsibility is linked with blame instead of needed information.	

Source: Quoted from Hollands, J. (July 30, 1997). How to Recognize a Healthy Organization. Los Altos, CA: *Los Altos Town Crier.* Retrieved June 18, 2000, from the World Wide Web: http://www.losaltosonline. com/latc/arch/9731/Business/3jean/3jean.html.

FIGURE 8.3   Characteristics of Organizational Health

parents, administrators, custodians, and students. Similarly, administrators complain about uncaring teachers and a nonresponsive community. In these organizations, conflict is just below the surface. The slightest provocation is all that a teacher needs to initiate a grievance. The mentality of these organizations is that people frame relationships in terms of allies and enemies. Everyone is defensive. Everyone is protective of his or her personal interests. In these organizations, members create a self-centered world in which survival of the fittest governs interactions. Organizational health is a complex phenomenon. It is the gestalt of five interrelated factors. These five factors contribute to the maintenance of organizational health when optimally operating. Each of these factors in Figure 8.3 represents an essential lesson in the school organization's continuous renewal.

Constructive change happens in healthy organizations in which each of these five interrelated factors optimally operates. The effective leader focuses on all five areas. He or she knows that as each area becomes healthier it positively affects the other areas. In effect, the leader works with members to construct an organizational culture that understands how to maintain a healthy environment.

Lesson Three: Effective Leadership Is Power

Dr. Jenkins reflected on the notion of organizational health. It was not a perspective that he considered when teaching his students. In fact, he reflected, he had never considered it.

He looked at Jo Ann. "I have not considered the notion of organizational health; my approach seems so simplistic. The leader builds a community of learners; he creates a learning organization; he educates the members to his vision. It is supposed to work. You're making it complex; I am beginning to see how organizational health is a multidimensional, highly complex construct."

"Your approach wasn't simplistic, Dr. Jenkins. You had a part of the picture, but you didn't have the whole picture. The first lesson regarding organizational health is leadership. There is no denying its importance. To understand how leadership relates to organizational health, Dr. Jenkins, you have to view the school organization as a living organism. Imagine each administrator, teacher, staff member, student, parent, and community member as the blood cells that flow throughout your body. The blood cells do not wander aimlessly; they flow in a predesigned pattern. These cells bring nourishment to the body's vital organs when the body is healthy. They fight potential disease; they bring healing to wounded members. Each of these cells acts interdependently and independently with one mission: to sustain the body's health. Body leadership operates out of the central nervous system that controls all functions, making multiple decisions at rapid speed. This is analogous to leadership. The leader is akin to the central nervous system. He operates with one function: His mission is to serve the needs of the school community and to sustain the health of the school organization."

Effective Leadership and Organizational Health.   Effective leadership is a power-driven core component that contributes to organizational health. In healthy organizations, the leader's primary function is to monitor the organization's health. In the form of an analogy, the leader has the organization hooked to the life-monitoring system. She constantly monitors the instruments, checks the pulse and blood pressure, and runs a variety of tests designed to ascertain the organization's health. The leader moves swiftly to intervene if any test indicates a potential challenge.

How effectively the leader moves to address potential challenges shapes the perceptions of the leader held by members and stakeholders. The perceptions of members and stakeholders determine the leader's effectiveness. A brilliant person may be a poor leader if the brilliant person does not meet the needs of the members or stakeholders. A person with average intelligence, but one who understands the needs of her constituents and stakeholders, wins membership respect. This type of leader understands paradigm trends. Some people may refer to this as vision, but it is more than vision. Leaders with vision may lead their organization in the wrong direction, whereas leaders who have an intuitive feel for forthcoming challenges, prepare their organization for the challenge, long before the challenge arises. When the challenge arises, the organization is ready; it meets the challenge as if it were a common occurrence. This type of proactive response contributes to member confidence in themselves and in the school's leadership. Self-confident people are mentally healthier opposed to those who are passive and depressed. One challenge faced by the leader in renewing organizations is the acquirement of sufficient resources for renewal.

The effective leader, concerned with the renewal of her organization, uses her power to provide resources for the members. She understands that organizational renewal is impossible with limited resources. In healthy organizations, members do not have to ask or advocate for resources. The leader anticipates their needs. This leader somehow, even in times of scarcity, finds ways to attract resources. She positions her school so that the school board, community, and parents become staunch allies in the struggle to acquire necessary resources. As a result, teachers and students, unconcerned about resources, focus on instructional achievement. When adequate resources are available, the leader focuses on the needs of people.

Effective leadership gives priority to the needs of people. The leader understands that people count more than does the organizational attainment of objects. In a counterintuitive sense, effective leadership attains organizational goals by focusing first on people. It is the reverse for leaders obsessed with attaining organizational goals while relegating people to a means-driven status. This leader lacks empathy. She never understands that her focus causes her failure. Management expert Warren Bennis states:

> The men I spoke with also talked of empathy, however. . . . Empathy isn't simply the province of artists. Former Luck Stores CEO Don Ritchey said, "I think one of the biggest turn-ons is for people to know that their peers and particularly their bosses not only know they're there but know pretty intimately what they're doing and are involved with them on almost a daily basis, that it's a partnership, that you're really trying to run this thing well together, that if something goes wrong our goal is to fix it, not see who we can nail."[14]

The effective leader, who believes in continuous renewal as a vehicle for constructive and progressive change, works with and through people. This leader anticipates the constituents' needs and acts proactively to meet these needs.

Lesson Four: It's All about Attitude

Dr. Jenkins had not had this much fun in a long time. He marveled at the wisdom of his former student. He wanted to learn more. He decided to press on. "The metaphor of the human body representing the school organization is powerful. Certainly, a person would not take a hammer and intentionally smash his finger. A healthy person would not take an overdose of drugs. Our health is vitally important. It seems to me that this metaphor helps us to understand that we have a critical role in sustaining organizational health. In nurturing the organization's health, we provide a thriving environment. This seems so simple, yet I do not see it being done. What is the problem?"

"We seem to be caught in a trap, Dr. Jenkins. I believe, however, there is a way out of the dilemma. I like to read the works of the father of American psychology, William James. He still has many lessons for us to learn. I memorized a quote from James. He states: 'The deliberate adoption of a healthy-minded attitude has proved possible to many who never supposed they had it in them; regeneration of character has gone on on an extensive scale; and cheerfulness has been restored to countless homes.'[15]

"It's all about attitude, Dr. Jenkins. Attitude is individual and collective. Each person takes an individual attitude toward life, work, play, or every other experience that he or she may encounter. The organizational culture also possesses a collective attitude formed over the life of the organization. If Dr. James was right, and I believe he was, a positive attitude, full of self-expectancy, is crucial to organizational health. We are both aware of Hawthorne experiments and the proof they give us of the teacher's attitude toward his students. I want to stress, however, that the attitude I find in schools begins with the leader. If the leader is pessimistic, then you can be certain that the faculty will be pessimistic. If the leader is optimistic and filled with a sense of positive self-expectancy, you will see this attitude mirrored in the teachers. When this attitude is mirrored in the teachers, it is also mirrored in the students and the community. It is marvelous to behold."

The Relationship between Renewal and Attitude.   Attitude " . . . is defined as a manner, disposition, or feeling about a person, event, or thing. Recognizing the three components of every attitude may be helpful: (1) the cognitive or knowledge part (what you know, think, or believe about the person or situation), (2) the feeling or evaluative part (what emotions you have towards the person or situation), and (3) the behavioral part (your actions with the person or in the situation)."[16] Attitude affects all of us throughout our lives. It shapes behavior and behavior reinforces attitude. Organizations, like people, project attitudes through policies, rules, rewards, and sanctions. The organization's attitude represents the collective consciousness of the organization's membership and culture. The notion of attitude is difficult to grasp because it is not tangible; we have to look beyond the action to find the attitude associated with the action.

According to Mackey, a *Minneapolis Star Tribune* columnist,

> Harvard psychologist William James put it this way: The greatest discovery of my generation is that a human being can alter his life by altering his attitudes of mind. Can we actually enhance our lives by altering our attitudes? Does success or failure have anything to do with mental attitude? The answer is a resounding "yes." . . . Let me tell you about two young women who decided to quit their jobs at a community hospital. They were tired of dealing with ungrateful, complaining patients, backbiting between employees and an apathetic administration. Before they quit, they decided to try an experiment: They vowed to go out of their way to help and be polite to everyone they encountered. No matter how someone looked at them, talked to them or treated them, they overwhelmed people with encouragement, courtesy and appreciation. Before long, an amazing transformation took place. Patients didn't seem so miserable, staff even smiled at each other and the administration seemed surprisingly interested in their affairs. The two women experienced a basic law of nature: For every action there is an equal and opposite reaction. The very situations that caused frustration were reflections of their own attitudes. . . . It's like the old farmer who was celebrating his 90th birthday. He'd seen it—the Dust Bowl, years of flooding rains and scorching heat, banks foreclosing on mortgages on every farm in the county. But through it all, he'd remained positive and determined, even downright cheerful. His family and friends pressed him for his secret on maintaining his optimism. "It ain't [sic] so hard," he said with a twinkle in his eye. "I just learned early on to cooperate with the inevitable."[17]

Attitude determines behavior. The effective leader who concentrates on continuous renewal knows that his attitude toward people, events, problems, and every aspect of life needs to be constructive, positive, and optimistic. Race, gender, age, ethnicity, or other categories do not obscure his mind. He assists each member of his organization to strive toward his or her full potential. He knows that an organization full of people attempting to maximize their potential results in a continually renewing organization that meets the needs of its members and stakeholders. This leader allows no ground for pessimism in his continuously renewing organization. Although setbacks occur, he becomes a source of motivation. He becomes the standard by which members measure their competence. This leader creates an optimistic attitude by his attitude, actions, and dynamic energy.

The effective leader's attitude is resilient and optimistic. There is no hesitation or fear of failure. The effective leader agrees with Max Moore's comments regarding optimism:

> Optimists expect to do well and to keep getting better. They feel no need to be perfect or do a job perfectly. They do not have to mow the lawn magnificently, just well enough. They do not need to write to their friends with unprecedented wit and skill; they just need to say things clearly. By setting realistic goals and standards for themselves, optimists succeed more often, thereby reinforcing their optimism and motivation. . . . Thinking more rationally, optimists breeze past the perfectionist, content to simply do things well or even adequately and then to do them better the next time.[18]

Each aspect of renewal has a constructive, renewing, optimistic thread woven into its fabric. The leader, for example, when confronted by a teacher complaining about a parent, states: "What is the challenge we face? How can we constructively work this out to meet the parent's needs as well as yours?" This approach, over time, teaches faculty that they are part of the problem solution process. They frame problems in win–win solutions. Attitude is an important element in the continuous renewal of the school organization.

Lesson Five: Leaders Link Actions and Policies to Change

"I've seen it a thousand times, Jo Ann. I've seen it in my graduate students, the athletic teams at the university, and in society in general: Attitude is everything. When my attitude is positive, upbeat, and constructive, my work becomes fun and people enjoy being around me. When my attitude is poor, I am cranky, pessimistic and people begin to move away from me. I blame it on them; however, it is really my fault. I see how this fits into the organizational schema and how it is an important part of organizational health. How does all this fit into the organization's actions?"

"You're a fast learner, Dr. Jenkins. A healthy organization acts healthy. You can tell the difference, in most cases, between a healthy person and an unhealthy person. Listen to the conversation, observe the behavior, and watch how the healthy person walks and talks. It is far different from that of an unhealthy person. An organization is no different. Healthy organizations promote healthy actions and policies. Unhealthy organizations promote defensive and destructive actions and policies. Chris Argyris calls these unhealthy organizational actions defensive routines. I have seen defensive routines in every unhealthy social organization. I have seen it in families, churches, schools, universities, university classes, and in numerous private sector operations."

"What do you mean by a defensive routine?"

"Let me use a personal example. How do you feel when you submit a manuscript for publication in an academic journal and have the manuscript rejected with numerous criticisms? I'll bet you're angry. I'll also bet that you don't run around the university sharing the rejection and criticisms with your colleagues. When that happens, you are experiencing a defensive routine. Individually and organization-ally, we all use defensive routines whenever we feel that we are threatened or likely to be embarrassed.[19] In effect, we hide our problems and attempt to deny them. We develop a series of actions meant to cover up, rather than to resolve, the problem. This isn't healthy for an individual or an organization."

Renewal and Organizational Policies and Actions.   An organization's actions and policies either contribute to renewal or lead to entropy. Renewing organiza-tions make sure that actions and policies are just, fair, and encourage tolerance.

Is the Action or Policy Just?   In renewing organizations the actions and policies meet the test of justice. The test of justice implies that every action is consistent among all members. It also implies that all actions and policies appropriately address each situation. A principal, for example, who demands that a teacher rewrite an entire lesson plan within twenty-four hours to conform to state achieve-ment testing is being unjust. The principal who offers to work with the teacher and provide the teacher with appropriate resources to learn how to write a lesson plan incorporating learning objectives that ensure student preparation for the state achievement test is being just. Justice implies an appropriate relationship between the organization's action and the event to which the organization responds.

Is the Action or Policy Fair?   In renewing organizations, all actions and policies meet the test of fairness. The test of fairness implies that each person receives equal treatment; there are no favors offered to special-interest groups. Two people, from different backgrounds, with different organizational roles, receive the same treat-ment. It does not matter to the leader if he likes one person more than he likes another person. His liking or disliking of the person has nothing to do with fair-ness. Fairness means that regardless of the situation, each person involved in the situation receives similar treatment.

Jo Ann Brimfield, the principal in our case study, reported that two teachers wanted to take their students on different field trips on the same day. Because it was near the end of the school year, she had enough resources to support only one field trip. She did not choose between the two teachers; however, she asked both teachers to meet with her to brainstorm alternative solutions. The result was that both teachers agreed to cochair a fund-raiser to secure the additional funding needed for both groups to take the field trips. Neither teacher received special treatment; both teachers felt they were part of a fair, just, and equitable solution.

Is the Action or Policy an Expression of Tolerance?   In renewing organizations, toler-ance is inherent in every action and policy. Tolerance means that the leader has the capacity to recognize and respect the beliefs and practices of the members of her school community. Because she has high levels of tolerance, she embraces diver-sity. She knows that students exposed to a widely diverse community learn toler-ance. She understands that people with different beliefs and practices broaden a learning community's perspective. A broadened perspective moves a learning organization toward greater inclusion. Renewing organizations tear down walls built for exclusion; instead, they encourage opportunities to promote inclusion. According to the Bertelsmann Group for Policy Research:

> In a tolerant society, there is less fear, hostility and violence, less dogmatism, hatred and fanaticism. Tolerance allows the free development of human creativity and is thus an essential and indispensable building block for democratic societies. The promotion of tolerance on a societal and individual level is therefore a matter of necessity. On the level of the individual, tolerance skills have to be actively fostered. On the level of society, the corresponding political and social framework conditions have to be created. These include respectful behavior towards each other and anti-discrimination rules. In addition, tolerance is a basic tenet of democracy, as it asks the central questions of how liberty and pluralism, rule of law and protection of minorities are guaranteed.[20]

In renewing organizations, the leader encourages opinions from members representing diverse backgrounds so she and her school community can learn from each other. This leader knows that learning does not take place in an environment filled with intolerance; an intolerant environment leads to entropy and eventual decay. It has no place in an organization undergoing continuous renewal.

Lesson Six: Reinvent Your Organization—Not the Wheel

Dr. Jenkins wrote furiously on his note pad. He immediately recognized how defensive routines played at the university. "Defensive routines are the antithesis of actions and policies that are just, fair, and tolerant. I have often criticized my colleagues, the university, and public schools for operating defensively. I never guessed that my actions mirrored those of my colleagues and institution. I don't want to operate that way; I want to have a constructive attitude; I want to teach my students how to renew their schools and make them healthy organizations. Once you recognize defensive routines and take corrective action, how do you construct and nurture a life-sustaining atmosphere?"

"Something is missing, Dr. Jenkins! I have walked into schools and other organizations in which the best word I can use to describe the atmosphere is toxicity. It is devastating to be in those environments. Your energy is drained. People are defensive, angry, and pessimistic. I believe that one of the critical elements of renewal and transformation of the organization rests in renewing and energizing the organization's atmosphere."

Jo Ann paused for a moment and waited for a response from Dr. Jenkins. He smiled at her and motioned her to continue. She felt energized; she was speaking with passion. "The leader does more than any other single person to create a school atmosphere conducive to learning, growth, and change. A great leader reinvents the organization—not the wheel. I like the metaphor of the space station as a way of explaining what I mean about organizational atmosphere. The leader is the astronaut. The astronaut creates an environment for survival in space. The environment or atmosphere must meet the needs of all astronauts. The astronaut regulates the environment to meet the optimal growing conditions of survival for those occupying the space station. Applying this to the school organization, the leader takes a personal interest in the people in his organization. His philosophy of personal concern is contagious. It spreads to assistants, lead teachers, department chairpersons, and teachers. A sense of solidarity develops among members. This sense of solidarity among members leads to a healthy sense of community."

The Workplace Atmosphere.   The workplace atmosphere provides the optimum environment for member productivity. Atmosphere refers to the gestalt of the environment and its impact on the organization. Healthy organizations possess the following four characteristics:

1. They maintain an environment of listening.
2. They have an absence of fear of reprisals or sanctions.
3. They reward and recognize effective performance.
4. They create an inclusive community.

Healthy Organizations Maintain an Environment of Listening.   A remarkable transition has occurred over the last twenty years. The transition was brought about by a combination of economic and political forces. On one hand, nations such as Japan challenged the United States to economic prosperity. The efforts of Japanese leaders caught the United States industry by surprise. Soon Americans were buying more goods, especially automobiles, from Japan than they were from U.S.-based companies. One of the Japanese secrets was the involvement of workers in production decisions. Japanese leadership felt it was critical to success to seek employee feedback. On the other hand, the global political movement toward greater democratization accelerated. Citizens began to demand a greater say in their government. These two forces worked their way into organizations. We now know that successful organizations consider employee input essential and make few decisions without consulting employees in the decision-making process.

Involvement begins by listening to employees. If the leader trivializes a teacher's suggestion, for example, the teacher feels marginalized and seldom offers further advice. The effective leader creates an environment that encourages sharing and listening. He does this informally and formally. In an informal sense, the leader encourages his faculty, staff, and students by observing what is happening and then entering into conversations with members. Members share firsthand knowledge of problems and potential solutions. They feel important because the leader took the time to listen.

In a formal sense, the effective leader uses many devices to encourage sharing and listening. The leader conducts focus groups, meets formally with school and community-based groups, randomly calls stakeholders, and uses technology to communicate efficiently and effectively. The leader knows that effective communication and the creation of a listening environment is done through interpersonal contact. This work, although time consuming, is the most effective way to create and sustain a healthy organizational atmosphere.

Healthy Organizations Have an Absence of Fear of Reprisals or Sanctions.   A healthy organizational atmosphere is free from fear of reprisals or sanctions. In repressive environments, risk taking is minimal; members do not want to risk for fear they may fail. Failure, in these environments, brings swift and certain reprisal. In a risk-free environment, members feel safe from personal attack from leadership or colleagues.

The leader takes responsibility for creating an environment devoid of the fear of reprisals or sanctions. She creates this environment by collaboratively working with teachers, staff, and students, to develop a set of rules and policies to guide interactions. The process she uses to develop safe environmental rules and guidelines becomes the model for teachers to use in their classrooms. A safe environment is created through practice. As members of the school community practice, they learn how to work within the guidelines they establish. They also learn how to monitor behaviors that threaten their safe environment.

Healthy Organizations Reward and Recognize Effective Performance. In a healthy atmosphere, the organization, leadership, and members reward and recognize superior performance. Superior performance becomes a model to emulate, not something to envy or the source of jealousy. Each member's superior performance is cause for celebration. Tom Peters states:

> The construction of public forums for the recognition of achievement is closely entwined with listening. Among other things, well-constructed recognition settings provide the single most important opportunity to parade and reinforce the specific kinds of new behavior one hopes others will emulate. Thus, recognition activities become a key listening and communication device, beyond their straightforward motivational influence on those being recognized.[21]

Focus on performance demonstrates respect for the human capacity to tap into existing potential. As members improve their performance, they feel better about themselves and their mission. They begin to feel part of an important enterprise. Focusing on and continuously rewarding superior performance reinforces leadership goals because the recognition of superior performance is done by measuring performance against widely recognized standards, not personal or intuitive values. Superior performance, when recognized and rewarded, sets the standard for performance within the organization. This performance transcends the personal likes and dislikes the leader may have toward members. The effective leader realizes that, in the end, all that matters is how well each person performs in his or her specific role.

Healthy Organizations Create an Inclusive Community. Healthy organizations create an inclusive community. An inclusive community addresses the primary need of human beings: the need to belong. Human beings want to belong. They want to be a part of a social fabric by which they feel they contribute to the unit's well-being. The leader takes responsibility for creating conditions for continuous renewal of a healthy sense of an inclusive community. She recognizes that continuous renewal is dependent on the sustainability and health of the relationships formed among and between members of the organization. Mark Van Doren states: "The connectedness of things is what the educator contemplates to the limits of his capacity. No human capacity is great enough to permit a vision of the world as simple, but if the educator does not aim at the vision no one else will, and the consequences are dire when no one does."[22]

Focusing on community is important work. Organizational health requires the sacrifice. Without the sacrifice, there may be temporary independence, but any independence is lost without a community to sustain and nurture it. The effective leader knows that meeting this challenge will allow her school community to flourish.

Lesson Seven: Renewing Organizations Are Self-Actualizing Organizations

Dr. Jenkins looked up from his note pad. It was filled with notes and diagrams. A cursory examination of his notes would give someone the impression that Dr. Jenkins was putting a puzzle together. He finished his coffee and said, "You haven't mentioned values. I think they are key to this model you've put together. Where do values fit into the picture? I'm sure that a healthy atmosphere has a set of values at its base. Effective leaders have a set of core values; effective organizations have a set of core values. I'm surprised that you haven't mentioned values."

"Dr. Jenkins, I've been mentioning values all morning; I haven't explicitly used the word. I've spoken about the importance of people. I've spoken about community. I've spoken about atmosphere. In every lesson there is hidden a set of values. I haven't mentioned values for two reasons: (1) It is important that each school community discover its own values. Values will differ from school community to school community. The work in discovering a common set of values reinforces a sense of community. (2) I look at values a little differently. On one hand, as an individual, I have a set of core values. These core values help me to identify who I am. On the other hand, my school organization espouses a set of core values. These values interpret the school organization to the community. Community members know what to expect from my school because teachers and administrators refer all decisions to our core set of values. If the decision doesn't reinforce the core set of values, the decision is not made. Beyond this traditional way of examining values, I refer to Maslow's hierarchy of needs. When we focus on assisting people to acquire higher levels of basic needs, we are espousing values. I think Maslow's hierarchy of needs has some appropriate applications to the school organization setting."

Maslow's Hierarchy of Needs and Renewal.   Maslow's hierarchy of needs helps to explain human motivation. As Maslow indicates, primary needs must be met before the person can move to a higher level (see Figure 8.4). The further the person moves along the hierarchy of needs, the more fulfilled the person; the person who proceeds through all levels ultimately becomes self-actualized. By concentrating on Maslow's hierarchy of needs, the leader gets a better sense of what it takes to sustain continuous renewal within an organization and sustain constructive change. How can the leader expect faculty, staff, and students to think about continuous renewal if they are trapped in the lower levels of the hierarchy? Understanding the hierarchy of needs allows the leader to develop strategies to move his school from level to level until the school organization becomes self-actualized.

Maslow's list of basic needs apply personally and organizationally. Physiological needs are at the lowest level. These focus on our physical needs. How can

FIGURE 8.4 Maslow's Hierarchy of Needs

LEVEL OF NEEDS	BASIC NEED
Level Five	Self-Actualization Needs
Level Four	Esteem Needs
Level Three	Belonging and Love Needs
Level Two	Safety Needs
Level One	Physiological Needs

we teach if we've had nothing to eat? How can we learn when our stomachs are empty? What occurs if the classroom doesn't have proper ventilation? What about rest-room facilities? Are they updated? Is there sufficient time built into the schedule to allow students and teachers to use the facilities? Unless physiological needs are met, students do not give learning a priority, nor do teachers give teaching a priority. It is impossible to build a healthy organization without a proper foundation.

The leader, once assured that he has taken care of the physiological needs of the members of his organization, focuses on safety needs. Safety needs refer to a complex set of issues. These issues include school discipline; emotional threats from parents, colleagues, administrators, students, or teachers; plant safety issues related to stairwells, walks, steps, and other similar topics. The leader assures parents that their children are safe. Once members feel secure; they no longer are defensive. Their primal instincts for survival soften and they move toward a higher value, belonging needs. The effective leader, working with the community, develops a safe school plan.[23]

School community members, once their physiological and safety needs are met, want their belonging needs met. Belonging needs are met through the formation of an inclusive sense of community. One way to bring people together is through the process of story sharing. My personal experience of teaching a change class demonstrates how important the concept of story sharing is to the forming of community. Through the process of story sharing, members discover that they are more similar than different. They discover that each person's journey is marked by pain and joy. Craig Abrahamson tells us, "While thinking is certainly a complex activity, thinking depends very much on storytelling and story understanding. People remember what happens to them, and they tell other people what they remember. It is this sharing that can enhance an understanding of what occurred, both to the teller, as well as to the listener."[24] Leaders can employ the power of story sharing to enhance a sense of community by using faculty meetings or small group sessions as a means of encouraging each person to share his or her story. It is time-consuming, but it works—people identify with each other at deeper and more personal levels. As they identify more deeply with each other, barriers break down. The leader facilitates the acceleration of the breakdown of barriers that segregate, separate, and isolate through story sharing. The greater the sense of belonging members have in the organization, the greater the sense of health by members and the organization.

Maslow places esteem needs next in his hierarchy. He states that these needs "may be classified into two subsidiary sets. These are, first, the desire for strength, for achievement, for adequacy, for mastery and competence, for confidence in the face of the world, and for independence and freedom. Second, we have what we may call the desire for reputation or prestige."[25] It is at this level that the leader finds the resources—human, financial, and material—to assist members of the school organization to feel competent. No teacher purposely goes to school to create harm. Every teacher desires to be successful. Many teachers, however, are far from successful. The reason may be aptitude or attitude. The leader, working to create a continually renewing organization, moves to make everyone successful. Some teachers and staff are self-motivated; they don't need to be told how to find the resources to be successful. Other teachers need guidance. The effective leader understands these differences. She doesn't let people drift aimlessly. As more staff members achieve this level, their competence influences students and the community. The more competent they feel, the more they seek higher levels of competence. It is a self-fulfilling cycle.

The ultimate level in Maslow's hierarchy of needs is self-actualization. At this level, a person discovers what he does best and uses this in the way an artist plies his craft. When a person, for example, comes to the realization that his destiny is to become a leader, he will express his leadership artistry without thinking of what he is doing. He knows that he belongs in the school community as a leader. Others will easily recognize him because he plies his craft effortlessly. This is true for the leader as well as the teachers. Arrival at this stage requires inner reflection, personal growth, and a developing comfort with oneself. In an organizational sense, it is as if the organization, as a whole, understands that the sole purpose for its existence is to serve the needs of its stakeholders.

Dr. Jenkins wondered where the morning went. He sat mesmerized by Jo Ann Brimfield. He didn't realize that he had so much to learn. He stood up and shook Jo Ann's hand. "Jo Ann, I feel overwhelmed. You've given me a lesson in what I should be teaching my students. I can apply this to my classes at the university and to my life as well. I don't know where I've been all these years."

"Don't be so hard on yourself, Dr. Jenkins. After all, you were my professor and you inspired me to learn. You always said that your primary goal was to be a learner and a teacher. I think that is an important goal for anyone who desires to lead an organization into a continuous renewal pattern. Continuous renewal means that change is a part of life. Our goal is to become a continuously renewing human being contributing to the renewal of organizations and our social structures. Thank you for being my catalyst."

CONCLUDING POINT

There are seven lessons to continuous renewal.

1. People are the secret to success.
2. Create healthy organizations.
3. Effective leadership is power.

4. It's all about attitude.
5. Leaders link actions and policies to change.
6. Reinvent your organization—not the wheel.
7. Renewing organizations are self-actualizing organizations.

Mastery of these seven lessons is crucial for the leader. Each lesson is a piece to the puzzle for the creation of a continuously renewing school organization. Without a philosophy of continuous renewal, change becomes change for the sake of change. When the leader focuses on renewal, the leader looks to reenergize the school and assists members in reclaiming and redefining their mission. The school organization teems with vibrancy. It is alive. It is dynamic. Those who understand and master the seven lessons of change realize that they are alive and are constantly creating and recreating themselves. By mastering the seven lessons of change, the leader discovers that she is part of a process whereby she becomes the catalyst for change, growth, and continuous renewal.

SUGGESTIONS FOR ACTION

- Determine how much you trust the people in your organization and seek their counsel. Plan to involve the people in your organization.

- What is the health level of your organization? Assess the status of your school's health and identify what is being done to sustain that health. Identify the barriers to good health in your school. Is it attitude? Is it defensive routines? Is it lack of support? Or, is it the lack of leadership?

- To what extent do you understand the members of your school and their individual needs? Identify each teacher or staff member. Describe the teacher or staff member's strengths and weaknesses. Ask the teacher or staff member to identify his or her strengths and weaknesses. Work with the teacher or staff member to provide a competence plan. *Leadership through Excellence* is an excellent resource for the leader in guiding people toward higher levels of competence.[26]

- What are the prevailing attitudes in your school organization? Are the attitudes that are reflected in the teachers' lounge a reflection of the administrative attitudes? Consider changing attitudes and embracing more optimistic, healthy attitudes.

- Can you identify the defensive routines that operate in your organization? The best way to do this is to work with a group of people and ask them to recall the step-by-step behaviors that occurred when the organization felt a threat or risk of embarrassment.

- Does your organization have a structure by which members formally share stories? Create an opportunity for faculty to share stories. Use a simple question such as "Share the story of a teacher who made a difference in your life." Develop other questions to continue the story sharing exercise at future faculty meetings.

- Where is your school organization on Maslow's hierarchy of needs? What percentage of members, teachers, and staff would you place at each level? Ask for input from members of your school community. Collaboratively develop strategies to move the entire organization toward self-actualization.

CHANGE FACTORS

TERM	HOW TO USE IT	WHAT IT MEANS
Attitude	The leader realizes that stakeholders constantly monitor his or her attitude. The leader maintains a can-do, optimistic attitude at all times.	Attitude refers to the cognitive predisposition toward an object, fact, or context.
Civility	The leader models civility in his or her interactions with every member of the organization and external stakeholders.	Civility refers to the respect, courtesy, and politeness afforded others in all interactions.
Effective performance	The leader encourages members to improve personal effectiveness. Effective performance is recognized and rewarded.	Effective performance is a phrase that refers to work behavior that excels, achieves, or surpasses quality standards, and meets the needs of stakeholders.
Inclusive community	The leader leaves no one behind or out. The leader encourages an array of views in a diverse and inclusive learning community.	Inclusive community refers to the wide-ranging efforts of members to expand the community borders to include as many people as possible regardless of differing opinions or viewpoints.
Metaphor	The leader uses metaphors to communicate to members. By using appropriate metaphors, the leader incorporates images that have embedded within them the shared values and vision of the organization.	Metaphor refers to a literary device whereby one uses an image, symbol, or other object to represent something that is abstract and acts as an analogy.
Misaligned cultures	The leader identifies and understands each of the organizational cultures present in his or her school organization. The leader works to facilitate communication between and among groups to sustain cultural alignment.	Misaligned cultures refer to the three organizational cultures that exist in all organizations. Misalignment occurs when members of the various cultures take it for granted that their cultural perspective is the sole perspective.

Reinvent the organization	The leader encourages members to discover ways to achieve their mission. He or she understands that as contexts change approaches must change.	Reinvent the organization refers to attitudes and actions taken by members of vibrant organizations to addresses dynamic contexts.
Renewal	The leader realizes that continuous renewal is his or her responsibility. As a result, the leader creates conditions for the school organization to become a learning community focused on continuous renewal.	Renewal refers to sustained learning and growth to maintain the vibrancy of the organization and its members and to fulfill its mission to its stakeholders.

NOTES

1. Gardner, J. (1964). *Self-Renewal.* New York: Harper & Row, p. 5.

2. Gardner, J. (1994). National Renewal. Article adapted from remarks to the 100th National Conference on Governance, November 12, 1994, Philadelphia, PA. Retrieved August 14, 2001, from the World Wide Web: http://www.cpn.org/sections/new_citizenship/national_renewal.html.

3. Gardner, J. Ibid.

4. Brantley, B. (June 16, 2000). Verily, He Talks the Talk. Theater Review. *The New York Times* 159, no. 51, 421: (B1, B6).

5. Ackoff, R. (1986). *Management in Small Doses.* New York: John Wiley, p. 142.

6. Schein, E. (1985). *Organizational Culture and Leadership.* San Francisco: Jossey-Bass, p. 40.

7. Schein, E. (1999). Three Cultures of Management: The Key of Organizational Learning in the Twenty-first Century. MIT: The Society for Organizational Learning. Retrieved June 10, 1999, from the World Wide Web: http://www.sol-ne.org/res/wp/10011.html.

8. Ornish, D. (1999). *Love and Survival.* New York: HarperCollins, p. 139.

9. Hesselbein, F. (Summer 1997). The Power of Civility. *Leader to Leader,* no. 5. Retrieved August 14, 2001, from the World Wide Web: http://www.druckerfoundation.com/leaderbooks/L2L/summer97/fh.html.

10. Maslow, A. (1954/1970). *Motivation and personality* (2nd ed.). New York: Harper & Row, p. 196.

11. Bohm, D. Bohm Dialogue. Retrieved August 14, 2001, from the World Wide Web: http://www.muc.de/~heuvel/dialogue/index.html.

12. The seven traits of healthy people, quoted directly from Dreher, H. (1995). *The Immune Power Personality.* New York: Dutton, p. 188.

13. Quoted from Hollands, J. (July 30, 1997). How to Recognize a Healthy Organization. Los Altos, CA: *Los Altos Town Crier.* Retrieved August 14, 2001, from the World Wide Web: http://www.losaltosonline.com/latc/arch/9731/Business/3jean/3jean.html.

14. Bennis, W. (1989/1994). *On Becoming a Leader.* Reading, MA: Addison-Wesley, pp. 156–157.

15. James, W. (1997). Varieties of Religious Experience: A study in human nature. Being the Gifford Lectures on Natural Religion. Delivered at Edinburgh in 1901–1902 [On-line]. Available http://www.csp.org/experience/james-varieties/james-varieties.html. Accessed: 15 August 2001.

16. Mental Health.Net. Developing Attitudes That Help You Cope. *Psychological Self-Help.* Retrieved August 10, 2001, from the World Wide Web: http://mentalhelp.net/psyhelp/chap14t.htm.

17. Mackey, H. (May 11, 2000). Performance Depends on Attitude, Not Aptitude. *Minneapolis (MN) Star Tribune*, p. 2D.

18. Moore, M. (1990/1997). Dynamic Optimism. *Extropy*, no. 8. Retrieved August 14, 2001, from the World Wide Web: http://www.extropy.org/do.htm.

19. See Argyris, C. (1992/1999). *On Organizational Learning* (2nd ed.). Malden, MA: Blackwell Business Publishers, p. 56.

20. Bertelsmann Group for Policy Research. (2000). *Tolerance: Basis for Democratic Interaction.* Gütersloh, Germany: Bertelsmann Foundation Publishers, p. 12.

21. Peters, T. (1987). *Thriving on Chaos: Handbook for a Management Revolution.* New York: Harper & Row, p. 370.

22. Van Doren, M. (1990). In Boyer, E. (1990), *Scholarship Revisited: Priorities of the Professorate.* Lawrenceville, NJ: Princeton University Press, p. 19.

23. See Calabrese, R. L. (2000). *Leadership for Safe Schools: A Community Based Approach.* Lanham, MD: Scarecrow Press.

24. Abrahamson, C. E. (Spring 1998). Storytelling as a pedagogical tool in higher education. *Education.* Available: [Online] http://www.britannica.com/magazine/article?content id=58571&query=abrahamson. Accessed: 15 August, 2001.

25. Maslow, A., *Motivation and Personality* p. 45.

26. Calabrese, R. L. (2000). *Leadership through Excellence.* Boston: Allyn & Bacon.

INDEX